Secondhand China

 FLASHPOINTS

The FlashPoints series is devoted to books that consider literature beyond strictly national and disciplinary frameworks and that are distinguished both by their historical grounding and by their theoretical and conceptual strength. Our books engage theory without losing touch with history and work historically without falling into uncritical positivism. FlashPoints aims for a broad audience within the humanities and the social sciences concerned with moments of cultural emergence and transformation. In a Benjaminian mode, FlashPoints is interested in how literature contributes to forming new constellations of culture and history and in how such formations function critically and politically in the present. Series titles are available online at http://escholarship.org/uc/flashpoints.

SERIES EDITORS: Ali Behdad (Comparative Literature and English, UCLA), Editor Emeritus; Judith Butler (Rhetoric and Comparative Literature, UC Berkeley), Editor Emerita; Michelle Clayton (Hispanic Studies and Comparative Literature, Brown University); Edward Dimendberg (Film and Media Studies, Visual Studies, and European Languages and Studies, UC Irvine), Founding Editor; Catherine Gallagher (English, UC Berkeley), Editor Emerita; Nouri Gana (Comparative Literature and Near Eastern Languages and Cultures, UCLA); Susan Gillman (Literature, UC Santa Cruz), Coordinator; Jody Greene (Literature, UC Santa Cruz); Richard Terdiman (Literature, UC Santa Cruz), Founding Editor

A complete list of titles begins on page 245.

Secondhand China

Spain, the East, and the Politics of Translation

Carles Prado-Fonts

NORTHWESTERN UNIVERSITY PRESS | EVANSTON, ILLINOIS

Northwestern University Press
www.nupress.northwestern.edu

Copyright © 2022 by Northwestern University.
Published 2022 by Northwestern University Press. All rights reserved.

Printed in the United States of America

10 9 8 7 6 5 4 3 2 1

ISBN 978-0-8101-4476-7 (paper)
ISBN 978-0-8101-4477-4 (cloth)
ISBN 978-0-8101-4478-1 (ebook)

Cataloging-in-Publication Data are available from the Library of Congress.

He emprès aquest camí, no pas pensant en els resultats que en podré obtenir que seran, gairebé segur, mediocríssims, potser nuls, potser negatius—llevat de produir-se alguna cosa impensada. He emprès aquest camí per vèncer la dificultat d'emprendre'l—exactament parlant.

And that's precisely why I have chosen this path—not with an eye to the results that might accrue, which will almost certainly be third-rate, non-existent, or perhaps counterproductive—unless something unanticipated happens. I chose it precisely for the difficulty of the path that I must overcome.

—Josep Pla, *The Gray Notebook*
(trans. Peter Bush [New York: New York Review Books, 2013], 549)

Contents

Acknowledgments

This is a book about hegemonies, and I feel I should make my own position explicit before the reader begins to read it. *Secondhand China* explains how China has been imagined in Spain through the mediation of ideas about the East previously originated in languages such as English, French, or German. In essence, it is a book about how the ways in which we make sense of the world are subjected to hegemonic languages that impose certain mindsets about other, distant cultures and about how these impositions are negotiated in each local context. This book itself is a consequence of these hegemonies still very much at work today: it is a book about China in Spain that has been written by a Catalan scholar in the English language.

For someone who lives and works mostly in Catalan and Spanish, who believes in the richness of multilingualism, and who is very concerned about how the monopoly of the English language is impoverishing the world academic ecosystem, writing a book about this topic in English feels ironic and, I must confess, quite uncomfortable. But it goes on to show that, just as it was the case during the chronology covered by the following chapters, cross-cultural conversations on a global scale are still being held only in a few dominant languages—nowadays mostly in one. If you want to participate in these conversations (in comparative literature, translation studies, global history, or the humanities in general), you have to leave your reluctance aside. It is difficult—if not almost impossible—to participate in these global conversations using a language that is not English. It is so difficult, in fact, that writing a scholarly book in English may be something taken for granted. Millions of scholarly books in English are written, published, read, and discussed all around the world, after all. But for scholars who are not English native speakers—and particularly those who work outside Anglophone institutions—writing in English is not taken for granted. There are thousands of humanities scholars who work under the hegemony of the English language (the most epidermic of the hegemonies) and for whom, I presume, writing in English creates similar contradictions and uneasiness.

For those who are lucky enough to work in their mother tongue, it may be difficult to understand the anxieties that working in English creates in many non-Anglophone scholars. It is not simply a question of publishing scholarly books or articles. In fact, that might be the easiest part—once the manuscript has been accepted, copy editors and proofreaders take good care of it, iron out all inaccuracies, and create an illusion that naturalizes the whole process. The problem lies elsewhere—especially if you work in noncanonical cultures or areas of knowledge: trying to navigate the "native-speakerism" of Western academia; trying to frame your "peripheral" contribution in an adequate perspective to make it significant for "central" readerships; trying to catch the attention of a publisher without the symbolic credential of an Anglophone institution; trying to convince reviewers to be graceful with the infelicities in your text; trying to erase your accent in conferences and talks so it does not delegitimize the ideas you are trying to convey. Even sending a short email can take quite a while: Is this the right word? Is this a genuine expression? Doesn't this sound awkward? Isn't this a false friend? I am sure many non-Anglophone scholars will recognize themselves in many of these situations and daily microdilemmas. Of course, you can always find ways around them: nice Anglophone colleagues are always willing to help out; some editors and reviewers have become more sensitive to these issues; translators or proofreaders can be hired at an early stage—and some departments (if you are lucky to be affiliated to one) even subsidize their cost. Or you can just spend a lot of time writing and rewriting and becoming a perpetual foreign language learner—always a humbling experience that, I honestly believe (no ironies here), turns you into a richer person and a better human being. But the unbalance is always already there—and it is quite painful, especially in disciplines that are supposed to enhance pluralism and combat all sorts of hegemonies.

Some Anglophone readers may think I am exaggerating. I am not. Language in the humanities is not just the channel through which we express certain ideas. Language *is* a crucial part of those ideas too. And so when your ideas deal precisely with the politics of language and you are working outside your mother tongue, the blurring between form and content leaves you overconscientious and insecure. While writing this book about issues of language and hegemonies related to China and cross-cultural representation in my own dubious English, I often experienced the feeling that I was being pulled by the same forces I was describing, which still regulate scholarship and cross-cultural academia. Building my criticism with the same fabric I was criticizing, I was often reminded of the potential futility of my arguments and of my own peripheral position. Nothing new, to be sure: these are feelings that lay at the very core of the subaltern predicament.

That is why I want to thank those non-Anglophone scholars in the humanities, particularly those who work outside Anglophone institutions, who have published their books in English. I thank them for having coped with their own insecurities and anxieties and for having pushed their projects to publication. Their books helped me become more aware of my own subalternity, and their example helped me cope with it. I do not know whether *Secondhand China* will be of similar help for future scholars. But I do hope that, at least, it will shed light on the nature and scope of our subalternities—showing how intricate, latent, and powerful they still are.

I first learned about cross-cultural hegemonies, the politics of languages and cultures, and China and the Sinophone world from Shu-mei Shih, Seán Golden, and Harriet Evans. I thank them for their intellectual sharpness, scholarly commitment, and personal support. In my own teaching I am guided by their example. I thank my present and former undergraduate and graduate students for the opportunity they offer me to pay off a small part of the debt I acquired with my teachers.

This book grew up as part of a larger collective project about the interactions between China and Spain that I have been privileged to carry out with my colleagues from the ALTER research group based at the Universitat Oberta de Catalunya in Barcelona. We began this larger project more than ten years ago. At that time, we wondered whether the lack of studies about the interactions between China and Spain in the nineteenth and twentieth centuries was due to a lack of interactions between the two countries (as conventional accounts used to argue) or a lack of scholarly attention (our hypothesis). Since then, one of the most fascinating things about developing this larger project in general and writing this book in particular has been witnessing how an archive is created and grows up right in front of your eyes beyond your most optimistic expectations. Our hypothesis proved right, and references, images, memorabilia, contacts, and personal stories started coming in. The *Archivo China-España, 1800–1950* (ace.uoc.edu) holds now more than 1,100 items and, as an open-access digital archive, has received more than 170,000 page views from more than 35,000 users in more than 30 countries around the world. This book has therefore been most fortunate to cover the journey with the best company. I thank my colleagues from the ALTER research group for being such a friendly and stimulating intellectual community: Carles Brasó, Rubén Carrillo, Montserrat Crespín, Mònica Ginés, Ivan González, María Íñigo, Etienne Lock, Lluc López, Maialen Marín, David Martínez, Siwen Ning, Xavier Ortells, Rocío Ortuño, Antonio Paoliello, Manuel Pavón, and Alberto Poza. The balance between our large collective project and our "small" individual projects on related issues has been extremely fruitful. I can't recommend this balance enough for research groups—particularly in Europe, where institutions are pushing researchers in the humanities to replicate lab conventions from the hard sciences and, as a consequence, scholars are being alienated from much-needed single-authored intellectual projects driven by a deep, critical, creative, and horizontal engagement.

This book would not have been possible without the help from many people. I want to particularly thank David Martínez and Xavier Ortells for their expertise and their kindness. David gave the project an unswerving support from the beginning, read many drafts of the manuscript, and offered not only valuable feedback but also—and most importantly—incalculable common sense. Xavier provided tons of materials, an unsurpassable mastery of the sources, and a keen critical insight. Many other colleagues and friends have read or listened to portions of this book, as conference papers, lectures, finished chapters, unfinished drafts, or ideas scattered over formal or informal conversations. They have provided invaluable guidance. They include Brian Bernards, Paul Bevan, Robert Bickers, Susan Frekko, Albert Galvany, Blai Guarné, Margaret Hillenbrand, Evelyn Hu-DeHart, Rosario Hubert, Jorge Locane, Irene Masdeu, Joshua Miller, Tom Mullaney, Albert Nolla, Pau Pitarch, Alicia Relinque, Gayle Rogers, Carlos Rojas, Joaquim Sala-Sanahuja, Jiawei Wang, and Yue Zhang. Andreas Langenohl and John N. Kim organized an experimental conference on translating society at

Universität Konstanz in 2009 that was very influential for my thinking about many of the issues developed here. At Universitat Oberta de Catalunya, I thank Jaume Claret, Josep-Anton Fernàndez, Joan Fuster, and Teresa Iribarren, and Glòria Pujol. I particularly thank Marta Puxan and Neus Rotger for being an example of academic rigor, intellectual integrity, and personal generosity. At Universitat Pompeu Fabra, I thank Manel Ollé and Alex Coello as well as the students in my courses on Chinese history and culture, Sinophone studies, and East Asian languages and cultural contexts. At Cornell University I found an ideal environment to write many parts of the manuscript in two research stays during 2018 and 2019. I thank Naoki Sakai, Brett de Bary, Andrea Bachner, Nick Admussen, Joshua Young, Anne Blackburn, and Julia Chang for being wonderful hosts and providing valuable feedback at a crucial stage.

Chapters or portions of this project were presented in talks at the University of Oxford China Centre, the Edinburgh College of Art, the Foro Español de Investigación sobre Asia Pacífico, the Confucius Institute in Barcelona, the Department of Translation and Interpreting at Universitat Autònoma de Barcelona, and the Department of Arts and Humanities at Universitat Oberta de Catalunya. At the 2019 ACLA Annual Meeting I was part of a very inspiring seminar organized by Miaowei Weng with Jovana Zujevic, Yunning Zhang, Yihan Wang, Kathleen E. Davis, Yiyang Cheng, Blake Seana Locklin, Yeon-Soo Kim, Dinu Luca, Yun Lu, Adam Lifshey, and Zhou Meng. I am grateful to my audiences for the productive conversations that followed these presentations.

Funding for the research and writing of this book was provided by grants from Ministerio de Ciencia e Innovación (PID2019-108637GB-I00, 2020–2023), Ministerio de Economía y Competitividad (HAR2016-79995-P, 2017–2019), Chiang Ching-kuo Foundation (2015–2018), Ministerio de Ciencia e Innovación (HAR2012-34823, 2013–2016), and Agència de Gestió d'Ajuts Universitaris i de Recerca (2014–2017). Without their generous support, this project would not have been possible.

Some ideas from chapter 1 were previously developed in "Disconnecting the Other: Translating China in Spain, Indirectly," *Modernism/Modernity Print Plus* 3, no. 3 (2018), published by the Johns Hopkins University Press. Parts from chapter 3 derive from "Writing China from the Rest of the West: Travels and Transculturation in 1920s Spain," *Journal of Spanish Cultural Studies* 19, no. 2 (2018): 175–89, published by Taylor and Francis. Some passages from chapter 4 originally appeared in "China and the Politics of Cross-Cultural Representation in Interwar European Fiction," *CLCWeb: Comparative Literature and Culture* 19, no. 3 (2017), published by Purdue University Press. I am grateful to the publishers and editors for permission to republish that material here.

The comments and suggestions by the readers chosen by Trevor Perri were very encouraging and most helpful in guiding my revisions. I also thank Patrick Samuel, Faith Wilson Stein, Anne Gendler, Anne Strother, Carly Bortman, and the team at Northwestern University Press for their work on the book. Jessica Easto did a superb job as copy editor, and I'd like to thank Steve Moore for his masterful index. Naturally, any remaining shortcomings are my own.

I dedicate this book to my whole family and, particularly, to Olga, Martí, and Arnau.

Secondhand China

Writing the East from the Rest of the West

This book came to life when, in the middle of reading all sorts of texts about China published in Spain during the first decades of the twentieth century, I discovered a common feature shared by the following four publications. The first publication is a series of seven letters published in Barcelona by the journal *Hispania* between September 1900 and April 1901. Written by the Scottish diplomat John Harrisson, each letter appears under the rubric *La China moderna: cartas de un diplomático a su familia* (Modern China: Letters from a Diplomat to His Family). Each letter surveys several aspects of traditional Chinese culture and of the late-Qing politics and society that Harrisson encountered while serving at the British legation in Peking. Each letter is about three pages long. Since *Hispania* has a strong artistic and literary orientation, each page includes two or three beautiful sketches and photographs.[1] The second publication is *El enigma del despertar de China* (The Enigma of China's Awakening). Written by T. S. H. Thompson and translated by Fabián Casares, this book was published in Barcelona by Editorial Apolo in 1931. The book offers a panoramic view of 1920s China, split into several chapters dealing with traditions, rituals, feminism, Christianity, pedagogy, Malthusianism, communism, and literature.[2] The third publication is *El despertar de Asia* (Asia's Awakening). Written by I. Worski-Riera, this book was also published in Barcelona in 1931 by

Publicaciones Mundial. The book connects the contemporary situation in East Asia with the Russian Revolution and the leftist movements that were taking place around the world.[3] The fourth publication is a pair of pieces published in Madrid by Espasa Calpe in 1942: *Cómo me escapé de Siberia y conocí a Chiang-Kai-Shek* (How I Escaped from Siberia and Met Chiang Kai-shek) and *Cómo funciona el espionaje soviético en Extremo Oriente* (The Working of Soviet Espionage in East Asia). Written by Karol de Czola-Olai, these two pieces combine fiction, auto-biography, and reportage about the new Soviet Russia, Manchuria, and China between the late 1920s and the early 1930s.[4]

This book came to life when I realized that these four publications shared a fake authorship. "John Harrisson" [*sic*] is someone who in all likelihood never existed. I have not been able to trace the real author of the letters, but it is reasonable to believe that they were written by writers or staff working for the journal *Hispania*. "T. S. H. Thompson" and his translator "Fabián Casares" are also inventions. The real author of their book, it turns out, was Mario Verdaguer. A key figure in His-panic modernism and a friend of Federico García Lorca and Salvador Dalí, Verdaguer impersonated the voice of an English diplomat-cum-sinologist. "I. Worski-Riera" is also a fake. It is, in fact, the nom de plume often used by Augusto Riera when he wrote about Russia and Asia. And, finally, "Karol de Czola-Olai" is also a figure who almost certainly never existed. Some investigations suggest that it was the alias used by Spanish diplomat Julio de Larracoechea when he was trying to regain the favor of the new Franco regime after having been in political trouble while serving at the Spanish consulate in Shanghai.[5]

Why would a journal such as *Hispania* create a fake author and even a fake translator, since the letters include the signature "Traducción del inglés por A." (English translation by A.), to describe China's traditional culture and contemporary society? Why would an intellectual such as Verdaguer—avant-garde novelist, occasional poet, translator of Goethe, Zweig, and Mann—try to pass himself off as a British essayist to write about China? Why would a prestigious journalist such as Riera create an imaginary second author with whom he cosigned the pieces about the East? Why would a diplomat with a long trajectory in China such as Larracoechea sign as an obscure foreign writer when dealing with Chiang Kai-shek and East Asia? These puzzles ignited the research for this book, and the following chapters will follow some of these threads.[6]

To be sure, pseudonyms and heteronyms have been used in most cultures and literatures around the world for all sorts of reasons. Well-known figures quickly come to mind: Lu Xun used more than 140 pseudonyms (false names) due to political reasons, and Fernando Pessoa wrote under more than seventy heteronyms (new identities) to diversify his creative universe through different personalities. Translators have also traditionally relied upon invisibility or anonymity.[7] Things were not different in Spain, where writers, intellectuals, and translators have used pseudonyms and heteronyms consistently throughout history. In view of this tradition, there is no puzzle and the explanation to my questions seems rather simple: *Hispania*, Verdaguer, Riera, and Larracoechea used pseudonyms and heteronyms for purposes such as adding veracity to their accounts, hiding their true identity for social or political reasons, or adding an exotic, creative twist to their projects and biographies.

However, these examples acquired a fascinating new meaning to me when I connected them with other texts and data related to how China was represented in Spain at the end of the nineteenth century and during the first decades of the twentieth century. In 1899, for instance, Enrique Bendito published in Valladolid the novelette *Un viaje a Júpiter* (A Journey to Jupiter), a tale of two aristocrats who embark on a trip to outer space in the company of a Chinese philosopher. Even if the subtitle makes sure to attest that it was an "obra escrita en español" (a work written in Spanish), the main characters are Henry Hampill Yorkshire, Duke of Blane, and George Hampill Yorkshire, Duke of Maryland. Or, in 1931, Joan Crespi i Martí published in Barcelona *La ciutat de la por* (The City of Fear), an acclaimed novel about a Catalan young man who discovers Canton through the guidance of Mr. Lawrence, an enigmatic Englishman who seems to know everything about the place and who plays a key role in the novel's action.[8] Why did Bendito and Crespi i Martí give foreign characters—British, to be precise—the voice to represent China? The connection with the previous examples kept me wondering: Why would a depiction of China given by a foreign voice be more plausible or realistic to the Spanish reader? Why would a secondhand account be more attractive? Or, in other words, why would a translation—or what came to be presented as one—have more value than an original work?

In this book I claim that the answer to these questions transcends the biographical contingency or the curious anecdote. I claim that the use of pseudonyms, heteronyms, and foreign voices, in fact, reveals a certain discursive disposition to explain and understand China—its history, culture, people—in Spain. I claim that it was almost impossible to imagine China from the viewpoint of Spain without a foreign mediation—particularly British or French. This reality, I believe, addresses a central problem for comparative literature and cross-cultural studies.

This is a book about the indirect ways in which China was represented in Spain in the late nineteenth and early twentieth century. The writers, texts, and practices that we will encounter in the chapters that follow are, so to speak, writers, texts, and practices of their time. They lived in "a world connecting," of travelers and goods, railroads and fast ships, telegraph lines and photography, films and inexpensive publications.[9] In these writers, texts, and practices we will see reflected many of the characteristics that define the historical period that goes from the last decades of the nineteenth century to the end of World War II: a dramatic shrinking of time and space as a result of the revolution in communications and transportation; an accompanying acceleration in mobility of people, goods, and ideas; intersections and mutual constructions of the global and the local; a proliferation of technologies of mass production and consumption; or, particularly, the hegemonic power of the West under systems of modern statehood and imperialism. As "accounts and images of distant places multiplied and became accessible to all but the most remote of the world's inhabitants," though, "the very possibility of familiarity also bred strangeness. New connections highlighted all kinds of regional differences, and the awareness of difference could promote suspicion and repulsion perhaps even more easily than it facilitated understanding and communication."[10]

By focusing on the representations of China I shed light upon some complexities of this new world ecosystem. China played an important role in the reconfiguration of the world. China contributed to the new interconnections between goods, institutions, technology, and culture that were configured during this period. As a result, there was a sound interest in China in Europe and North America. Since the seventeenth century there had been a significant social and intellectual interest in China among European elites. But the following chapters will show how, starting around the end of the nineteenth century and, especially, during the first decades of the twentieth century, this interest became extraordinarily variegated and sustained beyond simple curiosity or the political and intellectual agenda of elites. The image of China throughout the West—the different ways in which it was viewed, perceived, discussed, and represented in literature and the arts or within the public sphere—was bestowed with an extreme richness and diversity.[11]

The following chapters will address some of the historical factors that explain this paradigm shift in the ways in which China was imagined in Spain but also, more generally, across the West: a new perception of China as a coeval reality in the modern world; an increased mobility of Chinese to Europe and Europeans to China; a public welcome of republican China into the world of democracy; a new era in media and technology—radio, telegraph, transpacific transportation systems, and communications; new journalist practices and new types of intellectual exchange; humanist concerns for gender and class issues at a universal scale; the spread of massive popular culture genres in literature and film. The following chapters will show how the circulation of images of China across the West during the first decades of the twentieth century became wider and how a complex mosaic of Chinese representations was formed. The sinophobic yellow peril and the sinophilic exoticism that had constituted the two extremes of the representational pendulum for centuries were still in operation. But these traditional poles now coexisted with other visions: compassion (for the consequences of the Boxer Uprising in 1900, for the dignity of Chinese peasants), sympathy (for the development of democratic institutions in the Republic of China, for the formation of the Communist revolution), empathy (for the status of Chinese women), admiration (for Chinese volunteers who took part in World War I or in the International Brigades during the Spanish Civil War), geopolitical interest (for China and Japan as sites in world-wide wars and communist revolutions), or commercial attraction (for China as a future market of four hundred million customers). Some of these visions had existed to some degree in previous periods, but what makes the first decades of the twentieth century unique is their coexistence, circulation, intensity, and pervasiveness. Even if important European figures and movements were later attracted to Chinese culture and politics—such as the British Left in the 1950s, Marxist humanists in the 1960s, or the *Tel Quel* group in the 1970s—the pluralistic epistemology that was in full operation at the beginning of the twentieth century has remained a unique interlude in the history of cross-cultural relations between China and the West.

Scholars working on sinographies, or "the particular forms of writing that produce and convey (within China as well as without it) the meanings of China," have shown how China's presence in the West was not simply a quantitative accumulation of signs and references.[12] As Eric Hayot, Christopher Bush, and many others have argued, China—or, more specifically, the *idea* of China or the ways of thinking about China—has been central in the development of Western aesthetic, cultural, and political projects of modernity.[13] In essence, these works on sinographies have insightfully pointed out the tension between the historical and the allegorical presence of China in the West.[14] This book is rooted in that very same tension. My goal is to explore the relationship between, on the one hand, the historical and material conditions that explain the presence of China in the world's geopolitical, social, and cultural developments, and, on the other hand, the uses of the "Chinas" that came to be represented as a result of such increased historical and material presence. My goal is to explore this tension without privileging the latter over the former. But, above all, my goal is to explore this tension by opening up a new set of concerns and reflections about translation, cross-cultural representation, and indirect or mediated knowledge about the world. Was China consistently present across the West? Was "China" imagined in similar ways across the West? How were these similarities and differences created? What do these similarities or differences within the West tell us about the ways in which China and the world were being imagined at the time? And what do they tell us about the configuration of the West itself?

In fact, the presence of China and the representations of "China" in Spain were both similar and different to what was taking place in other parts of Europe. On the one hand, China was as present in Spain as it was across Europe during the same period. As we will see in the following chapters, China was a consistent topic in Spanish society and culture during the first decades of the twentieth century. The coverage of China in Spanish newspapers and magazines was remarkable. Dozens of books related to China were published regularly. China was an important source of inspiration for major literary and intellectual figures, including Vicente Blasco Ibáñez (1867–1928), Pío Baroja (1872–1956), Luis de Oteyza (1883–1961), José Ortega y Gasset (1883–1955), Federico García Sanchiz (1886–1964), and Ramón Gómez de la Serna (1888–1963). On the other hand, China was represented in Spain from a position that differed from other Western points of view. Between the colonial empire that lasted until the end of the nineteenth century and the courageous republic that was internationally acclaimed in the 1930s (the two historical entities that probably define Spain in the international imaginary), there is a period when Spain shared many historical predicaments with China: both countries faced military defeats in colonial or semicolonial contexts, saw the spread of nationalist ideas and the fall of monarchies, suffered military coups d'état and the ruling of dictatorships, witnessed the proclamation of republics and were devastated by civil wars. A shared consciousness of a fin de siècle crisis pushed both Spain and China to find new solutions and to negotiate beyond the boundaries of a national culture that had become inconsistent with the new world order. While the historical parallelisms between the two countries are quite striking, it is even more striking that these similarities remained largely unnoticed at the time. Why, given the potential for projecting a singular cross-cultural imagination of China, did Spain not produce a discourse that differed—in scope and magnitude—from the discourses on China produced in the West? Why didn't these shared historical predicaments between Spain and China even produce an alternative imagined global community of some sort?[15] To be sure, these are gigantic questions that could be answered in many different ways—or even dismissed as belonging to alternative history. But what is surprising, in my view, is that this kind of interrogation was never raised in Spain between the late nineteenth century and the early 1930s when the historical parallelisms were taking place.

This book will offer a partial answer to the question of why the connections between Spain and China did not emerge at that time. The answer can be found in the most important feature that characterizes the representations of China in Spain: most knowledge about China reached Spanish readers *indirectly*, as discourses on China arrived into European national contexts mostly via pivotal centers such as Britain, France, or Germany. Spanish illustrated magazines based their pieces on China on articles previously published in British or French magazines.[16] Newspapers' reports on China relied almost exclusively on information released by foreign agencies such as Reuters, United Press, or Havas. About 25 percent of the books related to China that were published in Spain between 1890 and 1940 (including poetry, fiction, and nonfiction) were acknowledged translations of English or French originals; the rest relied heavily on foreign sources as well, even if they were not always acknowledged.[17] Works by French or British sinologists and experts on China or East Asia such as Jean-Pierre Abel-Rémusat (1788–1832), Stanislas Julien (1797–1873), Guillaume Pauthier (1801–1873), L'Abbé Huc (Évariste Régis Huc, 1813–1860), James Legge (1815–1897), Herbert Giles (1845–1935), Charles Vignier (1863–1934), Paul Pelliot (1878–1945), and Arthur Waley (1889–1966) were well known, widely available, and common currency among Spanish cultural elites, even if these works were rarely translated into Spanish or Catalan. Relying on

Western sources to learn about China was assumed as a natural thing to do. Spanish writers even exhibited their English and French sources with pride. A secondhand China was more desirable than the original. In fact, a secondhand China was probably the only China they could conceive.

Such intellectual dependence, and the kind of hegemony it entails, may pass unnoticed for several reasons. For instance, it was—it still is, in fact—assumed quite naturally. At the time, it was accepted, even enthusiastically embraced, by cultural agents. Today, it may seem anecdotal or quantitatively unremarkable, and it remains comfortably located within an unproblematized "Western" subject that relates homogeneously with China as its object. However, the following chapters will reveal how the representations of China shaped this kind of intellectual hegemony, which has ended up being undetectable. This book will provide evidence that shows how this dependence remained consistent—and even increased—throughout the decades.

Such intellectual dependence may also pass unnoticed as qualitatively insignificant—a logical consequence of the cultural hegemony derived from the geopolitical context of Western modernity. It could also be argued that fake translations or pseudotranslations of Chinese works did not take place exclusively in Spain. In the eighteenth century, for instance, a large number of pseudotranslations, or texts originally written mostly in English or French, claimed to be translations from one or more Oriental languages. These pseudotranslations "affected the stereotypical notions of what it meant to be 'Chinese.'"[18] It could also be argued that translating from French translations was in fact very common in Spain in the nineteenth century. Russian literature, for instance, also arrived into Spain mediated through French translations of Russian works.[19] It could even be argued that all representations of China—or of any other culture, for that matter—are always indirect and problematic after all, regardless of their context of circulation. Our understanding of the distant other, we could claim, is almost never firsthand but always mediated through agents such as travel writers, journalists, or diplomats whose representations were probably also the result of previous representations—and even embedded in certain hierarchies of class, gender, or ethnicity that could be considered additional mediations as well. In other words, if we live in a perpetual chain of indirectness and *différances*, what is significant about the indirect representations of China in Spain in the late nineteenth and early twentieth century?

In my view, the chapters that follow illustrate at least two significant features. First, the cases I will examine show something meaningful in their indirectness. My point is not to demonstrate that translations that were "direct" were better or more accurate. While China was only known secondhand, I am not assuming that a better knowledge through primary contact was missing. My point is not to demonstrate that indirect knowledge of China was a phenomenon restricted to Spain either. In fact, it flowed different ways as well: some of the most influential popular books on China in interwar Britain, for instance, came in translation from German (Egon Erwin Kisch's *Secret China*, Vicki Baum's *Hotel Shanghai* and *Nanking Road*) or French (Henry Champly's *The Road to Shanghai*, André Malraux's *Man's Fate*).[20] Rather, my point is that these Spanish and Catalan texts attempted to *do something* through their secondhand-ness. Writers used the indirect representations of China to connect themselves to Europe in a moment of national crisis, to singularize their subjectivity and find their own national voice, or to put forward proposals for political and cultural modernity. Indirectness was not a by-product of their creative practices but rather a crucial, defining aspect of their intellectual projects. In other words, there was an important political dimension embedded in the act of representing China for Spanish readers through representations already existing in English or French. Second, as a scholar coming from Chinese studies, I want to also show that the indirectness of these cases was possible because China remained always the object in the equation. Writers used China for many purposes—which in the end, were not that related to China after all. Echoing Eric Hayot's claim about the nature of the mandarin in the "hypothetical mandarin" (the parable used to exemplify the connection between morality and emotional and physical detachment), we could say that it matters that the indirectness was related to China because its being Chinese means that its being Chinese doesn't matter.[21]

By looking at the indirect representations of China in Spain, I show how translation and cross-cultural representation contribute to discourses of domination and subjection.[22] I explore the effects of this indirect way of representing China. I argue that the secondhand production and consumption of images of China in Spain in the late nineteenth and early twentieth century reinforced the cultural hegemonies inside and outside the West. In other words, I argue that Orientalism was an instrument of hegemony not only between the West and the Rest but also within the West itself.[23]

Needless to say, the significance of this argument transcends the particular relationship between Spain and China. The indirect nature of the representations of China in Spain reveals the intricacies of imagining other, distant cultures around the world—even in historical contexts with a potential for mutual cross-cultural empathy, such as the ones we will explore in this book. The indirect nature of the representations of China in Spain requires us to reconsider the politics of language and translation in any form of cross-cultural representation. The chapters that follow suggest, for instance, that we should not measure the degree of engagement between cultures according to things like the number of translations existing between them or the number of images of one culture circulating into another. While the abundance and diversity of representations of China circulating in Spanish and Catalan languages may give the impression that there was a close engagement between China and Spain in the first decades of the twentieth century, the origin and, particularly, *the use* of these representations throw any kind of engagement with the Chinese other into question and reveal a subjection to discourses unrelated to China.

This is a phenomenon that informs us about very contemporary practices too. The cultural and literary markets in Spain and Catalonia today essentially follow the patterns of Anglophone or Francophone publications. Translations of Chinese literary works (and of works from many other "peripheral" literatures) into Spanish and Catalan tend to be commissioned only after a successful reception of the translation of the same works in the English or French market. Many publishers in Spain and Catalonia neglect the search for new voices—even in their own language—and prefer to comfortably wait and see what has worked in these central cultural markets.[24] Thus, while I fully share Ngũgĩ wa Thiong'o's claims to "read globalectically" and "approach any text from whatever times and places to allow its content and themes [to] form a free conversation with other texts of one's time and place," I do not share his confidence in translation as "the language of languages" that "opens the gates of national and linguistic prisons" and as "one of the most important allies of world literature and global consciousness."[25] The chapters that follow will rather show the opposite: translation is in fact part of the "linguistic feudalism" that may affect our potential globalectical reading of the world. The story of the representations of China in Spain shows how the linguistic feudalism that has settled to the bottom of the contemporary global literary and cultural circuits was created decades ago and even affected languages such as Spanish, which wa Thiong'o, as many of us, would consider part of the "aristocracy" of world languages.

I am writing this book from what, complicating Stuart Hall's famous formulation, could be considered the Rest of the West, and I believe we still need to rethink how we produce knowledge about the different cultures of the world—and beyond the China–West dichotomy in particular. At a time when labels such as "global studies," "global history," "world history," or "world literature" seem to dominate conferences, journals, curricula, and academic job openings, I believe there are questions that remain quite unaddressed and explanations that should still be reconsidered: Who produces knowledge about (distant) cultures? How does that knowledge get distributed and legitimized across *multiple* cultural contexts? How does that import knowledge overlap with local predicaments? What is agency in the transnational terrain of the cross-cultural politics of power? How can we cope—conceptually, methodologically—with these complexities?

The central problem examined in this book addresses these questions and highlights realities that transcend binary models of analysis. The indirect representations of China in Spain that were subordinated to British and French hegemonic discourses about China call for an understanding that, on the one hand, acknowledges the existence of dialectical polarities but, on the other hand, unsettles the binary model of centers and peripheries, West and Rest, self and other. Spain is an ideal laboratory case for investigating the puzzling, multidirectional, ambivalent, sometimes even contradictory power relations that characterize cross-cultural interactions and that may be in operation, to a greater or lesser extent, in the hybrid hegemonies and subordinations between languages and cultures around the world.

To be sure, revealing the multidirectional power relations in which Spain was involved between the late nineteenth century and the 1930s enriches our understanding of Spain's imperial decline and illuminates political, cultural, and ethnic issues related to Spain's national identity.[26] These multidirectional power relations also contribute to a more nuanced understanding of Spain's historical transformation in relation to other imperial transformations in Europe. Recent historiographical works have revised this relationship. Josep Fradera has compared the different transitions from imperial monarchies into modern nations that took place around the nineteenth century. He has insightfully used the term "imperial nation" to highlight a certain continuity—rather than a sharp break—throughout this process.[27] Fradera argues that "empires reshaped themselves while modern nations emerged" and that the essential struggle that characterized this transition was the metropolis's domination of the peripheries by different strategies (special regimes or dual constitutions, subordinate political representation, denial of representation).[28] As we will see, this transition from empire into modern nation was also reflected in Spain's cultural sphere. The following chapters will show how there was also a continuity of the imperialist mindset when it came to imagining distant cultures such as China. The ways of imagining China show that "the Spanish case was not the exception but the rule as it transformed the old empire into a liberal capitalist society with the aim of participating in divvying up the world. Both by tradition and by right, Spain behaved as an imperial nation."[29] At the same time, however, the following chapters will also show a rather contradictory coexisting feature: this remaining imperialist mindset in Spain was nurtured by a subordination to the discourses on the East that were produced in Britain or France. In other words, while Spain still assumed a symbolic position of a world metropolis, Spain was subjected to a subordinate position when it came to creating discourses about the world—and about China or Asia, in particular.[30]

But exposing the multidirectional power relations in which Spain was involved at the time also enriches phenomena that transcend the Spanish context. The representations of China in Spain arising in this context of multidirectional power relations concern broader Hispanophone and Lusophone contexts too. Indeed, the study of the interactions with China and Asia has become one of the most vibrant developments in Latin American studies in recent years and has revealed important cross-cultural encounters, connections, and influences unexplored so far.[31] Some contributions have used these unexplored connections to imagine new epistemological frameworks aimed at a global or transnational significance. Pedro Erber, for instance, has examined the connections between Japanese and Brazilian art and taken contemporaneity as a departure point to move beyond models of center and periphery in our understanding of global culture. Paulina Lee has shown how Chineseness was a critical discourse within debates about Brazilian national identity to suggest a different understanding of hemispheric histories of racial difference. Junyoung Verónica Kim has proposed Asia-Latin America as a method to examine the politics of knowledge and the persistent impact of the "West" in encounters between peripheries, which still prevents the fulfillment of the Global South project.[32] We should not be mistaken by Spain's historical position as colonizer in Latin America before 1898 and therefore isolate Spain from these discussions. To begin with, because, as Alejandro Mejías-López has suggested, the "inverted conquest" of *modernismo* connected Latin America and Spain in unprecedented ways between 1880 and the late 1920s—a period which almost overlaps with this study.[33] But also because, by alerting us of the intricate role played by (indirect) translation under these encounters with Asia, the representations of China in Spain can contribute to a collective and more nuanced discussion about alternative modernities and epistemologies that considers the linguistic and discursive hegemonies underneath periphery-to-periphery flows. In the linguistic dependence of the past, we can probably find the roots of the theoretical, epistemological subordination of the present.

Even more generally, the multidirectional power relations exemplified by the Spanish case highlight the role played by translation and the representation of other, distant cultures "as a constitutive, rather than a constituent" element of global and world history.[34] Translation was not a mere instrument of transnational interchanges but a key driving force in the imperial transformations of the nineteenth century and the new cultural and political hegemonies that consolidated in the twentieth century. It may not be an exaggeration to suggest that, underneath most of the connections traced by recent impressive works in global and world history, translation and cross-cultural representation lay as crucial infrastructures with important discursive implications.[35]

How, then, should we conceptualize the cross-cultural interactions arising in contexts of puzzling, multidirectional, ambivalent, sometimes even contradictory power relations exemplified by the case of Spain in the late nineteenth and early twenty centuries? We may think that postcolonial studies, comparative literature, or global literary studies have already done so, as their scholarship is already beyond dichotomies—conceptually or methodologically. Or that East/West, West/Rest, even colonizer/colonized, are now shopworn binaries. As a scholar standing in different "peripheries" (Catalan language, Sinophone literature, Spanish university), I am not so certain. To be sure, the cultural turn and the theoretical discussions in these fields have been questioning Eurocentric perspectives for many years now.[36] To be sure, works in East-West studies by Shu-mei Shih, Lydia Liu, Haun Saussy, Eric Hayot, Christopher Bush, Karen Thornber, and many other scholars have offered sophisticated and deeply nuanced arguments that question these binaries. However, it seems to me that East-West scholarship has mostly remained in a comfort zone that easily equates the West with Anglophone and Francophone contexts and that, while often paying attention to the unbalanced politics between East and West, forgets that the interaction with the East reinforced unequal power relations within the West too. It is just as inaccurate to homogenize "the Rest" as it is to think about "the West" in such a homogeneous way.[37] In other words, while scholarship has certainly left such broad generalizations behind and West/Rest is not really current vocabulary, Hall's formulation remains quite active. An underlying West/Rest assumption still blinds our understanding of the hierarchies between cultures and neutralizes the power imbalances taking place within each of these two broad divisions—or even in more complex (nonbinary, triangular, or multidirectional) relations. A few scholars like Naoki Sakai, James Hevia, and Dipesh Chakrabarty have called for a dislocation or provincialization of the West.[38] But we need to substantiate their claims. We need studies that engage in East-West discussions by complicating our understanding of the West from outside the Anglophone and Francophone perspectives but that, at the same time, do not fall into incommensurable localisms that refute the undeniable impact of the Anglophone and Francophone systems upon other Western contexts too.

The diffusionist or world-system theoretical models that now dominate our understanding of how literatures and cultures interact around the world do not seem to help much in this situation.[39] These models—which scholars these days either follow or take as a reference to be refuted—are characterized by their expansionism and the naturalization of the inequalities between cultures. These models privilege modernist texts, replicate the circulation of capital, and do not respect diversity in equality. Being supported with lucrative funds coming from institutions that attach an increasing relevance to digital humanities, these models have now become authoritative. From these models derives a strong emphasis on circulation, which has monopolized the study of translation and cross-cultural representation in recent decades. Attention to circulation has emphasized flows, transfers, and all sorts of fluid entanglements as important features that characterize the interactions between cultures. But the usage of circulation as a metaphor for this epistemological understanding of how cultures relate has also been quite erratic.[40] As a consequence, the West/Rest binary assumption remains latent.

Some reactions against the diffusionist or world-system theoretical models have claimed for the need to focus on the historicity and materiality of literary practices and leave the theoretical contributions in the background—or leave them aside completely.[41] The quest for a common theoretical ground, they argue, should eventually arrive in a utopian time and for the moment we should all concentrate on our specific, local realities. I believe, however, that scholars should not remain confined to the archives and that theoretical discussions should neither be postponed nor abandoned. We need them right now, too, since this kind of withdrawal relegates scholars from peripheral contexts to the role of native informants—a role very much welcomed by the diffusionist models they are trying to combat. If we are serious about setting up an honest dialogue among different cultural contexts and scholarly traditions, we must persist in our quest for common conceptual tools. All scholars and all contexts should be potential contributors to the discussion about how we understand the world and the different parts that define that world in interrelation.

This book is an attempt to contribute to these conceptual and methodological discussions in several ways. First, I suggest a way to deal with the "incommensurability of theory and archive" that characterizes the problems described previously.[42] The following chapters encompass a variety of textual examples of how China was imagined, understood, and discussed in Spain. This means that, instead of focusing only on explicit translations, I focus on many kinds of representations of China—most of which were dependent on translations but were not translations themselves. This also means that, instead of focusing only on canonical works of fiction or poetry, I include also nonfiction writings, popular literature, and texts with a hybrid nature—combining travel writing, journalism, and fiction, for instance. Such a variety of textual realities tries to reflect the dense, heterogeneous, and simultaneous ways in which China was present in Spain. Such a variety of textual realities strives to make the archive richer and to elaborate conceptual observations from such rich heterogeneity. I have followed this bottom-up methodology instead of accommodating only a few of these textual realities to top-down frameworks provided by world literature or world-system theoretical models. Here is a significant fact that, as I am writing this introduction at the end of this project, still keeps me quite astonished: had I only looked at the translations, either direct or indirect, from Chinese into Spanish in the period analyzed, I probably would have reached the conclusion that China was barely present in Spanish society.[43] However, as the following chapters will show, by opening up the archive to a variety of works that represented China in one way or another, my conclusion is, in fact, the opposite.

Second, I propose that the notion of indirect translation should be expanded from its original linguistic sense to a broader—yet interrelated—dimension at both discursive and cultural levels. Scholars in translation studies have typically focused on indirect translation as "any translation based on a source (or sources) which is itself a translation into a language other than the language of the original, or the target language."[44] Yet despite recent attention in some translation studies discussions, indirectness remains a largely unexplored phenomenon.[45] The following chapters show how indirectness and mediated knowledge can be a fruitful avenue of inquiry that supplements former critical scholarship not only on the role of translation itself but also on cross-cultural circulation and in comparative studies more generally.

Third, I extend the archive of sinographies by moving outside the Anglophone and Francophone contexts without forgetting the relevance of these central languages and geopolitical contexts. I suggest triangulation as a heuristic concept that relates theory and the archive. Or, in other words, as a pattern that connects the different agents intervening in cross-cultural interactions between China and locations outside the Anglophone and Francophone contexts. I share Karen Thornber's suggestive claim that "for understanding most literatures and cultures, particularly those of nineteenth- and twentieth-century empires and their aftermaths, it is essential to analyze how creative texts are transpatialized and how spaces are transtextualized."[46] But while I acknowledge that Thornber's notion of "contact nebulae" is evocative to describe the "vast networks of fluid transculturating spaces,"[47] I still think there are some mechanisms that patterned and shaped these fluid contact nebulae. I suggest that triangulation was one of these mechanisms. As scholars such as Jacob Edmond and Heekyoung Cho have shown, looking at the triangular relations between cultures and literatures illuminates issues that may otherwise remain hidden or naturalized.[48]

Inspired by Henri Lefebvre's work on human geography and by Shumei Shih's idea of "triangulation or tripling of the elements or agents brought into consideration for their actually existing dialectical relations," I propose a trialectical understanding of cross-cultural representation.[49] In *La Production de l'espace* (The Production of Space) Lefebvre argues that space can hide the reality of social power relations. A critical vision of space, then, needs a trialectical knowledge that combines perceptions, conceptions, and experiences.[50] According to Lefebvre, the triad does not always constitute a coherent whole:

> That the lived, conceived and perceived realms should be interconnected, so that the "subject," the individual member of a given social group, may move from one to another without confusion—so much is a logical necessity. Whether they constitute a coherent whole is another matter. They probably do so only in favourable circumstances, when a common language, a consensus and a code can be established.[51]

I resituate Lefebvre's notion of trialectics in the transnational terrain of cross-cultural politics of power. Trialectics reveal the politics embedded in many cross-cultural encounters. The China that will appear in the following chapters is the product of a similar perceived-conceived-lived triad in which each element of the triad relies on a different culture and political position: signs of China conceived through central Western power/knowledge and experienced within a Spanish local cultural imagination. This book aims, then, to unveil what, under the "favourable circumstances" provided by previous scholarship, may have seemed coherent: the singularities and incoherencies of imagining China from Spain under Western hegemonic discourses.

Finally, I suggest that translation hides or naturalizes the asymmetries that can be identified through a trialectical analysis. In other words: translation provides the "common language, consensus, and code" that turn these triangulations natural or unperceived. After all, as Naoki Sakai has argued, translation is a regime "organized around the schema of co-figuration." The chapters that follow show how translation as a "historical construct of modernity that has worked powerfully to project national/ethnic languages and the international world, only within which national languages are possible" transcends in fact a mere binary relationship between languages and cultures.[52] The chapters that follow, in sum, illustrate the workings of translation as a technology of cultural hegemony in a multidirectional way.

The book is structured in four chapters arranged in a loosely chronological order that covers the period between, roughly, 1880 and 1930. Each chapter employs historical approaches and close readings to examine the ways in which China was represented in the West and, more specifically, in Spain.

Chapter 1 explores how the representations of China were translated from European sources in the late nineteenth century. I examine the wide-scale causes and effects of representing China in Spain in such an indirect way. What were the material and discursive conditions for representing China from a peripheral Western location like Spain? Can we consider these secondhand representations indirect translations? Is the concept of translation suitable to explain these interactions? What are the implications of these oblique circuits of cross-cultural contact? I will approach these questions through the reading of three works that were not considered translations themselves but that were in fact heavily dependent on data, images, and perspectives translated from English and French sources. Enrique Gaspar's *Viaje a China* and *El anacronópete* (Travel to China, 1878-1882; and The Time Ship, 1887) and John Harrisson's *La China moderna: Cartas de un diplomático a su familia* (Modern China: Letters from a Diplomat to His Family, 1900–1901), a collection examined here for the first time, are illustrative examples of how the images of China in Spain depended on pivotal foreign sources and were projected through a variety of works and genres. We will see how the images of China in Spain relied on translation but were then reproduced in an array of forms that were not marked as translations themselves. I argue that, as a result from such a dependence on and erasure of translation, the discourse on China originated in the French and British colonial contexts was transplanted onto the social imaginary of a Spain in imperial decline. As hybrid, heterogeneous works with circulations mostly restricted within national borders, *El anacronópete*, *Viaje a China*, and *La China moderna* would probably pass unnoticed in discussions on world literature, translation studies, or comparative literature. They however illustrate how the dependence on and the erasure of translation contributed to the illusion of the West as a unified subject and kept the coherence of the trialectical relationship between China, Spain, and other European languages.

Chapter 2 reflects on the limits of this kind of secondhand cross-cultural imagination at the turn of the twentieth century. I show how the awareness of China as a coeval presence in the world around 1900 created new types of representations and concerns that coexisted with old patterns of representation. The overlap between these new and old images produced a keen concern for the truth about China. What was the "true China" that existed on the other side of the world? How similar, or how different, was this new "real China" from the "Chinas" that had been described in the past? How reliable were the Chinese voices who talked about China in the first person? I examine the tension between these new and old concerns. I argue that, in Spain, this concern for truth about a coeval China in the world increased the anxiety for

Spain's own geopolitical position. Yet, given the material and discursive context described in the previous chapter, was it possible to hold an independent Spanish view on China not influenced by other Western views? Was it possible to articulate a critical opinion against this indirect process of learning about China? I address these questions by looking into the Spanish translations of Chen Jitong's best sellers such as *Les Chinois peints par eux-mêmes* (The Chinese Painted by Themselves, 1894, translated into Spanish in 1901) and Fernando de Antón del Olmet's neglected book *El problema de la China* (The Problem of China, 1901). These works show how these kinds of critical insights were only partially possible. Chinese voices (real and fictional) were acknowledged indeed, and the secondhand access to knowledge about China was problematized—the actual trialectical nature of the representations of China in Spain became visible for the first time. Yet representations of China remained dependent on pivotal Western locations, which limited the scope of these critical voices.

Chapter 3 examines a new context for imagining China that emerged between the 1910s and mid-1920s. The catalog of representations of China became more complex in an unprecedented way. There were more images; images were more diverse; images involved more agents and were rooted in new epistemologies. As a result, China became an object of attention and multiple representations of China were put in competition among themselves. I look into how this new economy of representation interacted with the indirect patterns for representing China that were still in operation. How did this new economy of representation affect the ways in which China was imagined and written about in Spain? How was this competition between multiple Chinas played out in a national context where China had been imagined indirectly through the prism provided by other nations? What kind of representations emerged from firsthand experiences of Spanish authors who traveled to China, which were now more common in a more interconnected world, when these writers had learned about China indirectly, mostly through sources originally published in other Western languages? I explore these issues through the accounts written by authors who undertook literary travels to the Far East in the 1920s: Vicente Blasco Ibáñez's *La vuelta al mundo de un novelista* (A Novelist's Tour of the World, 1924), Federico García Sanchiz's *La ciudad milagrosa* (The Miracle City, 1926), and, particularly, Luis de Oteyza's underestimated novel *El diablo blanco* (The White Devil, 1928). I argue that the trialectical structure that had characterized the representations of China in Spain so far lost its internal coherence as tensions among the three vectors (a China conceived through Western discourses and experienced in a Spanish context) emerged. The three works show how these tensions produced a strong racial perception of China in Spain while a more plural and humane view toward China was taking shape in other Western contexts. The three examples also show how the dismantling of trialectics produced weak formal developments in these works' plot and structure.

Chapter 4 looks into the representations of China between the mid-1920s and the 1930s. I show how images of China and the Chinese were characterized by a combination of saturation, heterogeneity, and consumerism. At the same time, in Spain, China became embodied by Western agents to an unprecedented degree, and figures such as Pearl Buck and André Malraux introduced new sensibilities toward the Chinese people. In this context, I highlight the degree of adaptability of the representations of China in Spain. To do so, I focus on the Catalan context. Why were the representations of China in the Catalan language so different from the representations of China in the Spanish language? The question is even more puzzling given that the archive of representations of China that was available in Catalonia was not much different from the archive available in the rest of Spain. What does this difference tell us about the capacity for cross-cultural representations to adjust to different localities even within national contexts and across national languages? I address these questions through the reading of two Catalan works that have not been previously analyzed by scholarship: Joan Sacs's essay "Àsia" (Asia, 1927) and Joan Crespi i Marti's novel *La ciutat de la por* (The City of Fear, 1930). Both texts show how Catalan intellectuals and writers were particularly active in incorporating China in their own projects, both elitist and popular, often aimed at distancing themselves from the Spanish literary circles. They also show how the connection with China remained mediated by European discourses and voices. Influential Catalan intellectuals were keen to incorporate China into their works but were even more eager to flaunt their English and French sources. I finally argue, as a final reflection that provides further explanation to many of the examples seen in the book, that throughout all these processes of cross-cultural representation, "China" was an empty signifier with a ductile signified. "China" supported the code-switching between the different Chinas coexisting in the West. "China" accommodated to multiple, often contradictory demands arising from different historical contingencies—even in neighboring cultural and linguistic contexts such as Spain and Catalonia. In sum, "China" could be used by anyone and could mean pretty much anything.

The conclusion highlights the ambivalent role played by translation in cross-cultural representation and how a critical understanding of other, distant cultures should be aware of translation's ambivalence. I emphasize how the simultaneous dependence on and erasure of translation creates two illusions that should concern many fields in the humanities: the illusion of the West as a homogeneous subject vis-à-vis a China that remains always its object, and the illusion of translation as a neutral connection between cultures. I speculate that translation appeals to many fields across the humanities precisely because it controls but conceals an ethnographic gaze and the kind of politics underneath cross-cultural interactions that will be explored later. I close the book by suggesting that, while we obviously must rely upon translation to learn about foreign cultures, we need to enlarge our archives, diversify our languages, and challenge our epistemologies in order to aim for a more equal understanding of the world's complexity. This is the methodological—and ethical—approach used in the chapters that follow.

CHAPTER 1

"Illusion Is More Beautiful Than Reality"

Late February, 1884
  Yasnaya Polyana, Tula, Russian Empire

Leo Tolstoy writes in a letter to Vladimir Chertkov, his closest friend: "I sit at home with fever and a severe cold in the head, and read Confucius for the second day. It is difficult to realize its extraordinary moral height."[1] In the last period of his life, Tolstoy suffered a deep religious crisis. In the late 1870s he decided to abandon his literary career and begin a quest for spirituality that sparked his interest in China. His interest grew from spirituality to other topics, such as politics. Tolstoy sympathized with China as a nation that had suffered the invasion of Western powers. His criticism of the Eight-Nation Alliance intervention in Beijing that put an end to the Boxer Uprising in 1900 was harsh. Tolstoy studied China until his death in 1910.

Tolstoy's library hosted fifty-four books, pamphlets, and periodicals related to the East. Of these, thirteen are directly related to China. Tolstoy's diaries and correspondence reveal, at least, twenty-six additional publications dealing with China that reached Tolstoy at one time or another.[2] Tolstoy's interest in China was particularly influenced by two books: Thomas Taylor Meadows's *The Chinese and Their Rebellions*, a work on Confucianism and the Chinese examination system published in 1856, and Eugène Simon's *La Cité chinoise* (The Chinese City), a hyperbolic—and controversial—account of the virtues of Chinese society published in 1885.[3] But Tolstoy became well acquainted with other works by prominent sinologists, such as Jean-Pierre Abel-Rémusat, Stanislas Julien, Guillaume Pauthier, and James Legge.[4] Tolstoy's library reveals two important features that characterize the knowledge about China in late nineteenth-century Europe, which frame the questions discussed in this chapter. First, any European intellectual had plenty of knowledge about China at hand—even if he lived in a rather peripheral location in Europe. Second, most of this easily available information about China was originated in pivotal European centers: of the thirty-nine publications on China read by Tolstoy, nineteen were written in English, ten in French, seven in Russian, and three in German.[5]

Tolstoy's interest in China was not an oddity. Tolstoy's library exemplifies a common interest in China across Europe at the end of the nineteenth century. Plenty of public and private libraries in London and Paris, Berlin and Torino, Moscow and Barcelona, hosted similar—or even greater—collections related to China. Like Xavier de Maistre's narrator in his memorable *Voyage autour de ma chambre* (Voyage around My Room, 1794), readers were learning about China without leaving the walls of their libraries. But de Maistre's parody was not a parody, after all: books and libraries were indeed the common geographies for encountering China. Tolstoy's library also shows how China was being imagined, understood, and discussed across Europe through sources mostly written in English and French. Relying on English and French sources to learn about China was an assumed practice that did not bear any negative connotation.

Such interest for and indirect access to China was shared in mid- and late nineteenth-century Spain. Foreign sinological works were occasionally translated into Spanish and published as translations.[6] Foreign sinological works were sometimes explicitly quoted by Spanish authors or summarized in articles that provided update reviews of what was being published or discussed in places such as England and France.[7] But, most commonly, knowledge about China was translated from English and French sources and disseminated into Spanish texts without mentioning its origin. Appropriations and imitations were common practices across Europe, particularly during the Romantic period. These were not considered plagiarism as long as there were substantial changes, such as amplifications, or a different emphasis.[8] Illustrated periodicals shared a similar process when publishing contents about China: pieces were first identified in English, French, or German journals and magazines and later copied, summarized, or adapted in pieces aimed at Spanish readers. These "new" pieces were usually not signed. Engravings were also copied and incorporated, often in pieces dissociated from the original context in which they had been published.[9] It is important to note that this modus operandi was not limited to those who wrote about a China that was more than five thousand miles east of their editorial offices in Barcelona or Madrid. Diplomats like Adolfo de Mentaberry (1840–1887), Enrique Gaspar (1842–1902), and Eduard Toda (1855–1941) who *did* travel to China and wrote profusely about their firsthand experiences also relied heavily on English and French sources that usually remained uncredited in their works.[10] Again, this was not a simple exercise of extraction and copy. Their books, articles, and talks implied diverse strategies of translation and adaptation.

See the case of Adolfo de Mentaberry. He had a very short stint as primer secretario at the Spanish legation in Beijing: he arrived in Beijing on November 3, 1869, but at the end of December he was called back to Madrid due to the serious financial crisis suffered by the government.[11] Back in Spain, he gathered his impressions in *Impresiones de un viaje a la China* (Impressions of a Travel to China), which was published in 1876. We do not know whether Mentaberry's library looked like Tolstoy's library. But we do know that Mentaberry wrote *Impresiones de un viaje a la China* while working at the well-stocked library of the State Department, "una de las mejores bibliotecas del país de la cual se servían los diplomáticos para preparar sus destinos" (one of the best libraries in the country, which was used by diplomats to prepare their destination posts).[12] Probably spurred by the frustration of having his career as a diplomat interrupted, Mentaberry seasoned the book with poignant critiques against the Spanish government: he lamented Spain's apathy, lack of political intelligence, and incapacity to build a strong presence in China.[13] Yet, other than these criticisms, *Impresiones de un viaje a la China* is the archetypical travel account penned by a European traveling to the East. Mentaberry shows the usual fascination for the geographies he sails through from Marseille to Hong Kong; the conventional doses of chinoiserie in describing the society and culture he encounters after landing in China; and the almost prototypical frustration at finding a China that is quite different from the China he had read about but that nonetheless does not obscure his Orientalist vision.[14]

Impresiones de un viaje a la China is also an archetypical example of the secondhand nature of the Spanish accounts of China. Mentaberry relied heavily on works by experts, particularly for the parts about Chinese history, society, and culture. He explicitly mentioned, or even quoted, most of them.[15] But he omitted other borrowings, such as Ludovic de Beauvoir's *Voyage autour du monde: Australie, Java, Siam, Canton, Pekin, Yeddo, San Francisco* (Voyage around the World: Australia, Java, Siam, Canton, Peking, Eddo, San Francisco), which had been published in three volumes—two in 1867 and one in 1872. A comparison between the two works shows many parallel passages, in which Mentaberry translated, adapted, and amplified de Beauvoir's account.[16] The China in Mentaberry's account—just as the China in the Spanish illustrated periodicals—was a China that had been previously published in another language—English or, mainly, French. This secondhand China reveals the hegemonies, agencies, and mechanisms of cross-cultural circulation in nineteenth-century European culture.

What concerns us primarily in this chapter are the wide-scale causes and effects of representing China in Spain in such an indirect way. In this chapter I show how the image of China in Spain in the late nineteenth century heavily depended on data, images, and perspectives taken from pivotal English and French sources and how these were adapted and projected through a variety of works and genres. We will see how the image of China in Spain relied on translation but was then reproduced in an array of forms that were not marked as translations themselves. I argue that, as a result from such a dependence on translation, the discourse on China that originated in the French and English colonial contexts was transplanted into the social imaginary of a Spain in crisis. The dependence on and the erasure of translation contributed to create the illusion of the West as a unified, coherent subject.

A follow-up question that we will also raise is: How do we incorporate the politics of this type of indirect representation—so common in the nineteenth century but still present, under different forms, in our present day—into a meaningful discussion of translation and cross-cultural interactions? Comparative literature and translation studies have mainly focused on the circulation of translated works and derivative issues such as authorship, mediation, or equivalence. However, as the examples discussed in the following pages will show, the focus on translated works may reveal insufficient and inadequate. The variety and complexity of actual cross-cultural interactions may overflow notions such as authorship, mediation, or equivalence. I therefore share with scholars like James St. André the need to rethink our object of study.[17] In this chapter—and in the rest of the book—I probe into the indirect, trialectical nature of cross-cultural interactions with the goal of encompassing their variety and complexity. I ultimately argue that it is only through a broader corpus of literary and cultural representations and a bottom-up methodology that accommodates the theoretical reflections to the empirical findings (and not the other way around) that we can find insight into the central question of this book: the processes by which the knowledge about China was projected and legitimized in different locations across the West.

To better understand the fundamental changes in the ways in which China was represented in Spain during the late nineteenth and early twentieth century, let us go back to the mid-nineteenth century and see how China was perceived in Europe and in Spain at that time.

SPAIN, CHINA, THE PHILIPPINES

The first global best seller about China was written in Spanish. Juan González de Mendoza's *Historia de las cosas más Notables, ritos y costumbres del gran Reyno de la China* (The History of the Great and Mighty Kingdom of China and the Situation Thereof) became "the most widely read general history of China" after its publication in Rome in 1585.[18] González de Mendoza's work, based on firsthand accounts by friars Gaspar de Cruz and Martin de Rada, had a large impact across Europe in the late sixteenth and seventeenth centuries.[19] But things had certainly changed by the mid-nineteenth century. Spain was not a hegemonic language in Europe, and China had permeated into both the intellectual and the popular culture spheres in Britain and France.[20] As James St. André writes in *Translating China*, "Just as Mendoza's work shaped seventeenth-century understanding of Chinese and was the main source for the various philosophical speculations about it, [Jean-Baptiste] Du Halde's *Description géographique, historique, chronologique, politique, et physique de l'empire de la Chine et de la Tartarie chinoise* (A Geographical, Historical, Chronological, Political, and Physical Description of the Empire of China and of Chinese Tartary, 1735) became the touchstone for eighteenth-century discussions of the language and all things Chinese more generally."[21] And the study of China was later systematized by the first scholars who were not part of the "scholarly missionaries."[22] Robert Morrison (1782–1834), Julius Klaproth (1783–1835), Jean-Pierre Abel-Rémusat, John Francis Davis (1795–1890), and Stanislas Julien made the knowledge about China more widely available across Europe in English, French, and (in fewer cases) German. In 1815 the Collège de France began teaching the Chinese language. The Société Asiatique and the Royal Asiatic Society of Great Britain and Ireland were established in 1822 and 1824. Scientific journals were founded around the same time: the *Asiatic Journal* in 1816, *Journal asiatique* in 1822, *Transactions of the Royal Asiatic Society of Great Britain and Ireland* in 1824. These scholarly developments turned into translations and essays that added to popular works that featured China in one way or another—texts with an outside Chinese observer such as Jean-Baptiste de Boyer Marquis d'Argens's *Lettres chinoises* (Chinese Letters, 1739–1740) or Oliver Goldsmith's *The Citizen of the World* (1762), or collections of Oriental fiction such as Thomas-Simon Gueullette's *Les Aventures merveilleuses du mandarin Fum-Hoam: Contes chinois* (The Marvelous Adventures of Mandarin Fum-Hoam: Chinese Tales, 1723).[23]

This increasing knowledge turned into polarized visions of China in Europe. The tension between sinophilia and sinophobia was the most important aspect that defined the representations of China before the changes we will examine in the following chapters. In the eighteenth century, China had been a model for philosophers such as Leibniz, Quesnay, and Voltaire, who had expressed their admiration for Chinese culture and for what they perceived as a secular society that could be an example for European Enlightenment. But the French Revolution weakened those accounts of fascination. In the nineteenth century, depictions of China as a decadent society became more prominent, and the understanding of China became more contemptuous. Negative images of China proliferated due to a combination of factors: the cult of chinoiserie—one of the foundations for sinophilia—decayed in the nineteenth century; the Opium Wars left China in a position of weakness in the 1840s; the complicity between racialist sinophobia and the imperialist drive turned China and the Chinese into an object of domination; merchants and missionaries traveled more freely across China and their experiences brought about new kinds of perceptions.[24]

In the mid-nineteenth century, the remnants of sinophilia were fiercely attacked by "an increasingly harsh series of portrayals of Chinese scheming, danger, unreliability, and viciousness."[25] In the nineteenth century, images such as Daniel Defoe's corrosive attacks on China in the second part of *Robinson Crusoe* (1719) and George Anson's travels during the 1740s became very popular across Europe. These negative visions of China circled back to philosophy too. The China in works such as

Johann Gottfried Herder's *Ideen zur Philosophie der Geschichte der Menschheit* (Outlines of a Philosophy of the History of Man), published between 1784 and 1791, and Hegel's lectures on the history of philosophy, given between 1805 and 1830, shows that, by the mid-nineteenth century, sinophobia had been systematized and had a certain intellectual depth as well.[26] These polarities will be eroded in the late nineteenth century, when as we will see, the types of representations of China will become more diverse and complex. But in the mid-nineteenth century these polarities, which James St. André has aptly characterized as whiteface and blackface, monopolized the ways of thinking about China in places like London, Paris, and Weimar.[27]

Were these general, polarized perceptions of China shared in Spain too? How similar and how different were the ways of imagining China in Spain from the ways China was imagined in these European contexts? To be sure, the scholarly study of China did not develop in Spain as it did in France and England in the mid-nineteenth century. At that time, we can't find any Spanish equivalent of the diplomats-turned-sinologists such as Morrison or Davis; nor can we find philologists-turned-sinologists such as Abel-Rémusat or Julien. A comparison between the scholarly works on China published in France and Spain in the first decades of the nineteenth century is striking.[28] As a result, these foreign scholarly works fixed the discourses on China that would remain dominant even when, as we will see, Spanish diplomats started writing about China on the basis of their firsthand experiences in the late nineteenth century.

The lack of a Spanish scholarship on China did not prevent a general interest in China in Spain that was both created and satisfied through English and French publications. The cultural and literary developments in Spain were very much dependent on the importation of English and, particularly, French works and literary trends. As Elisa Martí-López has argued, "in the mid-nineteenth century all commercial publishing resources were invested in promoting and disseminating the French novel in Spain." The French novel, and by extension the French literary trends, "saturated the Spanish literary market and determined the habits and expectations of Spanish readers."[29] This movement influenced the representations of China in Spain too. Frequent references to China appeared in Spanish illustrated periodicals, for instance. Siwen Ning has offered a meticulous analysis of how China was present in major journals during the mid- and late nineteenth century and how these journals relied on pieces previously published in English and French periodicals.[30] In *Semanario Pintoresco Español* and *El Museo Universal*, for instance, China was the Asian country that received the most extensive coverage.[31] While articles were initially focused on traditional and picturesque aspects and displayed Orientalist images of China, events such as the Opium Wars or the world's fairs added new interests in current affairs and a new kind of scientific attention.

While, as I will argue later, there was a common underlying epistemology in Spain, England, and France that allowed these imported images of China to fit naturally in the Spanish context, these kinds of cross-cultural, cross-linguistic movements occasionally produced significant variations. The translation of Joseph Méry's *Anglais et Chinois* (English and Chinese) into Spanish offers a case in point.[32] *Anglais et Chinois*, originally published in French in 1843, is a light tale about the adventures of Melford, a young English sailor, in Canton. The novel mainly treats China as a foil. Set in 1806, the plot includes some details about Chinese culture and society but mostly centers on Melford's ability to remain faithful to his wife (and children) in England while he runs into all sorts of unexpected adventures in China. *Anglais et Chinois* is a vivid work that includes some satirical images of England and the English coming from a witty French author. Yet in the Spanish translation of Méry's novel, *Ingleses y chinos*, China is not a simple foil and taken more seriously than in the French original.

Anglais et Chinois was translated into Spanish by the painter Ramon Martí i Alsina, who remains uncredited.[33] Martí i Alsina supplemented his translation with a fifteen-page appendix with twenty-nine endnotes related to China and Chinese culture. He declares that he felt compelled to add this information that was not present in the original due to the lack of reliable, scholarly knowledge about China in Spain. This knowledge includes superfluous information about topics such as rice, for instance, and information about controversial topics such as infanticide.[34] Martí i Alsina explicitly mentions two works that he used as the main sources for these additions: Auguste Wahlen's *Moeurs, usages et costumes de tous les peuples du monde* (Manners, Uses, and Costumes of All the Peoples of the World, 1843) and Dumont d'Urville's *Viaje pintoresco alrededor del mundo* (A Picturesque Journey around the World, 1841) and he quotes extensively from them.[35] He occasionally mentions Clément Pellé, Abel-Rémusat, and Davis as well. As a result, Méry's text in Spanish becomes more "sinified" than in its French original. These additions were even publicized on the book's cover: "Ingleses y chinos. Novela histórica escrita por Mery. Seguida de algunas notas históricas añadidas por el Traductor" ("English and Chinese. Historical novel written by Méry. Followed by some historical notes added by the Translator"). *Ingleses y chinos* illustrates not only the interest in China and the concern for reliable information on China in Spain but also—and especially—how the systemic dependence on foreign sources to fulfill this interest could even change the kind of images of China introduced to Spanish readers.

The only Spanish work (written by a Spaniard and published in Spain) in the mid-nineteenth century that deals specifically with China and remains unaffected by the influence of English or French sources was written from the Philippines. Luis Prudencio Álvarez y Tejero, who never set foot in China, wrote *Reseña histórica del gran imperio de China* (Historical Review of the Great Empire of China) in Manila, where he worked as a lawyer for fourteen years.[36] The book was published in Madrid in 1857 and was sold by subscription—a method that also testifies to the emerging interest in China in mid-nineteenth-century Spanish society.[37] Álvarez y Tejero's goal was to fulfill the general interest for China in Spain by writing a book accessible for a wide readership—beyond the specific circles of missionaries and diplomats. Unlike the translator of Méry's novel and unlike the examples we will encounter in the following sections and chapters, Álvarez y Tejero did not rely on foreign sources to write *Reseña histórica del gran imperio de China*. He does often refer to previous works, which he quotes directly without revealing the original source.[38] But neither English nor French sources are explicitly quoted and there are no traces (such as the transliteration of Chinese names) that he relied on them.

Interestingly, however, Álvarez y Tejero's access to China was equally indirect. He tells us how his own experience in Manila put him in "contacto directo con testimonios presenciales de la evolución del imperio chino" (direct contact with eyewitness accounts of the evolution of the Chinese empire), who provided what he considers direct sources:

> Las noticias todas están tomadas en su mayor parte de los mismos chinos, de misioneros que han predicado el Evangelio, algunos años en aquellos países y remotas regiones, y de algun particular viagero que ha pisado algunos puntos del imperio empero que todos los datos adquiridos en esta forma han sido rectificados con repeticion, interrogando muchas veces detenidamente sobre ellos á los chinos que residen en Manila, teniendo despues el ímprobo trabajo y paciencia necesaria de formar, cotejar y repetir apuntes . . . (10)

> *The information is all taken for the most part from Chinese themselves, from missionaries who have preached the Gospel for some years in those countries and remote regions, and from a few travelers who have trodden some parts of the empire. Thus all the data acquired in such a way has been verified repeatedly, carefully interrogating many times the Chinese residing in Manila. Afterward I have had the hard work and patience necessary to form, collate and repeat notes . . .*

Reseña histórica del gran imperio de China reveals two important aspects for our purposes. First, Spain's colonial presence in the Philippines naturalized the indirect ways of learning about China. Álvarez y Tejero himself acknowledges how Spain's colonial presence in the Philippines enabled the gathering of his sources (9). The Philippines was considered a reliable proxy—a transition zone, part of Spain but also part of China, where firsthand experiences in China could be turned into reliable secondhand accounts that kept their legitimacy as genuine and authentic. This, however, had certain limitations. Álvarez y Tejero mentions the limitations of not being a "testigo ocular" (eyewitness [221]) and of such indirect contact with China. He confesses the many contradictions and confusions about China that can be found in sources and witnesses (8). He therefore does not promise to explain "the true China," but a China as exact as possible, a knowledge "al menos muy aproximado á la verdad" (at least very close to the truth [9]). His words reveal a concern for authenticity, but at the same time, an acceptance of the impossibility to reach it given the indirect access. As a result, current events are excluded from the discussion and China is, in a way, removed from the present: "Tratar de esto [acontecimientos actuales en China] seria sobradamente prematura, y tanto mas, cuanto que no tenemos noticias exactas y fidedignas de tales sucesos. . . . nuestro relato no va á entrar ahora en nada de los acontecimientos presentes" (To deal with this [the current events in China] would be far too premature. Even more so since we do not have exact and reliable news of such events. . . . our story will not go now into any of the current events [5]). In other words, given the indirect access to China, China is relegated to the past and to be only partially understood. Johannes Fabian's proverbial denial of coevalness is therefore produced here not only through the equivalent of an anthropological representation but also by an explicit acknowledgment of a deflected approach.[39]

Second, besides facilitating the gathering of sources, Spain's colonial presence in the Philippines had a deeper impact for representing China. Spain's colonial presence in the Philippines enabled a colonial (even if indirect) vision of China that was epistemologically similar to the colonial vision of China that emerged from English and French metropolitan centers. It seems plausible to assume that, given Spain's willingness to see the East as a colony, the visions of China held in European metropolises at the time found easy accommodation in the Spanish context. On the pages of *Reseña histórica del gran imperio de China*, China is described in ways that do not differ much from other English or French works of the same period. Without relying on English and French sources, Álvarez y Tejero juxtaposes the same polarized visions of China that were dominant in England and France. On the one hand, China is praised for its history, geographical extension, and degree of urbanization; for its meritocracy, education, and civil service; and for its morality, laws, and ethical principles. On the other hand, China is criticized for an underdeveloped science, an excess of ceremonies and courtesy protocols, and its geographical isolationism. Chinese people are described as greedy and submissive. They are often described in an animalized way and under a strong racialized discourse that would later evolve into Spanish versions of the yellow peril, which was also understood through the Philippines connection.[40] To be sure, these coincidences could be explained by the fact that many of these images of China go back to texts by European missionaries that were equally available in Spain and in other European contexts. However, my point is that centuries later we can still find a shared colonial view toward the East that sustains this imagery in a new geopolitical context. For Álvarez y Tejero, "Europe" is the actual point of reference or contrast with China. Sentences like "No se ven en China los estensos cercados que tenemos en Europa" (We don't see in China the large, fenced enclosures that we have in Europe [102]) are quite common throughout the depictions of China's geography and products. References to Spain, or even to the Philippines, are much less frequent.[41] This framework explains some of the features we will find in the texts discussed here.

If the images of China in Spain in the mid- and late nineteenth century were mostly imported from English and French sources (as shown by the translation of Méry's novel) and were embedded in a propensity to consider the East as a colony (facilitated by the Philippines, as shown by Álvarez y Tejero's book), the question that naturally follows from this is: What happened after 1898, then?

On May 5, 1898, Lord Salisbury famously declared that "one can roughly divide the nations of the world into the living and the dying."[42] Salisbury's speech echoed all over the Spanish media.[43] Social Darwinism had arrived into international geopolitics and it was clear on which side Spain was. Spain's geopolitical position in the late nineteenth century experienced a traumatic shift. The loss of Cuba and the Philippines in the summer of 1898 did not really have economic consequences, since the cost of the war was absorbed by repatriations and the keeping of export activity.[44] The psychological impact, however, was enormous. The loss of the colonies might have been expected but not at such a fast pace.[45] In May, the Spanish navy lost the battle at Cavite; in July, Spanish soldiers surrendered in Cuba; over the summer, harbors and train stations across Spain were filled with returning soldiers, "una impresión penosa que se convirtió en la imagen más cercana y visible de la derrota" (a painful impression that became the closest and most visible image of defeat).[46]

Why did the images of China written around 1898 and onward remain consistent with the images of China in Europe—even if Spain had a different geopolitical position in Asia and in the world?

To be sure, Spaniards' imperial mindset did not change so quickly. And if Spanish colonialism in the Philippines had enabled a colonial look toward China and the East, it could also be argued that keeping that colonial mindset *after* 1898 was a way of facing the actual loss of colonial power. Qing Ai has qualified this mindset as "imperial nostalgia."[47] She has shown how cross-cultural interactions with China (in travel writing, for instance) kept the colonial outlook alive— while, of course, in more complex or ambivalent ways. These answers clearly fit within Josep Fradera's insightful argument on the "imperial nations" and, as I mentioned in the introduction, on the historical process through which empires reshaped themselves while modern nations emerged.[48] Yet I still find these answers based on the continuity of the imperial mindset insufficient. In the following sections (and chapters) I provide a supplementary answer that focuses on the imported nature of these images of China and excavates the material and discursive realities underlying such permanent colonial attitudes toward China held by Spanish writers and intellectuals. In the late nineteenth and early twentieth century, China becomes "la cuestión palpitante, el asunto del día" (the burning question, the topic of the day).[49] Even if appeals to ignorance and lack of knowledge about China were tropes conventionally used to enhance the interest of many pieces, current political affairs in China were examined on hundreds of pages on a daily basis. Chinese cultural aspects were featured prominently as well. Yet the extensive coverage of China in Spain continued relying mostly on English and French sources.

VIAJE A CHINA AND EL ANACRONÓPETE

Late nineteenth-century diplomats were probably the main projectors of images of China in Europe. When the general understanding of China became so dependent upon imperialism and geopolitical Darwinism, diplomats' visions emerged as particularly relevant. The diplomat assembled and put into practical terms the concerns of the philosopher, the missionary, and the businessman. These "part-time" or "hyphenated" official-sinologists, "who stole time from their regular duties to introduce the China they knew to the West," guaranteed the coverage of all the new concerns: institutional, economic, cultural, and religious.[50] Their visions and accounts shaped the creation of images of China that were later disseminated in popular literature and other cultural forms.

Spain never had a solid diplomatic presence in China in the mid-nineteenth century, despite the opening of its first general consulate in 1853 and despite the fascinating figure of Sinibaldo de Mas (1809–1868). Mas actively participated in several diplomatic missions, opened the Spanish legation in Beijing in 1864, and ended up working as an agent for the Zongli Yamen—the department in charge of foreign policy for the Qing Empire.[51] Mas wrote extensively about China in French. His works reached Spain and acquired a certain prestige, particularly among diplomatic circles. But he was an isolated figure until the end of the nineteenth century, when other diplomats such as Eduard Toda, Juan Mencarini (1860–1939), Luis Valera (1870–1926), and Fernando de Antón del Olmet (1872–1955) started writing about China in Spanish on the basis of their firsthand experiences. These writings had a wider circulation.

Enrique Gaspar was one of such diplomats. A child of actor parents, Gaspar had the ambition of becoming a professional writer and playwright. But in 1869 he joined the Spanish diplomatic corps in need of a regular income to support his family. Gaspar was initially posted to southern France and Greece, where he continued his writing career. In

1878 he was appointed Spanish consul in China, and he served in Macau and Hong Kong until 1884.[52] Like many diplomats, Gaspar wrote about his experiences in China. Unlike most of them, Gaspar wrote about his experiences in China in two extremely different genres: travel writing and science fiction. On the one hand, *Viaje a China* (Travel to China) is a conventional travel account originally published in the newspaper *Las Provincias* between 1878 and 1882. In this work Gaspar gathers his thoughts about the journey to China and about several social and cultural aspects of China that he encounters upon his arrival. On the other hand, *El anacronópete* (The Time Ship) is a science-fiction novel that, written in 1881 and published in 1887, predates H. G. Wells's well-known *The Time Machine* by almost a decade.[53] In this work a group of characters travel across time and space in a machine that takes them back to, among other places, China during the Han dynasty in the third century. In 1887 *Viaje a China* and *El anacronópete* were compiled in a single heterogeneous volume that also includes a third piece, *Metempsicosis* (Metempsychosis), which is unrelated to China.[54] The three pieces form a collection about travel across humanity: fictional travel across time, real travel across space, and a more metaphysical kind of travel.[55]

Viaje a China and *El anacronópete* provide a perfect example of how the image of China was disseminated across a variety of works and genres in late nineteenth-century Spain. They also illustrate an important shift in the origin of the sources that were supporting those images of China. Thirty years after Luis Prudencio Álvarez y Tejero's *Reseña histórica del gran imperio de China*, the sources that feed the increasing presence of China in Spanish publications are different. To be sure, travel to China becomes less exceptional and personal experiences turn into an obvious important source. But, as we will see, these firsthand experiences are negotiated with secondhand sources that remain as important as before—or even more so.

In the late nineteenth century, works from the first generations of laic and/or professional sinologists such as Morrison, Klaproth, Abel-Rémusat, Julien, and Pauthier became available and reached a wider circulation in Spain. Yet these new works did not substitute the old works by the scholarly missionaries. In fact, many of the old works still remained mentioned—and their authority therefore renovated—in mid-nineteenth-century encyclopedic works that became important in later decades. Works such as Cesare Cantù's *Storia universale* (Universal History, originally published between 1840 and 1847, translated into

French between 1845 and 1854, and into Spanish—by the same publisher who published Gaspar's works—in 1854) and Pierre Larousse's *Grand Dictionnaire universel du XIXe siècle* (Great Universal Dictionary of the 19th century, published between 1866 to 1876) exemplify this mixture in the references to China.[56] On the one hand, these encyclopedic volumes include references to works by scholarly missionaries like Jean-Baptiste Du Halde (1674–1743), Jean-Joseph-Marie Amiot (1718–1793), and Pierre-Martial Cibot (1727–1780). On the other hand, they incorporate references to newer works by Morrison, Abel-Rémusat, Julien, and Pauthier.

It is probably safe to assume that, as a frequent visitor to libraries, clubs, and scientific societies in Hong Kong and Macau, Enrique Gaspar had an easy access to the knowledge gathered in all these works—even before they reached Spain. He refers to the British and their clubs, salons, and reading rooms, where he could find "todos los periódicos notables del mundo y una biblioteca rica en obras sobre la China" (all the world's important newspapers and a library rich in works about China [266]). *Viaje a China* and *El anacronópete* make intensive use of these materials, and, in fact, Gaspar reveals some of his sources. For instance, in *Viaje a China* he clarifies that it would be too long to describe the style of a certain ceremony and therefore "haremos un resumen de lo que el historiador Cantù y otros sinólogos cuentan sobre el particular; advirtiendo de paso que estos usos siguen practicándose hoy en China casi en absoluto, pues sabido es que el estacionamiento constituye la base de su carácter" (We will summarize what the historian Cantù and other sinologists tell about this topic; we will note in passing that these uses are still followed in China today almost without exception, since it is well known that stagnation is the basis of the Chinese character [121–2]). Gaspar borrows heavily from Cantù, both directly (121, 374) and indirectly—from Cantù he quotes works from other scholars such as Giambatista Pedranzini da Bormio (108). Gaspar also borrows heavily from Stanislas Julien (129–31), Julius Klaproth (355), and Ernst Behm and Hermann Wagner's *Die Bevölkerung der Erde* (World Population), whose China data are taken from Armand David (354).[57] On other occasions Gaspar acknowledges relying on sources but does not reveal them. For instance, when discussing China's finances, Gaspar states that he is relying on English accounts since the English are "los más versados en la contabilidad china" (the most knowledgeable in China's data [354]). And on other occasions Gaspar incorporates the information from his sources without any kind of acknowledgment. Passages on graphology, for instance, are based on Juan Bautista Carrasco's *Mitología universal* (Universal Mythology), which used works by figures such as Nicolas Trigault (1577–1628), Du Halde, and Joseph de Guignes (1721–1800) as sources (296), but these sources remain mostly uncredited.[58]

Such transitions between explicit and implicit references, acknowledged and unacknowledged sources, appropriations and rewritings, were not Gaspar's idiosyncratic choices. These were quite common in writings about China. We can find similar tendencies in other Spanish diplomats who wrote about China around the same time such as Fernando Garrido (1821–1883), Adolfo de Mentaberry, Eduard Toda, and Luis Valera. While "during the eighteenth century, a gradual heightened awareness of issues regarding authenticity emerged" and the modern sense of authorship was formed between 1750 and 1800,[59] these Spanish writings on China did not seem to raise any suspicion. In fact, the Spanish writings about China in the late nineteenth century seem to confirm Elisa Martí-López's analysis of Spanish popular literature in the mid-nineteenth century when "translation, imitation, and original writing were diffuse practices" and "their boundaries blurred by a practice of loose translation and original writing that constituted itself as a free reworking and reformulation of foreign (particularly French) materials."[60]

At the same time, however, authorship was an important issue in some writings on China. Emilia Pardo Bazán (1851–1921) is a case in point, as she was publicly accused of having plagiarized a classical Chinese tale. Pardo Bazán, who became interested in China and Japan due to her connections with European, particularly French, literary circles,[61] wrote two short stories set in China and inspired by Chinese classical tales. "Agravante" (Aggravating Circumstance, 1892) is a version of the classical "Zhuangzi Tests His Wife," first collected in seventeenth-century editions, some of them edited by author and compiler Feng Menglong (1574–1646). "El templo" (The Temple, 1901) is a free adaptation of empress Wu Zetian's biography (625–705).[62] "Agravante" was first published in *Nuevo Teatro Crítico* in March 1892 and later republished in *El Liberal* on August 30 of the same year. On the very same day that the story was republished, Juan Fraile Miguélez (under the pen name of Fray Juan de Miguel) accused Pardo Bazán of having plagiarized the story from Voltaire's *Zadig ou la destinée* (Zadig; or, the Book of Fate). The accusation was published in an open letter in *La Unión Católica*. Pardo Bazán replied with vehemence. The story, she argued, was in fact originally taken from Abel-Rémusat's *Contes chinois* (Chinese Tales) and was now almost universal currency:

Pero no es allí [en Abel-Rémusat] únicamente donde existe la tal historia, pues con sólo abrir (¡recóndita erudición!) el *Gran Diccionario Universal de Larousse*, que forma parte integrante del mobiliario de las redacciones, hubiese visto . . . que esa historieta es conocida en todas las literaturas bajo el título de *La matrona de Efeso*, y que igualmente se encuentra en la India, en la China, en la antigüedad clásica y en la inmensa mayoría de los modernos cuentistas, que dramática y sentenciosa entre los chinos, ha tomado en otras naciones, en boca de los narradores de *flabliaux* y en Apuleyo, Boccaccio, La Fontaine y Voltaire, sesgo festivo y burlón; y añade el socorrido *Diccionario*: "Esta ingeniosa sátira de la inconstancia femenil parece tan natural y verdadera, que se diría que brotó espontáneamente en la imaginación de todo cuentista, y no hay que recurrir a la imitación para explicar tan singular coincidencia."

De estas laboriosas investigaciones se desprende que el cuento es tan de Voltaire como mío, e hicimos bien Anatole France y yo en repartírnoslo según nos plugo, y hasta pude ahorrarme la declaración de su procedencia. En efecto, por mi parte, para remozar esa historia, no la he leído en Voltaire ni en ningún autor moderno, sino en la misma colección de [Abel-Rémusat,] *Cuentos chinos*; y estoy cierta de que mi versión se diferencia bastante de las demás.

Si entrase en mis principios dar por mío lo ajeno, o sea gato por liebre, no juzgo difícil la empresa. Claro está que yo no había de ser tan inocente que ejercitase el instinto de rapiña en lo que cada quisque conoce—o debe conocer por lo menos, pues se dan casos, y si no ahí está el descubrimiento de *La Unión*—. Sobran libros arrumbados: el que quiera tener algo bien oculto, que lo guarde en uno de estos libros.[63]

But it is not there [in Abel-Rémusat] only where such a story exists. Just by opening (oh hidden erudition!) the Grand Larousse, *which is now part and parcel of any newsroom's furnishing, he would have seen . . . that this little story is well known in all literatures under the title of* The Widow of Ephesus, *and that it can also be found in India, in China, in classical antiquity, and in the vast majority of modern storytellers. This dramatic and sententious story for the Chinese has taken a festive and mocking bias in other nations, on the lips of the narrators of fabliaux and in Apuleius, Boccaccio, La Fontaine, and Voltaire. The handy Dictionary adds: "This ingenious satire of feminine fickleness seems so natural and true that it would seem that it spontaneously arose in the imagination of every storyteller, and one does not have to resort to imitation to explain such a singular coincidence."*

From these arduous investigations it follows that the story is as much Voltaire's as it is mine. And that Anatole France and I did well to distribute it according to what we wanted. And that I could even have spared myself the disclosing of its origin. Indeed, for my part, to revive that story I have not read it in Voltaire or in any modern author, but in the same collection of [Abel-Rémusat's] Chinese Tales; and I am certain that my version is quite different from others'.

If it were among my principles to claim as mine what is foreign to me, that is, to pull the wool over people's eyes, it would not be very difficult to do so. Of course, I would not be so innocent as to exercise the instinct of rapine in what every knowledgeable person already knows—or must know at least, because there are exceptions, such as the discovery made by La Unión. There are plenty of rumpled books: whoever wants to have something well hidden, just keep it in one of these books.

As it was expected, the controversy followed (Fraile Miguélez insisted, Leopoldo Alas accused Pardo Bazán of being too arrogant and ridiculed her justifications) and then faded away and remained a small anecdote in Pardo Bazán's intense social life and literary career.[64] But the controversy helps us to be more specific on the question of plagiarism and authority in relation to China as a topic. The controversy not only shows how knowledgeable *literatos* were about China (i.e., *Don't fool us!*), how available sources on China were (i.e., *Just check up your Larousse!*) or how easy it was to borrow from them. The controversy also shows that, while plagiarism (or generous borrowing) in relation to China may have been common and socially acceptable, it was noticed indeed. And that acceptability could be broken when it collided with literary prestige. Significantly, unlike Pardo Bazán, diplomats including Enrique Gaspar, Adolfo de Mentaberry, Eduard Toda, and Luis Valera were never accused of having plagiarized contents related to China. It was acceptable to borrow, adapt, and rewrite about China if you were a diplomat or if you were writing a scholarly work that was supposed to be reliable and exact. It was not if you were a "serious" literary author writing a sophisticated piece—which required a more honest acknowledgment of sources—as we will also see in chapter 4 in the case of Catalan poets translating classical Chinese poetry. In other words, the symbolic value of an original knowledge about China was inferior to the symbolic value of literary originality.

Let us go back to Enrique Gaspar's works. What kind of China do all these sources create in *Viaje a China* and *El anacronópete*? How is China represented within all these mechanisms? A quick look at the volume that collected both works in 1887 readily notices Francesc Gómez Soler's exoticist cover and illustrations, which suggest an exoticist attitude toward China.[65] The content of both pieces expands on this impression.

Viaje a China is a set of eleven letters written between September 1878 and December 1882 in Macau.[66] The letters are addressed to the editor of *Las Provincias* and were published in this journal before being collected as a book. The series is pure convention. It opens conventionally: Gaspar leaves from Marseille in Vapor Tigris on August 11, 1878, and arrives in China after thirty-eight days of travel. And it moves conventionally across all sorts of cultural and social aspects observed by Gaspar. Conventional descriptions include traditions such as weddings, burials, lantern festivals (310), fireworks (314), medicine and healers (310), and new year rituals (307); political issues such as coolie migration (272), the Manchus, the Manchu invasion and government structures (259, 356), political factions, and secret societies (356); topics in culture and education such as Chinese language (296), officials (338), and imperial examinations (276); and more domestic topics such as maids and servants (280–81), housing, and tea.

Throughout these descriptions, China is essentially portrayed as a backward culture. Chinese people are frequently animalized: "seres que parecen monstruos salidos del Averno. . . . Los niños . . . tienen el aspecto de monos; como el simio, rechinan los dientes, y como él tienen los pies y las manos aplastadas, y muy largas las falanges" (creatures that look like monsters out of the underworld. . . . Children . . . look like monkeys; they grind their teeth like apes, and also like apes, they have crushed feet and hands, and very long phalanges [243]). Gaspar considers Chinese people the epitome of ugliness: "De la raza macaense no sé qué decirte para darte una idea de su fealdad. . . . Imagínate un bull-dog con vestimentas humanas, y no te quedas atrás" (I do not know what to say about the Macanese race to give you an idea of its ugliness. . . . Just imagine a bull-dog in human clothing and you will not be much far from it [271]). A description (reinforced by a drawing on the next page) of a naked Chinese man, wearing only a pair of glasses, squatting above a barrel while reading the *Times*, epitomizes the double perspective from which China and the Chinese are exhibited: Chinese people are mysterious objects ready to be scientifically explained, and China makes futile—even ridiculous—efforts to overcome its own backwardness and reach Western modernity (252–53). Animalization goes hand in hand with a uniformity that erases the differences between men and women: "el chino es el ser que bajo una misma terminación y artículo comprende los dos sexos, masculino y femenino" (the Chinese is the being that, under the same ending and article, comprises the two sexes, male and female [258]); between cities: "El que haya visto una población china las conoce todas; su construcción es idéntica" (Anyone who has seen a Chinese city knows them all; its structure is identical [341]); and even between social classes, unlike everywhere else in the world, where you can distinguish someone from a high social class from someone from a low social class: "aquí no; todos son iguales . . . son ejemplares del mismo cliché" (it is not the case here; they are all the same . . . they are copies of the same cliché [280]). Backwardness is reinforced through dirt and uncleanliness. Sampans have a "toldo de bambú en la popa, chorreando mugre por todas partes y exhalando una fetidez insoportable . . . el perfume local, conocido por el europeo con el nombre genérico de 'olor de chino'" (bamboo hood at the stern, dripping dirt everywhere and exhaling an unbearable stench . . . the local perfume, known to Europeans by the generic name of "Chinese smell" [257]). Actresses are "bien vestidas y mejor peinadas (pero nunca limpias)" (well dressed and better groomed [but never clean] [350]).

The result of such combination of uniformity, animalization, and uncleanliness is a moral condemnation: "Este es el Cantón típico: miseria, basura, abyección" (This is the typical Canton: misery, garbage, abjection [344]). Opium addiction, gambling, ancient morals, and sexual discrimination are frequently criticized. Opium and opium dens are described in detail (940) as well as the government's efforts to fight them through taxes. "Sus efectos son espantosos" (Its effects are appalling) and "sus efectos son la atrofia y sus consecuencias la imbecilidad" (its effects are atrophy and its consequences are imbecility [334]). Gambling is also depicted in detail. Gaspar describes the vaisen (*weixing* in

Mandarin Chinese, lit. "surname guessing"), a gambling practice played in Macau that is based on betting about which candidates will pass or fail the imperial exams.[67] This game creates all sorts of irregular behaviors, as money is offered to examiners to fail certain candidates or to candidates to fail on purpose (275–76). Bound feet are a "bárbara costumbre" (barbarian custom [278]) and "la confusión de ambos sexos es degradante para el fuerte, que ve en la madre de sus hijos una esclava y no una compañera" (the confusion of both sexes is degrading for the strong one, who sees the mother of his children as a slave and not a companion [329]).

To be sure, these were all conventional criticisms. *Viaje a China* is also very conventional as it remains on the surface of landscapes and impressions. Gaspar's attention goes from here to there without fully engaging in the scenes he is describing. In fact, he openly praises superficiality as an aesthetic experience: "Siempre que puedo, me limito a la superficie, sin meterme en honduras, convencido de que la ilusión es más bella que la realidad" (Whenever I can, I limit myself to the surface, without going into depth, convinced as I am that illusion is more beautiful than reality [227]). He invites his readers to remain within "una función de fantasmagoría sin alardes de erudición" (a performance of phantasmagoria without any boast of scholarship [227]). Yet this kind of shallow travel writing is not innocent as it transforms the aesthetic into the political. Shallow travel writing combines vehement statements with moral condemnations. Shallow travel writing also differentiates Gaspar as a subject placed in the present from China as an object placed in a past that is both mystical and underdeveloped.

El anacronópete is a much less conventional work, even if it is also a work of its time. It was written in 1881 and published in 1887, just when "all commercial publishing resources were invested in promoting and disseminating the French novel in Spain" and when "the French novel saturated the Spanish literary market and determined the habits and expectations of Spanish readers."[68] The plot could very well have been imagined by Camille Flammarion or Jules Verne, two writers who were extremely popular in Spain at the time. Don Sindulfo García is a scientist who has invented the "anacronópete," a machine that can navigate across time and space. Don Sindulfo and a few friends (young Benjamín; Don Sindulfo's niece, Clara; Clara's maid, Juana; a dozen French prostitutes; and a squadron of Spanish hussars) enter this iron squared box and go back in time in search for different goals: Don Sindulfo's real motivation for having invented the machine is to move back to a period of history when it is socially acceptable to marry his own niece; the prostitutes and the hussars also want to live in more permissive times; Benjamín wants to find the key to eternal life. They travel from the Exposition Universelle in Paris in 1878 to the Battle of Tétouan in 1860, to the cities of Granada in 1492 and Ravena in 690, and further back to China in 220, Pompeii in 79, and the year 3000 B.C. The machine explodes when it reaches the day when God created the world. In spite of the imaginative creation of the time machine, then, the plot does not unfold according to scientific parameters. Traveling to different places provides an exotic landscape where the romantic relations between the Don Sindulfo and his friends develop, and their behaviors are satirized. Under the foil of a science fiction novel lies a work in three acts closer to a zarzuela or an operetta—genres that Gaspar had actually cultivated as an author himself.[69]

Travel to China takes place in act 2. Don Sindulfo and his friends arrive in China during the year 220 and spend forty-eight hours there. They ask for an audience with the emperor. Their depictions of the imperial palace and other places are full of fascination and recall Marco Polo's accounts. They ask the emperor to share with them the principle of immortality, which, according to them, has been discovered in China. But the emperor believes they are members of a dangerous Chinese sect. To prove their true Western origins, they show him "una pequeña muestra de los progresos operados por la civilización en los diez y seis siglos que nos separan" (a small sample of the progress made by civilization in the sixteen centuries that separate us [126–27]). The emperor then falls in love with Clara, and the travelers have to escape in a hurry. The anacronópete then stops working, but after a few moments of suspense, they finally make it work and move further back to Pompeii to keep searching for the formula of immortality.

Traveling back to a mythical past sets China as the object of fascination for its cultural legacy. Han China is described as a terrain where a battle is taking place between Laozi's metaphysics (shared by society at large) and Confucius's morality (shared by scholars and officials). There are also references to Buddhism, Nestorianism, and political rebellions. This ample context, which interrupts the characters' actions every now and then, is provided to the reader as "necessary" background information (105) to understand the social and political tensions encountered by the characters when they arrive at a court that, after General Cao Cao's failed attempt to unify China, is now ruled by the mandarins. Similarly, inventions such as the compass, bombs, and fireworks are

stressed as Chinese inventions discovered even before European sinologists' calculations (129). Benjamín then makes sure to mention that
pride makes Europeans unwilling to accept that these inventions were
discovered in ancient China (129). In sum, China is represented as a
great empire in the third century that has been unable to adjust to the
progress of history. Going back in time reinforces the idea that China
has remained in the year 220 forever. Visiting China from the future
proves Herder and Hegel right: China has indeed been stagnated in
the past. The China of the present is not very much different from the
China of the past. "La Europa del siglo XIX ante la China del siglo III"
(Nineteenth-Century Europe against Third-Century China), the title of
chapter 13, makes the contrast even more explicit.

Interestingly, despite their obvious thematic differences, *El anacronópete* and *Viaje a China* share a similar formal structure and a similar approach to China. Don Sindulfo and his friends move across Han
China just as Gaspar moved across late-Qing China. Their adventures
are often punctuated with excursuses on multiple aspects related to Chinese history and society. These are typically introduced with expressions
such as "Un poco de erudición fastidiosa aunque necesaria" (A little
tedious though necessary erudition [105]) and followed by long explanations taken—quoted, adapted, plagiarized—from the sources mentioned previously.[70] Out of these parenthetical disquisitions emerges a
scattered, superficial, impressionistic representation of China. This formal structure also projects an anthropological gaze toward China and
the Chinese. By moving freely along different chronologies (past, present, and future) but placing China always in the past, *Viaje a China* and
El anacronópete impose an allochronic vision of China that denies the
simultaneous existence of Gaspar and the China he is witnessing and
writing about.[71]

This allochronic representation of China activates the typical tension
between the real China experienced by the traveler in the present and
the mythical China of the past he has read about. Indeed, this is an overarching topic that runs through the different chapters of *Viaje a China*:

> Cuando desde Europa se le ocurre a uno pensar en China, se
> la representa en su imaginación como una inmensa tela de
> esos abanicos que llegan allí del Celeste Imperio. Por lo me-
> nos así me la forjaba yo. . . . Cerremos el abanico y abramos
> la puerta del hoy imperio tártaro. Vas a ver el desengaño que
> nos espera. (256)

When someone from Europe comes to think about China, it is represented in his imagination as an immense cloth from those fans that arrive to Europe from the Celestial Empire. At least that's how I forged the image of China for myself. . . . Let us close the fan and open the door of the present Tatar empire. You will see the disappointment that awaits us.

Aquello no es China; las casas que veo son las de mis latitudes, la gente con coleta que circula por las calles es la hez del pueblo uniformemente vestida, y yo necesito la tela del abanico, los colores, la luz, el recamo de oro, los bordados en seda, el Oriente, en fin, con sus mandarines, sus tropas, sus mujeres, su industria, sus diversiones, su vida peculiar. (263)

That is not China; the houses that I see are those of my latitudes, the people with pigtails who circulate through the streets are the scum of the town uniformly dressed, and I need the fabric from the fan, the colors, the light, the golden patch, the silk embroideries, the East, in short, with its mandarins, its troops, its women, its industry, its amusements, its peculiar life.

¡Horror! ¡Abominación! ¿Y para esto he empleado treinta y ocho días y me he expuesto a las contingencias de un viaje de tres mil leguas? . . . En vano sería buscar en Hong-Kong la tan deseada tela del abanico. (268)

Horror! Abomination! And for this I have spent thirty-eight days and exposed myself to the contingencies of a journey of three thousand leagues? . . . It would be in vain to search Hong Kong for the much-desired fabric of the fan.

What is interesting for our purposes is the clash—and hierarchy—of authorities that emerges from the representations of China in *Viaje a China* and *El anacronópete*. On the one hand, Gaspar's frustration for not encountering the fictional China he has read about shows an authority based on his firsthand experience in China. On the other hand, Gaspar still provides throughout both works a conventional, exoticist, impressionistic, allochronic representation of China based on previous (foreign) sources. The contrast with Álvarez y Tejero's book written a few decades earlier is quite informative about a shift in the politics regulating the sources for representing China. While Álvarez y Tejero valued firsthand accounts from others as a reliable source of authority and information, Gaspar, who does have the authority of a firsthand experience, limits his own views and mostly projects secondhand representations that come from foreign sources. For writers like Gaspar, these sources could actually be more *real* than the reality they were supposed to be experiencing in China. Textual secondhand China was taken as a fundamental truth. Personal firsthand experiences gave authority to question textual views or even the notion of veracity itself (*Viaje a China*, 294; *El anacronópete*, 130). But firsthand experiences did not fully reverse the authority of these secondhand accounts with a new, original discourse about China.

As a result of this combination of formal structure and textual authority, Spain shared a subject position alongside England and France vis-à-vis a China that always remained their object. Foreign sources on China were conceived of as shared capital, probably not even thought of as "foreign." It is striking how language is never an issue in the use of these sources, even if they may have been used in the original. English, French, or German appear as the natural languages to represent China, and neither their foreignness nor their suitability for the Spanish context is raised. This will continue to happen in later decades as well—as we will see in the next chapters. We will also see how, when the foreignness of these sources will eventually be raised, difference will then emerge and Spaniards in China will define themselves as different from Europeans in China. This self-differentiation will also unveil the hierarchy already at play at the time when Gaspar was writing his works and will habilitate a trialectical perception of China.

But that was not the case with Gaspar—nor in any other Spanish writer around the late nineteenth century. Their writings on China barely mention Spain.[72] Unlike the serious intellectual mediations we will see in chapter 2 and the travelers we will examine in chapter 3, neither *Viaje a China* nor *El anacronópete* mention any aspect related to Spain's political, diplomatic, or geopolitical contexts. This is even more remarkable given Gaspar's position as a diplomat. Spanish diplomats in China experienced the new geopolitical context with acute intensity. But Gaspar projects a unified vision of Europe and the Europeans. References to "Europeans" are frequent, usually casual, in *Viaje a China*: "Se me olvidaba consignar que los europeos deben ir provistos de algún frasco de esencia con que preservar el olfato de ciertas emanaciones" (I forgot to mention that Europeans must be provided with a bottle of essence with which to preserve the smell of certain emanations [350]). England remains as the point of reference as "conserje universal" (universal custodian [241]), a gatekeeper who surveys everything that is taking place in the world and acts as a referee when necessary.

In sum, between the authority of secondhand foreign sources and a formal structure that projects an allochronic China as an object, the West emerges as a subject that does not singularize the Spanish position. The China objectified by the English and French sources becomes objectified in a Spain that was not in a historical, geopolitical, or cultural context to exert that kind of (discursive) power. This economy of representation was dependent on translation but not conceived of as translation. This economy of representation turned Gaspar's firsthand experience in China irrelevant. Gaspar could have written the same kind of works from Spain without having ever set foot in China. This is exactly what we will see in the next section.

LA CHINA MODERNA

John Harrisson never set foot in China because John Harrisson never existed. But the person who made up his identity—most probably in a newsroom in Barcelona at the turn of the twentieth century—made sure to imagine him as a British diplomat. Harrisson penned a series of seven letters entitled *La China moderna: Cartas de un diplomático a su familia* (Modern China: Letters from a Diplomat to His Family), published in the journal *Hispania* between September 1900 and April 1901. Harrisson addresses four letters to his wife, Olga, and three letters to his brother Robert (or "Roberto").[73] Harrisson shares with them his experiences in China. He also provides more specific information about China to Robert, who is a member of the House of Commons and has ambitions to get the "honroso puesto de Secretario de las Colonias" (honorable post of Secretary of the Colonies [L2, 360]). Harrisson hopes that the information will become useful for Robert at some point in his political career.

While each letter ends with the short remark "Traducido del inglés por A." (English translation by A.), many evidences show that "John Harrisson" is a fake identity and the letters are pseudotranslations written by someone who gathered information from books and journals, mostly of British and French origin. To begin with, neither "Olga" nor

"John Harrison" (not to mention "Harrisson") sound like names of Victorian diplomats. Many other dubious details abound: the temperature is given in Celsius and not in the Fahrenheit scale (L3, 386); the equivalent of the Chinese currency in taels is given in francs and not in pounds, shillings, or pence (L2, 362); sometimes the content of the letter refers directly to the images published alongside the text (L1, 333); some passages had been previously published in Enrique Gaspar's *El anacronópete* (L6, 464). One of the strongest evidences is a hilarious case of mistranslation: Harrisson explains how the "Pi-Yung-Kung" or "Academia Clásica" (Classic Academy) forbids access to foreigners because, according to a Chinese official, "guardamos religiosamente el texto completo del *Nine-King* o libro clásico, compuesto de lo más antiguo y selecto de la literatura china" (we religiously keep the full text of the *Nine-King* or classic book, composed of the oldest and most select of Chinese literature [L6, 465]). Without doubt, submerged in English sources, the person at *Hispania* trying to impersonate Harrisson's voice thought "nine-king" to be a Chinese expression rendered phonetically from the Chinese language when, in fact, it indicates a collection of nine ("9") classics or *king* (*jing* in *pinyin* transcription).[74] Besides these specific details, the letters lack verisimilitude and are full of affectation. Depictions of London and England are too stereotypical: "whisky legítimo, tan sabroso como el que se bebe en la cervecería de Barklay [*sic*], junto a nuestra casa de Londres" (legitimate whiskey, as tasty as the one drunk at the Barklay Brewery [*sic*], next to our London home [L5, 426]); "¡Cuántas veces tu y yo, siendo niños, allá en 'Hyde Park' o en 'Battersea,' hemos tirado de la trenza a algún magestuoso funcionario de la Legación de la China en Londres!" (How many times did we, as children back in Hyde Park or Battersea, pull the braid of some majestic official of the Chinese legation in London! [L3, 398]). No British person would write things like these to his family.

Despite such theatrical combination of forgery and fakery, *La China moderna* is not a parody. And the most significant thing about Harrisson's letters is that, precisely, there is no comedy implied: *La China moderna* takes the representation of China very seriously indeed. As we will see, *La China moderna* illustrates several features that characterize the representations of China in Spain at the turn of the twentieth century. *La China moderna* also shows how these representations were still projected through a variety of works and genres beyond scholarly sinological essays and "standard" literary translations. Moreover, *La China moderna* gives evidence of the reliance on foreign sources for representing China. A couple of decades after Enrique Gaspar's writings, the person behind the pen name John Harrisson used a similar, yet slightly more modern, set of sources. The mistranslation of "nine-king" indicates an English origin of some of these sources. Explicit references to Évariste Régis Huc (as "Padre Huc" [L7, 154]) or the romanization of names such as "Mandchou" seem to indicate the French origin for some others (L1, 332, 333; L2, 361). Some data explicitly refer to the *Almanach de Gotha*, the annual directory also published in French (L1, 333). The text is also supplemented with images by British painters such as Mortimer Menpes (1855–1938) and Arthur Paine Garratt (1873–1955) (L1, 334; L6, 464; L7, 153).[75]

I want to interrogate *La China moderna* in two directions that explore these aspects further. On the one hand, why does *La China moderna* take the impersonation of a British voice to such a theatrical degree? And what are the effects of this kind of fake authorship? To be sure, it was not unusual to use pen names or create fake authorships to talk about China. As James St. André has convincingly argued, we can even describe the act of "translating China" as a cross-identity performance.[76] However, Harrisson's letters take particular delight in elaborating the British persona and the British prism through which China is portrayed for a Spanish readership. What is the relation between this kind of foreign impersonation and the Chinese "reality" being described? On the other hand, why does *La China moderna* elude the Boxer Uprising of 1900? This is a surprising absence as the series of letters was published between 1900 and 1901, and the Boxer Uprising was widely covered by international media—also in Spain, where even a satirical magazine such as *La Esquella de la Torratxa* translated (nonsatirically) the Boxer manifesto.[77] Why are Harrisson's letters so removed from the contemporary events at a time when China, as we will see in the next chapter, had started being perceived as a coeval reality in the West?

In my reading of *La China moderna* that follows, I suggest that these two questions are intimately connected and can be answered by the historical process that, as we have seen in the previous sections, had solidified a kind of "textual" China for Spanish readers during the mid- and late nineteenth century. This kind of textual China was created by a combination between the indirect accounts that relied on foreign sources and the ethnographic gaze that subjected China to an allochronic position. As a result, this kind of textual China projected China as an enigma.

While in his very first letter Harrisson introduces China as a place that has already been described by many travelers and authors, he emphasizes the idea of China as an unknown, misunderstood reality. Harrisson puts Chinese language at the origin of this problem: the image of China that has reached the West has been based on "textual" materials written by officials and the elite. This has created a biased image of China that does not correspond to the reality he has witnessed and experienced: "Y ¡cuántos errores se divulgan!" (And how many errors are disclosed! [L2, 361]). There is no irony in Harrisson's words, but the irony is supreme indeed: John Harrisson, who never existed outside the text, blames a knowledge of China that is merely textual and stresses his own "first-hand" experience: "Con que, ya lo ves . . . A los que te digan, sin conocer *más que por el mapa* la China moderna, que el Celeste Imperio, en materias de adelantos modernos, vive aún en la época en que se edificaron las murallas famosas, puedes desmentirles en absoluto" (So, you see . . . To those who tell you, knowing modern China *only by the map*, that the Celestial Empire, in matters of modern advances, still lives at the time when the famous walls were built, you can prove them wrong completely [L5, 425; my emphasis]).

The enigma of this textual China requires not only a firsthand experience to be decoded but also—and more importantly—a *British* firsthand experience. This is even more significant as some Spanish expertise on China was already available at the time. At the turn of the century, access to China was not that exceptional any more. Since the opening of consulates in Macau (1854), Shanghai (1858), and Xiamen (1859) and the opening of a legation in Beijing (1864), Spain had had a minor but continuous diplomatic presence in China. From the 1880s onward, the Spanish community in China had always around three hundred residents. In 1899 the Spanish community had grown to, at least, 448 residents.[78] Moreover, late nineteenth-century China had hosted illustrious long-term and short-term Spanish visitors. Some of them were well-known figures in Barcelona, including Sinibaldo de Mas, Juan Mencarini, Eduard Toda, and Enrique Gaspar. Once back in Spain, many of them published works and gave public talks on China. Yet, despite the increasingly available firsthand accounts by Catalan and Spanish diplomats, missionaries, and businessmen, *Hispania* chose a British man as the fake author for *La China moderna*. A secondhand account (in translation) by a British voice had more value than a firsthand account by a Spaniard. Harrisson's cultural and symbolic capital as a British man legitimizes his representations of China. Harrisson emphasizes his own credentials as a China hand. He claims to be a good friend of "Príncipe Ch'un, séptimo hijo del emperador Tao-tchoun y padre del actual. Hijo y padre de emperador" (Prince Ch'un, seventh son of Emperor Tao-tchoun and father of the current emperor. An emperor's father and son [L2, 362]). He mentions his connections with Li Hongzhang, probably the most important Chinese political figure at the time. He also refers to real Western residents in China, such as Marquesa de Salvago Raggi, Spanish ambassador Bernardo Jacinto de Cólogan, and Stephen Wootton Bushell, the longtime physician of the English legation in Beijing. Harrisson seems well informed about the politics at the Chinese court and the tensions between Prince Tsai-Yi [Tuan] (L5, 424–26) and Dowager Empress Cixi (L5, 426). Harrisson also insists on the value of his firsthand experiences across all social environments. His accounts are based on "datos obtenidos *sobre el terreno* estudiando las cosas y hablando con gentes de todas las castas y cataduras" (data obtained *on the ground* by studying things and talking to people of all castes and moral qualities [L2, 360, my emphasis]). But it is Harrisson's Britishness that turns his implausible impersonation into a plausible representation. The investment in Harrisson's Britishness throughout *La China moderna* is so intense that if the letters were not focused on China the whole project would look like a parody.

Decoding the enigma of this textual China through the "translation" of a British account also facilitates the creation of a unified subject position. "Europe" is here the subject that includes Spain and that relates to China as its object. As was the case in Gaspar's works, Spain is never mentioned in *La China moderna* and topics such as the loss of the Philippines, which would point to Spain's critical geopolitics at the time, become obliterated. In other words, by representing China in translation the letters circumvent the reality of Spain's international weakness. By representing China in translation, the letters remain in a safer, unproblematic European position that still concedes a colonial view of China (and the world) from a higher position in the political hierarchy.

The enigma of this textual China also detaches China from its present—something that coincided with *Hispania*'s mission. As a journal modeled on the German *Jugend*, *Hispania* was a modernist publication not particularly interested in contemporary events.[79] It was rather interested in literature and art. The popularity of the Boxer Uprising might have encouraged the journal to create a piece on China. But the aesthetic interest in the China of the past was so prevalent that it was actually possible to avoid the Boxer topic of the present. The letters were published between the fall of 1900 and the winter of 1901, but they are dated in the summer and fall of 1898.[80] Dating the letters before the Boxer events allows Harrisson to avoid the topic.[81] The aesthetic interest in China also explains why the letters sometimes refer to the images on the side. Each letter is about three pages long, and each page includes one, two, or three images (sketches, lithographs, or photographs) that take up considerable space. The origin of the images is certainly foreign. Some of them are signed—for instance, by Mortimer Menpes and Arthur Paine Garratt—but most of them appear uncredited. While this kind of juxtaposition would break the verisimilitude of the project (to be sure, a letter in 1900 did not incorporate images in the way that Harrisson quotes them), the connection between text and images reinforces the aesthetic interest for *Hispania* readers.

In sum, the enigmatic, textual China represented in *La China moderna* in 1900 shares the same economy of representation that had dominated the images of China in Spain in previous decades. The textual China of the past still obscures the contemporary China of the very present. Harrisson's letters share with Gaspar's works the use of the ethnographic form to depict China. His letters share with *Viaje a China* (and *El anacronópete*) the voice of the traveler who projects an allochronic vision of a China that remains fixed in the traditional past. And the array of topics covered does not differ much from the topics we find in previous (and real) travel accounts. Harrisson's series begins with geographical accounts (L1, 331–32) and observations about politics (L1). It is followed by a brief introduction to the Chinese language, which is described as "uno de los testimonios más irrecusables de la gran antigüedad de la civilización china" (one of the most irrefutable testimonies of the great antiquity of Chinese civilization [L2, 360]). Then it continues with the conventional comments on customs and folklore: details about officials' nails (L4), tea (L5), the architecture and distribution of Chinese houses (L5 and L6), opium dens (L6), and food (L7). The way these topics are covered feeds the image of an underdeveloped society still living in the past. China appears as a distant place, set in Europe's antipodes (L1), as a "desdichada nación" (wretched nation) that lacks any progress (L1). Chinese people are described through racial stereotypes, from "el ser burlón por excelencia" (the mocking creature par excellence) who makes fun of foreign religions (L1) to "caricaturas vivientes" (living caricatures [L1, 334]). As in Gaspar's works, Chinese people appear animalized and repulsive: all Chinese look the same (L4, 399); "El chino es la antítesis de la belleza plástica, tal como la entendemos nosotros" (The Chinese are the antithesis of plastic beauty, as we understand it [L1, 334]). As in Gaspar's works, dirt is everywhere: from "mesones sucios" with "acre y penetrante hedor" (dirty inns with a pungent and penetrating stench) to "en aquel montón de andrajos y miseria, como espantoso estercolero, se revuelve la bestia humana, adormecida un momento en su vida de sufrimiento brutal, y, sin embargo, satisfecha de vivir" (in that heap of rags and misery, like a frightful manure dump, the human beast revolts, asleep for a moment in his life of brutal suffering, and yet satisfied with living [L7, 152]).

However, while the China represented in *La China moderna* in 1900 shares the same economy of representation and produces the same kind of conventional images of China that had been dominant in previous decades, it also includes some details that suggest that a different vision of China is emerging at the turn of the twentieth century. This is a less homogeneous and slightly more complex vision of China than the vision offered by Gaspar in the late nineteenth century. As more knowledge on China becomes available, the ethnographic boundaries of travel writing are modified by more critical nuances. Class, for instance, arises as a site for particularization: "lo que en China no tiene arreglo y lo que es origen de su mala fama en Europa, es la inmoralidad que viene de arriba" (the thing that has no solution in China and that is the origin of its bad reputation in Europe is the immorality that comes from above [L2, 361]). China's ruling administration is described as chaotic, corrupt, and nepotist, against the commonly assumed view of China as a meritocratic society: "A pesar de la decantada igualdad, que solo existe en teoría, sufre China la tiranía más abyecta de cuantos han oprimido a un pueblo" (Despite the aforementioned equality, which only exists in theory, China suffers the most abject of the tyrannies that have oppressed any people [L2, 362]).

These critical and more heterogeneous views often stand in contradiction with the more conventional and homogenizing views that were commonly assumed. Both sets of views coexist on the same pages. Chinese people appear both as animalized and polite, dirty and educated, repulsive and studious. Soldiers are depicted as brave, smart, and with good capacities to copy modern weapons—"Los chinos, sin embargo, tienen excelente madera de soldados. Las veces que han combatido a las órdenes de ingleses, franceses o españoles, se han portado con mucha valentía" (The Chinese, however, are made for being excellent soldiers. Whenever they have fought under the command of English, French, or Spanish, they have behaved with great courage [L6, 466])—and as a band of bandits and scoundrels who lack modern weapons—"Hasta hace poco, hasta la guerra con el Japón, los soldados, en su inmensa mayoría, carecían de fusil, haciendo el ejercicio con cañas" (Until recently, until the war against Japan, the vast majority of soldiers lacked a rifle and practiced with reeds [L6, 465]). All of these contradictions foreshadow the multiple signifieds that, as we will see in the following chapters, will be invested in the single signifier "China" during the first decades of the twentieth century. In Spain, such variety will end up reinforcing the legitimacy of the foreign authorial voice: China is such a contradictory, complex reality, so difficult to decode, that only a British or French expert can really make sense of it. The abundant knowledge will turn China into a more confusing, even more enigmatic reality— and Spanish readers will always prefer to rely on a Harrisson to have it deciphered.

La China moderna also includes some new minor observations about the channels for understanding China. Besides the (ironic) critical views about the reliance on textual or secondhand sources, Harrisson problematizes the indirect circulation of the visions of China through Japan. He interviews a mandarin who stresses the problems of understanding China in the West through the "translated" visions projected by the Japanese: "No es la China . . . con sus 600 millones de habitantes ese gallinero que os han pintado esos pérfidos japoneses después del traicionero golpe que nos asestaron. Hay muchas virtudes y hay mucho patriotismo entre los míos" (China . . . with its 600 million inhabitants is not that chicken coop painted for you by the perfidious Japanese after the treacherous blow they beat us. My people have many virtues and much patriotism [L4, 400]). Through the mandarin's native voice, China is represented as an unknown great society that has made important scientific contributions to the world:

> *No se nos conoce.* . . . Vosotros mismos, los ingleses, no concedíais a la China sino muy escasa atención y creo que ninguna simpatía; y, sin embargo, ¡cuán digno de consideración ese un pueblo que, como el chino, tiene 5.000 años de existencia histórica reconocida, que ha sembrado el mundo con sus inventos seculares y que posee una constitución política y social superior a la de Rusia y aun a la de otras naciones europeas! ¿Cómo tildarnos de bárbaros con nuestra agricultura, que sabe utilizar hasta el más pequeño rincón de tierra, con nuestros campesinos sobrios, trabajadores, enriquecidos

por el más gigantesco sistema de riegos que jamás se ha realizado en el mundo? (L4, 400, my emphasis)

We are not known. . . . *You, the British, did not pay to China but very little attention. You, I think, did not grant much sympathy to China. And yet, how worthy of consideration is a people who, like the Chinese, have five thousand years of acknowledged historical existence, who have sown the world with their secular inventions, and who possess a political and social constitution superior to that of Russia and even to that of other European nations! How can you call us barbarians given our agriculture, which is able to use even the smallest corner of the land; our serious, hard-working peasants, enriched by the most gigantic irrigation system that has ever been carried out in the world?*

Enhancing China's virtues turns into a way to introduce its geopolitical potential and the danger of the yellow peril: "y no está lejano el día en que, exasperados los hombres de raza amarilla por las extorsiones a que los someten ciertos individuos de raza blanca, repitan en Europa invasiones de otros siglos, menos bárbaras que las de entonces, pero mucho más formidables, porque tras la bandera del dragón irán millones de soldados" (and the day is not far off when the men of the yellow race, exasperated by the extortions to which they are subjected by certain individuals of the white race, will replicate in Europe the invasions of previous centuries, less barbarous than those back then, but much more formidable, because after the dragon flag millions of soldiers will follow this time [L4, 400]). While focusing on China's past and therefore still remaining within the boundaries of the conventional economy of representation, Harrisson connects China's strength in the past to China's danger in the present: connecting past, present, and future in such a way gives a new meaning to the allochronic regime.

Finally, another innovative aspect where *La China moderna* stands apart from the general views on China projected in mid- and late nineteenth-century works is the way it incorporates a (minor) self-criticism of the West. Several passages refer to situations such as a Westerner who kills a Chinese by accident while hunting and gets by with a simple fine; women that get mistreated; and offensive behaviors in pagodas. This encourages a self-criticism of Westerners' behavior in China: "*Nosotros* hemos abusado aquí de nuestra superioridad" (*We*

have abused our superiority here [L2, 361, my emphasis]). And also in
the West:

> A los chinos—y no es de ahora—les estamos tratando como
> a perros y no solo aquí, en su propia tierra, sino también en
> todas las ciudades de Europa y América a donde emigran
> para trabajar honradamente. Para nosotros—y ellos lo sa-
> ben y lo soportan—un chino es poco menos que un animal
> inmundo y así le tratamos. Por eso, cuando hablan de los
> europeos, ¡nos llaman los diablos blancos! (L2, 361)

> *We are treating the Chinese—and this is not something*
> *new—like dogs and not only here, in their own land, but also*
> *in all the cities of Europe and America where they migrate*
> *to work honestly. For us—and they know it and bear it—a*
> *Chinese is little less than an unclean animal and that's how*
> *we treat him. So, when they talk about Europeans, they call*
> *us white devils!*

Harrisson connects China's political awakening to the historical abuses
suffered during the Western intervention at the end of the second Opium
War: "Débese esto a la expedición anglo-francesa del año de 1860. De
las cenizas del palacio de Verano, incendiado y saqueado por las tropas
expedicionarias, nació el odio profundo que se tiene a los europeos"
(This is due to the Anglo-French expedition of 1860. From the ashes
of the Summer Palace, burned and looted by the expeditionary troops,
the deep hatred that we have for Europeans was born [L6, 466]). These
criticisms do not arise from Spain's geopolitical singularity (as we will
see in the next chapter), but rather from a general conception of "we"
or "Europeans" or "Europeans and Americans" (L4, 398; L4, 399). In
these self-criticisms, "the West" appears always as a unifying designa-
tion. Again, Spain is never mentioned. These criticisms project a division
of the world between the West and China, colonizer and colonized,
in which Spain is part of the West only by omission.

In this chapter we have seen how the image of China in Spain in the late
nineteenth century heavily relied on pivotal English and French sources
and how these sources were used widely and uncredited across all sorts
of works—not only in works explicitly marked as translations. Pseudotranslations such as *La China moderna* illustrate the strong dependence

on indirect translation that characterized works such as *Viaje a China* and *El anacronópete*. They also illustrate the legitimacy of speaking about China with an English or French voice.

Elisa Martí-López concluded that "translation, imitation, and original writing were diffuse practices in the 1840s and 1850s, their boundaries blurred by a practice of loose translation and original."[82] This chapter has expanded her conclusions by examining what happened when the object caught within these blurred boundaries and diffuse practices was a geographically and culturally distant one—as it was China for nineteenth-century Spaniards. We have seen how the trialectical relationship between China, Spain, and English or French sources had political effects—for not only the image of China represented in Spain but also the position of Spain representing China. As China was understood in Spain through the prism provided by these English and French sources, indirect representations of China contributed to integrate Spain within the Western subject position that kept China as its backward, noncoeval object. The hegemony of indirectness can therefore be explained by the complicity between, on the one hand, the epistemology that characterizes translation (i.e., a subject translating an object) and, on the other hand, the politics for representing the world within the West. Translation assumes the differentials of power that are intrinsic in the ethnographic look.[83] Translation contributes to projecting the image of a distant, backward object—even beyond the works explicitly considered translations themselves. Translation imposes a regime of cofiguration that, under a binary frame, simplifies the heterogeneity of each cross-cultural representation—its indirectness, its internal differences.[84]

We have seen how in late nineteenth-century Spain, translation and China, or China in translation, contributed to keep Spain within a unified Western subject. Going back to Enrique Gaspar's words, "illusion" that was "more beautiful than reality" was not only an allochronic China but also a unified West. The illusion created by translation turned this trialectical relationship invisible. In other words, viewing China through English and French sources was a naturalized process of cross-cultural representation. In the next chapter we will see how, at the turn of the twentieth century, while this dynamic remained strongly rooted in Spain's social imaginary, some concerns about Spain's singularity were raised and how this trialectical relationship started being perceived as such.

CHAPTER 2

"To Show the Real Truth"

July 23, 1900
  London, United Kingdom

Today is Monday and a memorial service is scheduled to begin in St Paul's Cathedral at 11:30 A.M. It has been one week, and Europe and North America are still in shock. On Monday, July 16, the *Daily Mail* reported that the diplomatic community under siege in Beijing's Legation Quarter had been annihilated by the Boxers on the night between July 6 and 7. The headline was "The Peking Massacre. All White Men, Women and Children Put to the Sword. Death Not Dishonour." The news spread like wildfire across European and American media. The *New York Times* added that the defenders "went mad and killed all their women and children with revolvers." The London *Times* expressed "the righteous cry for vengeance from the Western world." Obituaries were published. Messages of condolence were received. Then, just before the start of the memorial service in London, a short-ciphered telegram that had arrived in Washington on July 20 is given credibility: "In British Legation. Under continued shot and shell from Chinese troops. Quick relief only can prevent general massacre." The sender is Edwin H. Conger, United States minister to China. He was supposed to be among the victims reported one week earlier and the impact of the *Daily Mail* report was such that the telegram was initially taken to be a forgery— all diplomats in Peking were supposed to be dead, after all. But doubts arise, and the service in St Paul's Cathedral is cancelled at the very last moment.[1]

The anecdote has been told many times as one of the many dramatic events that punctuated the chronology of the Boxer Uprising and the siege of Beijing in the summer of 1900.[2] Arthur H. Smith, the famous author of *Chinese Characteristics*, was one of the sieged participants. In his account written a few months after the event, Smith summarizes how the alleged massacre reported by the *Daily Mail* changed the views about China around the world:

> The sensational details of the alleged massacre in the British Legation on the 7th of July, and the almost accomplished Requiem Service in St. Paul's, when followed by a knowledge of the principal facts, riveted the attention of all nations. The absolute novelty, the intense dramatic interest, the world-wide scope, and the far-reaching consequences of the events which have taken place in China, combine to differentiate the Convulsion in that Empire from anything in history, whether ancient or modern.[3]

The alleged massacre illustrates a new kind of relationship between China and the West. During the months of June and July 1900, the whole world was following the events in China very closely: "Affairs in North China ousted the Boer War from its hallowed position in the leading news column of *The Times* and were given a similar prominence by the Press of other countries."[4] The world was following the events in China on a daily basis because China was connected to the world through a new media environment. In fact, all accounts stress how direct communications with Northern China were interrupted and how dramatic that disconnection was: the telegraphic link with the legations in Beijing was cut on June 13; the link with Tianjin was cut on June 16; communication with the international relief force of two thousand men led by British Vice-Admiral Seymour was also cut, as it was attacked on June 18 and remained unable to communicate until rescued by a regiment of 1,800 on June 26. Connectivity, now lost, spurred the urgency of knowing what was going on in China almost in real time.

In fact, connectivity had already generated dark premonitions since early June. Diplomatic telegrams from Peking had made it clear that something tragic was about to happen. With direct communications interrupted at the end of June, rumors abounded about the fate of the legations and the Seymour Expedition. On June 29, two authentic communications from the legations were able to reach the outside world smuggled into Tianjin by a Chinese courier. One was dispatched on June 24 by Robert Hart: "Foreign community besieged in the Legations. Situation desperate. MAKE HASTE!!" Another was dispatched on June 25 by a missionary and reported the murder of Clemens von Ketteler, the German minister. Confusion increased in early July and rumors got gloomier—unconfirmed stories, mostly from Chinese sources in Shanghai or Canton. On July 6, the *Times* correspondent in Rome reported that "news of a general massacre in Peking had induced a 'painful stupor' throughout Italy."[5] On July 7, Reuters reported from Shanghai: "Prepare to hear the worst." Thus, the dramatic *Daily Mail* report of July 16 spread across this loaded terrain.[6]

My point is that connectivity—as imperfect as it was at the time—created the atmosphere, triggered the mistake, and finally stopped the memorial service to be held in London on July 23. In early August several capitals received with relief telegrams from their ministers in Peking. As Peter Fleming writes, "It was with a slightly mortified astonishment that the newspapers passed on the glad tidings to their readers."[7] The situation of the diplomatic community in Beijing's Legation Quarter had been and still was certainly critical, but they were still alive and resisting the Boxers' attacks. The international force led by British General Alfred Gaselee reached Beijing on August 14, and the Legation Quarter was finally relieved.

In sum, the alleged massacre vividly illustrates how, at the turn of the twentieth century, China had become a coeval presence in the world that was being observed through a new kind of attention. Compared to the context examined in the previous chapter, the change was extreme. As James Hevia argues, "by 1900, wholly new mechanisms of information processing were in place to exploit the story on a scale that had been unimaginable in 1860" and "delivered the sensational developments in China at a velocity and in a form that made information itself a spectacle, allowing for a vast expansion of vicarious audience participation in events."[8]

What concerns us primarily in this chapter are the effects of such a new awareness of China as a coeval presence in the world. Did the new mechanisms of information and the new understanding of China as a coexistent reality in the world bring about changes in the views on Chinese history, culture, and society? China was not (only) a remote location from which information was gathered and read under the form of ethnographic travel writings. China was here and now, interacting with Western citizens almost in real time. How was China imagined in this new context? A question that follows this and that we will also ask is: What consequences did this awareness of a coeval China bear on the representations of China in Spain? This question is particularly relevant since, as we have seen, China in Spain was dependent on an indirect—and therefore somehow delayed—circuit of representation. How was the tension between a coeval China and the mediated, indirect ways of learning about China in Spain played out?

This chapter shows how the perception of a coeval China that emerged in Spain at the end of the nineteenth century and the beginning of the twentieth century did not substitute the old patterns of representations of China that we saw in the previous chapter. New and old representations overlapped and were interrelated in a somehow contradictory way. On the one hand, the perception of a coeval China still remained within old representational patterns. While the material conditions that influenced the writing about China did change, some crucial representational aspects remained unchallenged. The alleged massacre reported by the *Daily Mail* offers clear illustrations. First, information about what was happening in Beijing arrived in Spain almost as fast as in England or France but still through the same circuit that pivoted around European (or Western) centers. The massacre was reported across a wide range of Spanish publications immediately after the *Daily Mail*'s report (sometimes quoting it in full) and only one day after Conger's telegram had reached the United States. Their sources were telegrams received from London, Paris, New York, or Brussels, usually quoting reports previously published by other European or American newspapers.[9] Second, China was still represented in opposition to "Europe" or "the West" as a unified subject that included Spain. The service scheduled in St Paul's Cathedral, for instance, was "for the Europeans massacred in Peking" and reports in the Spanish press referred to the massacre as "asesinato de europeos," "matanza de europeos," or "europeos asesinados" (killing of Europeans, massacre of European, or Europeans murdered). The Spanish Minister Plenipotentiary Bernardo Jacinto de Cólogan, the only Spaniard in Beijing at the time, was barely mentioned in the wide Spanish coverage of the event.[10] Third, ancient stereotypes still prevailed. In fact, it was an intense sinophobia that made it possible for most people to believe the fake report published by the *Daily Mail* and call for vengeance.[11] Intense sinophobia was expressed in characterizations of "el espíritu del pueblo chino" as "cerrado á toda influencia exterior, enemigo de todo lo extranjero, lleno de odio hacia toda civilización que no sea la suya, hacia todo progreso que esté en pugna con su fanatismo y ese absurdo é intolerable orgullo de raza que le hace creerse superior á cuanto fuera de él existe" (the spirit of the Chinese people as closed to all external influence, enemy of everything foreign, full of hatred toward any civilization that is not Chinese, toward all progress that is in conflict with Chinese fanaticism and that absurd and intolerable pride of race that makes Chinese to think about themselves as superior to everything else).[12]

On the other hand, the perception of a coeval China had other implications that were new. More information became simultaneously available in a new format. Reports on the Boxer siege in the Spanish newspapers, for instance, included several releases from different press agencies and foreign sources, all juxtaposed on the same page. These reports were preceded with sentences like: "Otras muchas referencias se han recibido del extranjero confirmando todos los sucesos ocurridos en Pekín, lean aquí ahora los telegramas recibidos" (Many other references have been received from abroad confirming all the events that occurred in Beijing, read here now the telegrams received).[13] As we will see, more heterogeneous representations of China and the Chinese became available too. In sum, representations of China—the knowledge about China beyond the Boxer incident—acquired a different volume, form, visuality, and materiality. And, as we will also see, the mechanisms through which China was being represented in Spain were questioned for the first time, and the singularity of the Spanish position vis-à-vis China (and the world) was added to the discussion—particularly after Spain's imperial defeat in 1898.

In this chapter I argue that the overlap between these new and old representations produced a keen concern for truth about China. What was the "true China" that existed right now on the other side of the world? How similar, or how different, was the real China from the "Chinas" that had been described in stereotypical travel accounts and still lived in the popular imagination and on libraries' bookshelves? How reliable were the Chinese voices that talked about China in the first person? To be sure, this was not the first time in history that China had been the object of inquiries about truth or authenticity. James St. André, for instance, has shown that early nineteenth-century translators of Chinese materials were increasingly preoccupied with authenticity.[14] Yet at the turn of the twentieth century, as knowledge about China became more available and displayed under multiple forms, this concern for truth became more urgent and intense. In this chapter I also argue that, in Spain, this concern for truth about a coeval China in the world increased the concern for Spain's geopolitical position. The concern for truth created the need to hold a genuine view of China that (apparently) differed from other Western views and that should help Spain in dealing with its own predicaments. I ultimately argue that, in this context, truth became a trope, almost a cliché, that updated the old interest for an enigmatic China that had prevailed in the ethnographic context of the nineteenth century and adapted it to the new informational context of the twentieth century without challenging the epistemological roots for representing China.

To be sure, representations of China had been contradictory in previous decades too. And transplanting information about China into Spain from English or French sources had not been done without raising occasional criticism during the nineteenth century.[15] The examples examined in the previous chapter show the formal tensions and conceptual ambivalences in representing China from Spain using the hegemonic European perspective. However, as the following sections will show, around the turn of the twentieth century the perception of a coeval China turned these critical reflections more visible, more acute, and much more concerned about veracity. This will be evident in the analysis of Chen Jitong's popularity in France and Spain in the last years of the nineteenth century and of Fernando de Antón del Olmet's critical book *El problema de la China* (The Problem of China), published in 1901. Both authors attempted to view China, the Chinese people, and Chinese culture in a new light. They show the possibilities and the limitations that emerged from a new type of interaction with China.

CHINA, HERE AND NOW

Let us move to December 13, 1894. We are at the Ateneo de Madrid, one of the main sites of intellectual life in Spain's capital. Ramón Auñón y Villalón (1844–1925), "capitán de navío" (naval captain) and, at the time, "diputado a Cortes" (deputy in the Spanish Parliament) is giving a public talk on the naval Battle of the Yalu River between China and Japan. This is a rather immediate analysis, as the battle has taken place less than three months before: on September 17, 1894. Besides its immediacy, there is something impressive in Auñón's analysis. It is very assertive and full of details. It surveys with precision aspects like the kind of vessels that took part in the battle and the type and amount of ammunition fired by each navy. It even has diagrams representing the movements and tactics followed by each squad. It is important to note that, even though Auñón talks with proficiency, he is far from an expert in East Asian affairs. He fought in conflicts in Africa and Cuba and will later serve as minister of the navy during the Spanish-American War in 1898. But unlike diplomats such as Enrique Gaspar, Eduard Toda, and Juan Mencarini, Auñón does not have direct experience in China. However, his talk—what he presents and *how* he presents it—illustrates a high degree of familiarity with the Chinese context. His talk illustrates that around the turn of the twentieth century the representations of China in Spain—and, more generally, in the West—are entering into a new phase.

This greater familiarity with China can be credited to developments in technology and communication. In the late nineteenth century, "vastly expanded transportation and communication systems linked the east coast of China into a global steamship and railroad network."[16] The Suez Canal was opened in 1869, and it decreased the travel time to China in a significant way.[17] By the 1880s, the telegraph system, established in China in the 1860s and initially connected only to the European treaty ports, had diffused widely through the country, primarily due to commercial interests. At the end of the century most of China's cities had become connected to a large telegraph network and, through this, to the world.[18] In parallel, as Steven Topik and Allen Wells have noted, "the advent of international wire services like Reuters in England, Havas in France, the Associated Press in the United States, and Wolff in Germany provided world news (really the news of the part of the globe they thought was important in Western Europe, North America, and various global cities) to the daily newspapers that were beginning to attract mass readerships in major metropolises."[19] All this was part of the "Great Acceleration" that took part in the late nineteenth century. As Christopher Bayly and many others have noted, the revolutions in transportation, communication, finance, and commerce brought about not only new transnational networks but also new cross-cultural sensibilities: "a flowering of efforts to reimagine the world as a single field."[20] This, of course, also implied reimagining China as part of this world. As Rebecca Karl summarized, "China had become more imbricated in the world and the world more imbricated in China."[21]

Broadly speaking, China was reimagined by two simultaneous processes that took place around the turn of the twentieth century: more knowledge about China became available and, more crucially, this knowledge was spread across a multiplicity of forms and readerships. In the last years of the nineteenth century, sinology was already an established discipline with professional scholars. Books on China were much more abundant than a century—or even a few decades—ago and, perhaps more importantly, were *perceived* to be abundant: "Some three thousand five hundred works have been written on China and are now accessible, many large libraries having from one thousand to one thousand five hundred titles on this subject."[22] Books on China reached wider readerships too. Take Arthur H. Smith's *Chinese Characteristics*, for instance. Originally published as a series of essays for the rather local *North-China Daily News* in the late 1880s, the topics "excited so much interest" not only among the international community in China but also in Great Britain and North America that the series was reproduced as a book in 1890 for a wider audience. By 1894 an enlarged edition with illustrations had been reprinted at least five times.[23] *Chinese Characteristics* was followed by *Village Life in China* in 1899. Both books were praised in general newspapers and journals such as the *New York Observer*, the *Independent*, and the *Nation*. In his account of the many books on China quoted previously, journalist Talcott Williams singles out Smith's books as "not only two of the *very* best books on China, but two of the *very* best books which have ever been published by *any* author on *any* country at *any* time."[24] The extensive press coverage of events in China, particularly during conflicts such as the First Sino-Japanese War in 1894 and 1895 or the Boxer Uprising— and particularly the siege of Beijing—in 1900, intensified that interest. Reports on China's political situation increased the interest for Chinese culture too. As we saw in the previous chapter, Spanish journals like *La España Moderna* or *Hispania* had special pieces on China and Chinese culture unrelated to the Boxers. Articles were generally accompanied by evocative portrayals of politicians and emperors.[25] Cartoons and comic strips testify how familiar Spanish readers were with Chinese politics: a "common" Spanish reader in 1900 had enough contextual information about China to recognize a politician like Li Hongzhang as a familiar face in a cartoon.[26]

In my view, however, the most remarkable shift in such a reimagination of China can be found not in the amount of information about China that became available in the West but in the new forms in which China was represented. Travelers' writings, missionaries' accounts, and sinologists' essays were joined by other forms of knowledge. In contrast to the long narratives of books and essays, telegraph connections produced short reports that appeared juxtaposed in newspapers that the reader had to put together. New visual mediums displayed the East too.[27] Photography was "one of the new potentially transnational 'languages' that emerged in the late nineteenth century," and China became part of the "desire to understand the world through photography." But, as Emily S. Rosenberg notes, photography also exemplified "the differentiated commonalities of this period," as images produced currents connecting the globe, but meanings of those currents became variable and multivocal.[28] As the epitome of the "exhibitionary nodes," world's fairs "constituted one of the most important nodes in the transnational currents of this period" and "became major cultural enterprises of global significance because their representations projected powerful imaginaries about the world, its diverse cultures, and its interconnectivity and divisions."[29] The exhibitions from China and Japan had had a great impact in the 1876 world's fair in Philadelphia, for instance.[30] In 1888 the China section was the most popular in the Universal Exhibition of Barcelona.[31] To be sure, cinema contributed decisively to these new forms and rhythms for representing the East.[32]

Moreover, new voices that represented China emerged—for instance, voices from Chinese citizens who were in the West or who wrote in Western languages and who were allowed a certain representational agency. In the next section we will examine the figure of Chen Jitong, but other examples can be mentioned: Gu Hongming (1857–1928) criticized sinologists like John Francis Davis or James Legge and, while his writings had a limited circulation compared to Chen's, they were reviewed in the *Times* and were important within sinological circles.[33] Western voices who were critical in the role that the West was playing in China emerged too. Reports of Western armies' looting after breaking the Boxer's siege triggered more nuanced representations beyond sinophobia. Pierre Loti's denunciation of Western armies' atrocities, Sarah Conger's expressions of compassion for the Chinese, and Mark Twain's support for the Boxers are perhaps the most well-known examples.[34]

In sum, China became more ubiquitous through a variety of agents and agendas, voices and formats. Analyzed in isolation, each representation—a talk here, an exhibition there, literary references somewhere else—may seem anecdotical.[35] But read together across genres, media, and formats, these representations started to create a remarkable mosaic of textual and material Chinas around the turn of the century— even before the explosion of representations that, as we will see in the following chapters, would take place around the interwar period, which has received more scholarly attention.[36]

This heterogeneous accumulation required the reader to do a certain critical processing. Take *La Correspondencia de España* on August 3, 1900, as an example. Page 2 is divided into six columns. The siege of Beijing occupies the space of five columns. Each column is divided into four or five short pieces, which make a total of twenty-three short pieces. These pieces had been telegraphed from different cities and correspondents: Berlin (Holdzman), London (Harry), Paris (Blasco), and New York (Azor). Other cities are mentioned as original sources of the information provided: Washington, Brussels, St. Petersburg, Hong Kong, Yokohama, Shanghai, Che Fu, Tianjin. The specific date and time for each dispatch is indicated in each piece—for example: "Berlin 2, 8° 8 m" or "Londres 2, 9° 35 m." The pieces also mention as sources "algunos periódicos" (some newspapers), "los periódicos de París y Londres" (Paris and London newspapers), or more specifically, the *Daily Mail*, the *Morning Leader*, the *Times*, the *Daily Express*, the *Daily Telegraph*, or the *New York Herald*. It is striking how China is conveyed through such a profusion of data, world referents, and short inputs. While such degree of detail gives the illusion of connectivity, the pieces are diverse, even contradictory, and each reader must compose his or her own picture of what is actually going on. This happened at the rather limited level of a single newspaper page. A similar exercise—obviously at a much broader scale—must have been required for anyone who was exposed to the different, heterogenous Chinas that circulated under different forms across cultural and social spheres.

In other words, China was a coeval presence in the world, but at the same time, China was a more fragmented reality that became more difficult to grasp. It is no surprise, then, that doubts were raised. The multiple, juxtaposed reports from the alleged massacre in the Spanish press are most illustrative when they include remarks such as: "De ser esto verdad . . ." (If this is true . . .) and "Imposible es sacar nada en claro de lo que allí sucede: las noticias que de allí se reciben son contradictorias, y lo que un día afirman, lo rectifican al otro, para volverlo á afirmar y rectificar en los siguientes" (It is impossible to get anything clear from what happens there: the news received from there are contradictory, and one day the news says something then the next day the information is corrected, and then the information is affirmed and corrected again in the following days") or "¿Verdad o mentira? Nadie sabe a qué atenerse en vista de las noticias que se reciben de China" (True or false? Nobody knows what to expect in view of the news received from China).[37] Doubts and concerns for truth could also be found beyond journalistic reports. Arthur H. Smith's opening to his famous *Chinese Characteristics* conveys the mood of the time:

> A witness when put upon the stand is expected to tell the truth, the whole truth, and nothing but the truth. Many witnesses concerning the Chinese have told the truth, but perhaps few of them have succeeded in telling nothing but the truth, and no one of them has ever told the whole truth. No single individual, whatever the extent of his knowledge, could by any possibility know the whole truth about the Chinese.[38]

Let us go back to the Ateneo de Madrid and Ramón Auñón's talk to point out another important aspect of this new environment for representing China—particularly from the Spanish context. Why does the Yalu battle between China and Japan matter to Spain, after all? We can answer the question through what Auñón says and—especially— through what he prefers to leave unsaid. Auñón's answer illustrates the ambivalent position of Spain in representing China in this new environment at the turn of the twentieth century. Throughout his presentation, Auñón had taken China—or the Battle of the Yalu River, to be precise—as an object to be examined from a European position. To be sure, this position was facilitated by the English and French sources from which he had gathered the information.[39] His talk, then, followed the conventional binary of China/West that, as we have seen in the previous chapter, had been assumed in the Spanish understanding of China throughout the nineteenth century. But Auñón concludes his talk with the following consideration:

> Y queda, finalmente, una última consideración sobre la cual sólo he de hacer indicaciones muy ligeras, porque una conveniencia patriótica aconseja no manosear demasiado estos asuntos en conferencias ó discusiones públicas. ¿Es de todo punto indiferente á España el resultado de esta guerra? Evidentemente que no.[40]

> *And finally, there is one last consideration about which I only have to make very slight indications, because it is not in the best interest of a patriot to tamper with these matters too*

much in talks or public discussions. Is the result of this war
completely indifferent to Spain? Obviously not.

Japan's victory and, as a result, Japan's control over the island of Formosa (or Taiwan) had become a serious menace for the Philippines, still
under Spanish domination: "Desde Formosa á Filipinas hay 60 millas;
desde España á Manila hay 10.000. Estos y otros que callo por sen-
timientos patrióticos serán los términos forzosos de futuros problemas
que habrán de resolverse en el extremo Oriente. Yo aquí sello mis labios
y pongo fin á mi trabajo" (Formosa and the Philippines are sixty miles
apart; Spain and Manila are ten thousand miles apart. These terms, and
others that I keep silent about due to patriotic feelings, will be the terms
of future problems that will necessarily have to be solved in the Far
East. I seal my lips here and end my work).[41] We can see here how the
situation in China unsettles the silence about Spain's irrelevant geopolitical position in the world. While, as we have seen, China had been
the object that kept Spain within the Western subject, China now also becomes a topic that habilitates a reflection on Spain's predicaments and
weakened position within the very same West. This association will become even more conspicuous after the Boxer Uprising, when Spain finally loses Cuba and the Philippines.

Auñón's restrained comment was followed by similar reflections by
other people connecting China's current situation with Spain's singularity. The most sophisticated literary one was by Luis Valera in *Sombras
chinescas: Recuerdos de un viaje al Celeste Imperio* (Chinese Shadows:
Memories of a Trip to the Celestial Empire), which has been insightfully
examined by Joan Torres-Pou.[42] We can read Valera's account of his
travel to China as primer secretario of the Spanish legation in Beijing
right after the Boxer Uprising from a double perspective. On the one
hand, he provides a universal reflection, an "ejemplo extraordinario de
las tensiones en que se debatía todo occidental—con un mínimo de con-
ciencia—al que le tocaba vivir de cerca los horrores del colonialismo
europeo" (extraordinary example of the tensions that any Westerner—
with a slight conscience—had to struggle with when he had to closely
experience the horrors of European colonialism), and on the pages of
Sombras chinescas we find "junto a su convicción de pertenecer a una
civilización superior, un fuerte sentimiento de culpa por las barbari-
dades causadas en nombre de esa civilización" (along with his convic-
tion of belonging to a superior civilization, a strong feeling of guilt for
the barbarities caused in the name of that civilization).[43] On the other

hand, Valera's critical reflection is facilitated by his singular position as a Spaniard. He is a "testimonio excepcional, ya que el suyo no es ni el discurso del colonizador ni el del colonizado ni el del descolonizado, sino el de un representante de una antigua potencia colonial que ha sido vencida y sojuzgada por otras potencias coloniales emergentes" (exceptional witness, since his is neither the discourse of the colonizer nor that of the colonized nor that of the decolonized, but that of a representative of a former colonial power that has been defeated and subjugated by other emerging colonial powers).[44] To be sure, similar critical reflections were raised by Mark Twain and Pierre Loti. And, given the trialectical representations of China in Spain described so far, we could sustain that, in fact, Valera exculpates Spain from colonialism just as Loti had tried to exculpate the French troops from looting in *Les Derniers jours de Pékin* (The Last Days of Pekin).[45] However, the relevant point here is that in Valera's work, as in Auñón's talk, China acts as a mirror for Spain: "en su viaje por el triunfo de las fuerzas internacionales, no solamente tiene presente la ausencia de España en China, sino su derrota, no pudiendo dejar de ver en el vencido un reflejo de sí mismo" (along his journey through the triumph of the international forces, he not only thinks about Spain's absence in China, but also about Spain's defeat; he cannot help but see in the defeated a reflection of himself).[46]

The criticisms raised by Spain's singularity were taken even further. *La Correspondencia Militar*, for instance, published the following piece in May 1901, which is worth quoting at length. The restrain in Auñón's words or the ambiguities expressed in *Sombras chinescas* disappear, and Spain's weakness are turned into a moral victory:

¿Lo recordáis? Surgió la cuestión de China, y las grandes naciones civilizadas mandaron al Celeste Imperio sus Ejércitos aliados, para en nombre de la humanidad restablecer el orden y no permitir las matanzas, los saqueos y el pillaje en menor escala. . . .

Los humanitarios soldados de los Estados Unidos, los correctos soldados alemanes, los intachables militares ingleses, japoneses, rusos y todos, en fin,—salvo raras excepciones— han profanado y abierto los vientres de las mujeres, han pisoteado con sus caballos los niños inocentes, han despedazado á los hombres, han saqueado los tesoros chinos, han destruido edificios, no han respetado nada y lo han profanado todo, sin temor á nada ni á nadie.

. . . las naciones que van á la cabeza de la civilización,— como por ejemplo los Estados Unidos, que intervinieron en Cuba en nombre de la humanidad para despojarnos,— cometen en la guerra actos de impiedad y realizan actos de salvajismo que España nunca pensó siquiera llevar á la práctica en las que fueron sus colonias.

El Ejército español jamás hubiera realizado esos hechos; los soldados de nuestra Patria nunca se hubiesen atrevido á profanar los cadáveres de les niños con las patas de sus caballos, y, sin embargo, España pasa ante el mundo por una nación atrasada y cruel, capaz de encadenar y torturar á los débiles con frialdades de verdugo de la Edad Media. ¡Así se escribe la historia y así se nos ha deshonrado á mansalva, cuando en España hay más generosidad y más nobleza que en esas naciones que sostienen que van á la cabeza del progreso, al impulso del humanitarismo!

¡No pensarán lo mismo ciertamente los hijos del Celeste Imperio, ni querrán los cubanos y filipinos, después de esto, que los Ejércitos aliados vayan á poner orden y á restablecer el humanitarismo en sus interiores discordias![47]

Do you remember? The question of China arose, and the great civilized nations sent their allied armies to the Celestial Empire, to restore order in the name of humanity and prevent killings, looting and smaller scale pillage. . . .

The humanitarian soldiers of the United States, the civil German soldiers, the faultless English, Japanese, and Russian military, all, in short (with rare exceptions), have desecrated and opened the wombs of women, trampled innocent children with their horses, torn men to pieces, plundered Chinese treasures, destroyed buildings, respected nothing, and desecrated everything, without fear of anything or anyone.

. . . the nations that are at the forefront of civilization— such as the United States, which intervened in Cuba in the name of humanity only to strip us—commit acts of impiety in war and perform acts of savagery that Spain never even thought of bringing to the practice in its former colonies.

The Spanish army would never have carried out these acts; our country's soldiers would never have dared to desecrate children's corpses with their horses' legs. And yet Spain is considered by the world as a backward and cruel nation, capable of chaining and torturing the weak as a cold executioner in the Middle Ages. This is how history is written and this is how we have been largely dishonored—when there is more generosity and nobility in Spain than in those nations that maintain that they stand at the head of progress and of humanitarianism!

There is no doubt that the children of the Celestial Empire will not think the same. There is no doubt that, after this, the Cubans and Filipinos will not want that the allied armies bring order and restore humanitarianism to their internal discord!

In sum, while the representations of China in Spain still depended on English and French material and discursive sources, Spain's singularity within the relations between China and the West is singled out. In other words, while a coeval China—and the mechanisms that sustained that coevalness—kept Spain connected with the European and Western centers, China also unveiled Spain's geopolitical fragility. This contradiction opened up new ways of thinking about China, which coexisted with the old allochronic understandings of China that were still applied to the coeval China of the present. The following sections will delve into these ambivalences that characterized the representations of China in Spain at the turn of the twentieth century.

LES CHINOIS PEINTS PAR EUX-MÊMES

Chen Jitong (1852–1907) was probably the most popular Chinese personality across Europe during the late nineteenth and early twentieth century. Through his writings, talks, and social activities, Chen played the role of cross-cultural mediator between China and the West. To be sure, as James St. André has argued, the figure of the visitor from China—or from another country—had been one of the Enlightenment's favorite tropes, as "viewing Europe through the eyes of a stranger allows Europeans to see that certain things they take for granted may seem strange to others, and the stranger's wonderment, amusement, or shock then causes Europeans to question the necessity of such practices."[48] However, Chen Jitong's case is significant because he was not an impersonation behind a pseudotranslation but a real visitor from

China indeed, who spent fifteen years in Europe. Chen learned French at the Fuzhou Navy Yard and in 1876 was selected to work as an interpreter in the legations that the Qing Empire had in Paris and Berlin. In 1877 Chen enrolled in the École libre des sciences politiques in Paris, where he studied international law. He then became chargé d'affaires at the Imperial Chinese Embassy in Paris. He stayed in Paris until 1891.[49] During his time in Europe, Chen became an extremely popular public figure. He was a regular speaker in salons. He collaborated with French writers, sinologists, and ethnographers. He contributed regularly to French newspapers such as *Revue des Deux Mondes*, *Le Matin*, *Le Monde*, *Revue des traditions populaires*, *Le Figaro*, *L'Echo de Chine*, and *Revue illustrée*.[50] Between 1884 and 1892 he authored seven books in French—most of them compilations of texts he had previously published in newspapers.[51]

The most important of his books—and perhaps the cornerstone of his project of cross-cultural mediation—was *Les Chinois peints par eux-mêmes* (The Chinese Painted by Themselves). It was originally published as a series of eighteen articles in *Revue des Deux Mondes* between May and June 1884 under the title "La Chine et les Chinois" (China and the Chinese) and came out as a book later that year. *Les Chinois peints par eux-mêmes* became a great success: eight editions were published in that same year, and it became an acclaimed book in French society. "Everyone has more or less read his book," asserted a reviewer.[52] Its popularity crossed national borders as it was quickly translated into English (1885), German (1885), and Danish (1886).[53] It is difficult to find any single work that had a bigger impact in the debates about China at the turn of the century across Europe.

Chen Jitong was an extremely popular figure in Spain too. Chen's prestige in the Spanish cultural sphere illustrates many of the dynamics and concerns that regulated the representations of China in Spain at the turn of the twentieth century. Chen's case illustrates how difficult it was to represent China outside the regime of translation and the binary framework (colonizer/colonized, subject/object) that was rooted in the Western imagination. In other words, Chen Jitong's popularity in Spain shows that, despite the singularization of Spain's position in its relationship with China expressed by Auñón or Valera, China in Spain was still mostly represented and understood through a trialectical connection via Britain or, in Chen's case, France.

Chen started appearing in the Spanish press in the early 1880s when he was acting as a military attaché in Berlin.[54] The Sino-French War, which was closely followed by Spanish newspapers, turned Chen into a recurring reference and increased the attention for his works and, eventually, for Chinese culture.[55] A typical example of this concatenation between geopolitical and cultural interests would be:

> Los últimos acontecimientos del Tonkin, que tan vivamente han impresionado á todos los amigos de Francia, han tenido á dar un carácter de actualidad á un libro que me envió hace algunos meses el editor de París Calmann Lévy, libro sumamente interesante, escrito por el coronel Tcheng-Ki-Tong [Chen Jitong]. . . . Mis ocupaciones no me permitieron leerlo entonces: los telegramas publicados estos últimos días por *El Imparcial* referentes al descalabro de los franceses en el Tonkin, me hicieron recordar que tenía ese libro en mi poder; lo he leído, y como para muestra basta un botón, trascribo un extracto que me he entretenido en hacer anoche de uno de sus capítulos, el consagrado al matrimonio.[56]

> *The last events in Tonkin, which have so impressed all the friends of France, have turned a book that the Parisian editor Calmann Lévy sent me a few months ago into a very timely reading. It is a very interesting book written by Colonel Tcheng-Ki-Tong [Chen Jitong]. . . . My occupations did not allow me to read it then: the telegrams published these past few days by* El Imparcial *referring to the collapse of the French in Tonkin reminded me that I had that book in my possession. I have read it and, as a small sample, I transcribe a passage that I amused myself to write down last night. It is from the chapter devoted to marriage.*

As Chen became a central character in the Parisian cultural and social life, he also became an object of fascination in Spanish media. If we look only at the translations of Chen's books published in Spain, we will receive a false impression: only *La China contemporánea* (Contemporary China, translation of *Mon pays, la Chine d'aujourd'hui* [My Country, Today's China]) and *Los chinos pintados por sí mismos* (The Chinese Painted by Themselves, translation of *Les Chinois peints par eux-mêmes*) were published in 1899 and 1901.[57] However, the interest in Chen was far from moderate: Chen's talks were reported—sometimes verbatim—in Spanish publications;[58] Chen's presentations at the Paris world's fair in 1889 on variegated topics such as water management, social organization, and typical costumes in China were also widely recounted;[59] Chen's series of articles for *Revue des Deux Mondes* was followed by several media, which mentioned, summarized, or even quoted in full Chen's originals;[60] the publication of *Contes chinois* (Chinese Tales) and *Les Plaisirs en Chine* (Pleasures in China) were celebrated in Spain just when these works were out in France—and even before they were translated into Spanish;[61] and some of Chen's essays and short stories were eventually translated in journals and magazines—most of them without any translator acknowledged.[62]

Along with the interest in Chen as an intellectual and cultural mediator, his personal life became an object of fascination too. Chen can probably be taken as one of the first cross-cultural celebrities—and example of how, as Topik and Wells have argued, the development of the telegraph and the increasing importance of news agencies homogenized many aspects of social life across cultures, including celebrities.[63] *El Liberal*, for instance, characterized Chen as follows: "Este chino, más conocido seguramente en Europa que nuestro decaido presidente del Consejo de ministros, y de seguro mucho más que nuestro ultramontano ministro de Fomento" (This Chinese, surely better known across Europe than our decaying President of the Council of Ministers, and surely much better known than our ultramontane Minister of Development).[64] Chen's witty remarks were often echoed in brief pieces.[65] His marriage with Marie Adèle Lardanchet was reported too.[66] When Chen was recalled to China in 1891 under the accusation of having profited from his official position by raising private loans, a general concern was expressed in the Spanish press and "sinister rumors" about Chen's fate abounded.[67] The resolution of his case was received with relief, as he would not be "decapitado ni ahorcado" (beheaded nor hanged).[68] Even Chen's role in the short-lived Republic of Formosa was announced.[69] It is no surprise that, after Chen's death, obituaries were published—some of them quite hyperbolic.[70]

Why was Chen so popular in France and Spain? Why were works such as *Les Chinois peints par eux-mêmes* so influential? Scholars have answered these questions by focusing on Chen's position as a cross-cultural mediator.[71] While Chen always presented himself as a Chinese official and signed as "General," he took up mediation between China and French cultures as a personal project.[72] Ke Ren argues that Chen "neither provided a nationalistic defense of an essentialized 'China' nor offered an 'Orientalized' (or 'self-Orientalizing') account that catered to the imagination of his Western readers."[73] Chen astutely bridged cultures through "the literary personas of autoethnographer, flâneur, and boulevardier, in addition to the Chinese lettré, as he cultivated a creative and cosmopolitan identity of a writer at home in both the mass press of fin-de-siècle Paris and in the literati values and sensibilities of late imperial China."[74] Chen's aim was to combat the negative stereotypes about China—particularly those spread by missionaries and travel writers. He claimed to have an independent view to describe the true China. That type of true China was particularly appealing as it was projected by a native Chinese speaker who was, in fact, a cosmopolitan voice: after all, his project to counterbalance dominant sinophobic perceptions was executed from the literary salons in Paris. In my view, however, Chen's popularity can be explained by the innocuousness of his approach. The combination of his legitimacy as native speaker and good-humored criticism of Western flaws under a cosmopolitan foil never really challenged the epistemological foundations of how the West was looking at China. Rather, he adapted to them.[75] While Chen countered the sensationalist views of missionaries and travelers with a more humanized vision of the Chinese people and a soft criticism of certain Western aspects, he never moved away from a binary, polarized framework that kept the West as the subject and China as the object. This is why his books were widely available, read, and reviewed. And this is why Chen's work became probably the most popular work that projected a vision of China in the last decades of the nineteenth century, which was spread across European contexts.[76]

Les Chinois peints par eux-mêmes illustrates these points. Chen explicitly declares in the preface that his goal is to provide an alternative vision of China to counter the negative images of the Chinese as despotic and barbaric people. To do so, he believes that he can take advantage of both his condition as native Chinese, which provides a reliable view, and his knowledge of European customs: "représenter la Chine *telle qu'elle est*, de décrire les moeurs chinoises, *avec la connaissance que j'en ai,* mais avec l'esprit et le goût européens" (to represent China *as it is*, to describe Chinese customs, *based on the knowledge that I have*, but also with European spirit and taste).[77] He actually flaunts this role as a cross-cultural guide quite poetically:

> Mon lecteur m'accompagnera, il entrera avec moi, je le présenterai à mes amis et il partagera nos plaisirs. Je lui ouvrirai nos livres, je lui apprendrai notre langue, il parcourra

nos coutumes. Puis, nous irons ensemble dans les provinces; pendant la route nous causerons en français, en anglais, en allemand; nous parlerons de sa patrie, de ceux qui attendent son retour.[78]

My reader will accompany me, he will come with me, I will introduce him to my friends, and he will share our pleasures. I will open our books to him, I will teach him our language, he will go through our customs. Then we will go together to the provinces; along the way we will chat in French, English, German; we will talk about his homeland, about those who await his return.

However, the chapters of *Les Chinois peints par eux-mêmes* do not paint a very different image of China and the Chinese compared to previous accounts by missionaries and sinologists. Chen depicts the conventional series of social, political, and cultural aspects that had characterized many ethnographic accounts of China: family, religion, education, literati, and so on. Chen depicts "a rational and 'harmonious' Chinese civilization" and "a well-functioning patrilineal society based on Confucian patterns of hierarchical social relations—not autocratic or despotic rule—that extended from the family to the state."[79] True: Chen seasons his account with bits of humor and occasional comparisons with French or European elements that act as counterpoints for a more relativistic perspective. But he counterbalances the negative visions of China's despotism, barbarism, and decline that had become dominant in late nineteenth-century Europe with an equally fictional China—a harmonious society that had fascinated the Enlightenment philosophers and that stays equally away from the European societies. In other words, Chen resists the reductionism of sinophobia with the reductionism of sinophilia. As a result, the two representational poles that had historically defined China as an object remain the same. It could be argued that this was nothing but a strategy. Jing Tsu, for instance, notes that Chen was aware of the potential of manipulating the representations of the Chinese other: "Even as he often lamented the false representations of the Chinese in Europe, Chen was fully aware of the value of manipulating that space."[80] My point, however, is that Chen's position—whether deliberate or not—remained within an epistemology that relied on difference. Chen's project as a cross-cultural mediator as well as the cultural and symbolic capital he acquired from it depended on the very same separation that he was trying to bridge. *Les Chinois peints par eux-mêmes* therefore did nothing but stress the difference between both parts of the world. Everything—from the persona he created for himself (he made sure to wear the official Qing robe and always sign as "General," for instance) to the content of his texts—was anchored by this gap.

The acclaim for Chen's life and works in Spain illuminates these points with even more clarity. The main reason that explains Chen's success in Spain is precisely Chen's polarization of China and France, which reinforced the existing cultural and political hierarchies. Chen is popular in Spain because he is as Chinese as French. Although he was praised for his external vision of the French life and for his "gran ingenio, no exento de sátira contra la vida parisiense" (great inventiveness, not without satire against Parisian life),[81] he was equally praised for his command of the French language.[82] Chen's work in Spain was not published as an exotic eccentricity but along with important figures such as Pardo Bazán who worked under a strong French influence. The translation of Chen's *Mon pays, la Chine d'aujourd'hui* was published in a series that included works by authors such as Tolstoy, Wagner, Zola, Goncourt, Dostoevsky, Turgenev, Balzac, Mérimée, and Stendhal.[83] The reception of Chen's works in Spain illustrates Chen's Frenchness and Chen's epistemological grounding, which in turn explains Chen's success in France.

Chen's popularity in Spain also illustrates other aspects related to the trialectical pattern that characterized the representations of China in Spain as well as the image of China arising from it. As the image of China was affected by the prestige and symbolic capital conferred by French writing, Chen's work was transplanted into Spain through a network of secondhand readings—a procedure that was even systematized in specific sections such as "Notas críticas" (Critical notes) and "Revista extranjera" (Foreign review).[84] Chen's success in Spain can also be explained by his amalgamation of points of enunciation. On the one hand, he embodied the geopolitical, the cultural, and the personal in the interaction between China and the West. Chen's figure facilitated the interaction among these different dimensions: China in international geopolitics triggered the interest in China as a culture and for Chen's personal life—and vice versa. On the other hand, as Chen occupied both a Chinese and a French point of enunciation, the double linguistic and cultural translation from Chinese into French and then into Spanish appeared to be simplified, creating the illusion of a closer—and more coeval—China. A concern for a coeval China is perhaps the most significant aspect of Chen's story—both in France and in Spain. Through Chen, China is perceived to be a coexisting presence in the world and to have a certain agency. It is a China that (apparently) can challenge myths and stereotypes.[85] It is a China that is asking to be understood—even if the "new understanding" provided by Chen is still anchored in the same old terms and within the same epistemological boundaries of the past.[86] This new China nevertheless opens up a moment of doubt, the need to find out what is going on. Chen provides answers but, even more importantly, intensifies the questions about what the truth about China is, who can tell this truth, and whether the Chinese themselves can reveal it. These questions underlie the fascination for Chen in Europe at the turn of the twentieth century. These questions perpetuate the same epistemological positions: China remains an object to be discovered by the West.

Chen Jitong declared that he wanted to "re-establish the truth" and warned that "a beau mentir qui vient de loin!" (he who comes from afar may lie!).[87] The concept of truth explains Chen's ultimate success: he simultaneously played the two categories that operated in the grammar that ruled the representations of China in the West at the turn of the twentieth century. As a Chinese in France, Chen is the object that raises new concerns and renews the quest for a truth about a China that is here and now. As a writer in French, Chen is the subject that provides old answers to these new concerns. Being himself subject and object at the same time, whatever he says must be true: "Sabe dar tal colorido, dibuja los tipos con tal verdad—á pesar de no conocerlos nadie—que basta leer una columna para convencerse que no puede menos que ser cierto lo que nos cuenta" (He is so able in giving that color, he is so skilled in drawing people with such truth—even if no one really knows these people—that it is enough to read a column to convince oneself that what he tells us cannot but be true).[88]

EL PROBLEMA DE LA CHINA

To be sure, Chen Jitong was not the only author who wrote about China and emphasized the importance of truth. As Felipe Fernández-Armesto has put it, "As the world got 'smaller,' travelers' tales grew taller."[89] The concern for truth and China was part of a general concern for learning about the world in an age when distances decreased and fictional accounts abounded. This happened in Spain too. Back in 1876,

Adolfo de Mentaberry's *Impresiones de un viaje a la China* had already warned that:

> El mentir de las estrellas
> Es muy seguro mentir,
> Porque ninguno ha de ir
> A preguntárselo a ellas.[90]

> *The lying of the stars*
> *Is a very safe lying,*
> *Because no one will go*
> *And ask them about it.*

In 1880, Fernando Garrido had reinforced the irony of *Viajes del chino Dagar-Li-Kao* (Travels of the Chinaman Dagar-Li-Kao) with observations such as: "Quédese el mentir, el contar patrañas, para los viajeros europeos, que explotan á sus crédulos compatriotas, hasta el punto de haber llegado á ser entre ellos proverbial la frase de 'a luengas tierras mentiras luengas'" (Let the lying, the telling of tales, be only for the European travelers, who manipulate their credulous compatriots to the point that the saying "lengthy lies to lengthy lands" has become proverbial among them).[91] Luis Valera also confessed that "la franqueza y la veracidad son cualidades inestimables, aunque, según algunos, poco frecuentes en los viajeros, y por esa misma razón, y a fin de que nadie pueda echarme en cara aquello de a luengas vías luengas mentiras, me he propuesto no apartarme un ápice de la verdad y hablar de todo con cabal franqueza" (frankness and truth are invaluable qualities, even if, according to some, rather infrequent in travelers; that is why, in order not to be accused of the old "lengthy paths lengthy lies," I made the purpose of not moving myself away from the truth, not even an inch, and speaking about everything with complete frankness).[92] But perhaps one the most acute and sincere reflections on the issue of truth can be found in Ramón Auñón y Villalón's account of the Battle of the Yalu River: "y agradecedme esta leal declaración, porque también pude haber adoptado el sistema de á luengas tierras luengas mentiras, y si alguna digo (*de lo cual no estoy muy seguro*) será porque yo mismo me lo he creído antes" (and thank me for this loyal statement, because I could very well have adopted the approach of lengthy lies to lengthy lands, and if I tell any (*of which I am not very sure*), it will be because I myself had assumed it was true).[93]

Fernando de Antón del Olmet shared this widespread concern for truth and China. Yet what is most striking about *El problema de la China* is the arrogance of his warning. Antón del Olmet claims many times that his book portrays "la verdad" about "este tenebroso asunto" (the truth about this dark topic), which he qualifies as the problem of China.[94] Being one of the most flamboyant writers about China in the 1900s, the serious tone of Antón del Olmet is quite dramatic. The gravity of *El problema de la China* contrasts with his own colorful and lively accounts as tercer secretario at the Spanish legation in Beijing between 1897 and 1900.[95] Such gravity seems to give credit to the absolute seriousness of China's problem—and to his truthful account of it.

Back in Spain right before the Boxer siege, Antón del Olmet used the knowledge and symbolic capital provided by his recent experience in China to become a regular contributor to a Spanish press that was eager to incorporate pieces on China after the Boxer events.[96] He also gave lectures in different cultural clubs and scientific societies. *El problema de la China* originated in one of these talks. Antón del Olmet gave it at the Real Sociedad Geográfica in Madrid on December 4, 1900. He later published it as a short book in the *Boletín de la Real Sociedad Geográfica*.[97] In his exposition Antón del Olmet insists so much on revealing the truth about China that he goes beyond the conventional remark. What is interesting for our purposes is how he connects this search for truth with a specific Spanish angle. His aim, he confesses, is to "vulgarizar" (vulgarize) his own knowledge about China and the events taking place there at the moment "en beneficio de la cultura nacional" (for the benefit of the national culture [21]). *El problema de la China* radiates both the urgency to correct the knowledge about China that is circulating across Spanish society and the need to do so for the sake of Spain's future. *El problema de la China* is the first elaborate remark on the indirect perception of China in Spain.

As expected, previous sources lay at the core of Antón del Olmet's criticism. According to him, the origin of the dominant misperception about China can be found in previous books. Their authors are either fantasists or ignorant. The former, usually having lived in China for too long, provide accounts that are too empathic with China and the Chinese: "los que han vivido en el Celeste Imperio muchos años, en fuerza del íntimo contacto con los chinos, dominados por la influencia del medio, convertidos en más chinos que estos mismos, por un fenómeno de óptica mental, pierden en absoluto la facultad de la visión clara y precisa, confundiendo los colores" (those who have lived in the Celestial Empire for many years, by virtue of intimate contact with the Chinese and too much influenced by the environment, become more Chinese than the Chinese; due to a phenomenon of mental optics they completely lose the faculty of clear and precise vision, they get the colors confused [23]). The latter, usually having learned about China from a distance, show a major "desconocimiento de la *verdad verdadera*" (ignorance about the *real truth*) and "forzosamente déjanse llevar de un prejuicio, de una idea sugerida; se engañan ante un aspecto transitorio, una apariencia particular; *prestan una excesiva confianza á ciertas fuentes dignas de poco crédito*" (let themselves be carried away by a prejudice, by a suggested idea; they deceive themselves before any transitory aspect, any particular appearance; *they believe too much in certain sources worthy of little credit* [23, my emphasis]). These shortcomings make it difficult to diagnose the real problem of China and prescribe an effective remedy.

Yet Antón del Olmet does not stop there. He delves into these problematic sources. In a systematic way, he divides them in two groups according to the author's national origin. On the one hand, he lists some of the most influential books on China written by Spanish authors throughout history.[98] He briefly reviews each work according to his idiosyncratic—and quite vague—notion of "truth." Each work is assessed by the author's capacity to offer a combination of personal and negative accounts of China. This allows Antón del Olmet to dismiss in one way or another all the works mentioned. He praises Sinibaldo de Mas's *La Chine et les puissances chrétiennes* (China and the Christian Powers) as "admirable" (remarkable) and "única obra de un diplomático español que en este género de estudios orientales es en el extranjero reputada por de grande autoridad" (the only work by a Spanish diplomat which has a strong reputation in the genre of Oriental studies due to its great authority) but also critiques de Mas as a victim of "fatal optimismo sinófilo" (fatal sinophilic optimism), which raises "ciertas reservas en lo que concierne al conocimiento de la verdad tal como es" (certain reservations about knowing the truth as it is [25]). He qualifies Eduard Toda's *La vida en el Celeste Imperio* (Life in the Celestial Empire) as "digna de consideración especialísima por la verdad absoluta de cuanto en ella se contiene" (worthy of special consideration for the absolute truth of all that is included therein) but dismisses it as "una obra de descripción, en la que no se emiten opiniones" (a work of description, in which no opinions are expressed [25]). He applauds Adolfo de Mentaberry's *Impresiones de un viaje a la China* for telling a "verdad absoluta" (absolute truth) but claims it is a "libro puramente narrativo" (merely narrative book [25]).

On the other hand, Antón del Olmet assembles an exhaustive list of foreign works on China, which he includes in the appendix—also arranged mostly according to the authors' nationality. No reviews are provided for these works. Only three of these works are discussed in the main text, as, according to Antón del Olmet, they represent the most mistaken views of China due to their excessive sinophilia. He qualifies Chen Jitong's *La China contemporánea* as "exquisita" (refined) but dismisses it as misleading, as it offers an image of China that is too pleasant and that has even become a genre (25). He attacks Eugène Simon's *La cité chinoise* as too fantasist and sentimental. He condemns Simon as one of the "panegiristas del pueblo chino" (panegyrists of the Chinese people [28]). Finally, his critique of Pierre Loti's "Una correspondencia desde Pekín" (A Correspondence from Peking) is so strong that he sets this work aside in a special section of the appendix, where he attacks it as an example of the kind of works that "lejos de enseñar, confunden al que no puede juzgar por otro medio" (far from teaching, they bring confusion to those who cannot judge by any other means [123]).[99]

To be sure, Antón del Olmet's ferocious criticism is aimed at reinforcing his own legitimacy as a capable analyst. He backs up his sharp remarks with frequent appeals to his own personal experience in China: "Los que hemos habitado largo tiempo en la China despojados de sentimentalismo y fantasías, y hemos podido confrontar por nuestros ojos esas fingidas imágenes y la realidad vivida, sabemos bien á qué atenernos" (Those of us who, free from sentimentality and fantasies, have lived in China for a long time and have been able to confront through our eyes those pretended images with the actual reality, we know well what to expect [28]). And he also adds that having lived in China is not enough for a truthful account. He clarifies that he has not turned his experiences into literary paintings, but as more "objective photographs" that provide that kind of "naked truth, real truth:"

> A los libros precedentes sobre China, pretenciosa galería de cuadros más ó menos caprichosos, he substituído una sencilla colección de fotografías instantáneas tomadas al natural. Mostrar la verdad desnuda, *la verdad verdadera*, ha sido el único pensamiento de este Ensayo, encaminado á difundir en nuestra Patria el gusto por las cosas que se salen del marco estrecho de la política local. (24, my emphasis).

Unlike the previous books on China, a pretentious gallery of more or less whimsical pictures, I offer here a simple collection of snapshots taken from nature. To show the naked truth, the real truth, the real truth—*this has been the only motivation of this essay, which is aimed at spreading in our country the taste for things that are outside the narrow framework of local politics.*

Photography was, as mentioned previously, a new language with a transnational potential,[100] and Antón del Olmet is keen to use the photograph metaphor—since no actual photographs are included in the book—to convey his personal, unmediated approach.

However, Antón del Olmet's systematic survey of the existing sources about China also reveals a concern that transcends his ostentatious display of legitimizing symbolic capital. The way he distinguishes the origin of the sources shows an unusual national singularization of Spain. Moreover, Antón del Olmet justifies the truthfulness of his account by his own nationality. As a Spaniard, he claims, he holds an impartial and independent view on China. This is a natural quality that does not require much: as a Spaniard "me he dejado llevar de una natural sinceridad, de una imparcialiad nativa. . . . Sin más esfuerzo que éste, sin hacer más que no hacer nada" (I have let myself be carried away by a natural honesty, a native neutrality. . . . Without any other effort than this, without doing anything except doing nothing [21]). What he implies, in other words, is a deliberate rejection of previous views, "algunos de ellos resultado de un estudio vasto u aun profundo, pero todos más ó menos erróneos como basados en un eje falso ó saliendo de un punto de partida equivocado" (some of them the result of a vast or even in-depth study, but all of them more or less mistaken as they are based on a false idea or coming out of a wrong starting point [23]). He claims that, as a Spaniard, he is at the right position to "ver las cosas como son y llamarlas por su nombre . . . *juzgando con nuestro juicio y no pidiendo prestados, para andar, los pies de otro*" (seeing things as they really are and calling them by their real name . . . *judging with our own judgment and not borrowing someone else's feet to walk* [21, my emphasis; see also 24]).

Antón del Olmet's determination is important because, for the first time in the history of the representations of China in Spain, it breaks the illusion of trialectics. *El problema de la China* not only evidences that the connection between China and Spain has traditionally been mediated but also claims that Spain's unmediated relationship with China could eventually be more reliable given the "neutral," "honest" position of Spain in China. In other words, Antón del Olmet's proposal illustrates how the new concern for China increased the perception of an autonomous Spanish view of China. Moreover, Antón del Olmet's determination is significant because *El problema de la China* also reveals the limitations of such a proposal—and therefore the degree of subordination to the secondhand connection between China and Spain. While Antón del Olmet did live in China and while the remarkable amount of data that he includes in his work could be seen as a kind of raw, photographic portrayal of China, his claim of not having relied on someone else's feet is (ironically) far from the truth.

Indeed, the weight of referential information in the second part of *El problema de la China* is massive: the sixteen-page account of China's history is extensive, and the eleven-page summary of statistics and data about contemporary China probably overwhelmed any general reader at the time. All this information was taken from foreign sources, which Antón del Olmet himself reveals to us. In an impressive bibliographical appendix, he mentions nine encyclopedias (including British, Larousse, and Cantù); several ancient books about China;[101] more than thirty books or authors who wrote on China in English;[102] more than thirty books or authors who wrote on China in French;[103] more than thirty books or authors who wrote on China in German from Germany and Austria;[104] and almost twenty books or authors who wrote on China in Russian, Italian, Portuguese, and Dutch.[105] He confesses that these works are the sources for the historical account he has provided in Part I of his essay. He also mentions that statistics were based on *Almanaque de Gotha de 1899–1901* (100–110). My point is that it is probably not that relevant that Antón del Olmet used these sources. Instead, what is most remarkable is that, despite his strong claims about the importance of having a direct Spanish access to China, *he still feels the need to exhibit these foreign sources* for his own "firsthand" account to be convincing.

Similarly, Antón del Olmet's insistence on truth and originality does not match the actual formal development of the text, which turns out to be rather conventional, quite similar to most of the books about China published in the previous decades. *El problema de la China* is divided in two parts. Part 1 includes a set of sections that analyze the Chinese empire and the different agents involved in Chinese society: "El Celeste Imperio," "Los boxers," "El pueblo chino," "El gobierno chino," "La dinastía Manchú," and "Los extranjeros en China" (The Celestial Empire, The Boxers, The Chinese People, The Chinese Government, The Manchu Dynasty, and Foreigners in China). They are examined in a referential way that is not much different from previous essays on China. A section on the different nations established in China, "Las grandes potencias en China" (The Great Powers in China), offers an encyclopedic account that includes small nations like Italy, Austria, Belgium, Holland, Portugal, and Spain (66–73). In a final section of Part I, "Filosofía del problema" (The Problem's Philosophy), Antón del Olmet concludes with some ethnographic generalizations that look at contemporary China through an allochronic perspective and contradict the book's innovative view of China as a coeval presence in the world (79). Part 2 is a heterogeneous combination of sections on Chinese history, statistics, official documents, and some remarks on Pierre Loti, mentioned previously.[106] In other words, *El problema de la China* keeps China as an object to be examined, diagnosed, mentored; the gaze is ultimately ethnographic; and the information is arranged according to conventional formal structures that provide coverage for old wide generalizations and stereotypical topics and issues. At the end of the day, then, *El problema de la China* is not much different from Enrique Gaspar's travel account or from John Harrisson's letters, for instance. Despite the author's pompous self-promotion, China remains locked in its old form.

One question that quickly follows from such an extensive use of foreign sources and reliance on an old epistemology in Antón del Olmet's project is: How do all these sources inform Antón del Olmet's "autonomous" vision of China? What is, in fact, the "real truth" about China that he is proclaiming on the basis of this epistemology? What is the problem of China, after all? And what kind of China emerges from his project? Is it a different China from the China that had been represented before in Spain or the West?

Antón del Olmet's main thesis turns out to be that China is an obstacle for the natural expansion of Western capitalist powers and their economies. China is blocking the development of progress and modernity at a world scale. This, he urges, must be solved as soon as possible. The Western nations must unite and intervene in China to provide peace for the global markets and the development of capital. Indebted to the theories of Herbert Spencer and social Darwinism, Antón del Olmet uses a poignant organicist metaphor to describe the relationship between China and the West: China is a corpse currently being dismembered by the Western nations who act as vultures:

El Imperio de la China era un cadáver acéfalo. Cada Settlement que otorgaba, cada bail que concedía, era un pedazo de
su cuerpo que una nación disecaba. Rusia, se había apodera-
do de su brazo derecho; Inglaterra, del izquierdo; de la pier-
na derecha, Alemania; de la izquierda, Francia. De la cabeza
quiso apoderarse el Japón, y, no encontrándola, se quedó
á la cabecera como hermano del muerto con derechos á la
herencia. Los Estados Unidos se apoderaron de una parte, y
hasta Bélgica, á la sombra de sus grandes hermanas de Europa, se apoderó de un pedazo. Italia quiso tomar su trozo
de león; Austria, prudentemente se mantuvo a la expectativa,
como Holanda, más modesta. Portugal, nuestro hermano, el
primero en descubrir la China para Europa, perdida su gran-
dez de otros días, se alejó de la presa, contemplando con do-
lor el espectáculo de las fieras de Europa apoderándose del
cadáver del coloso, y aprendiendo en tan brutal enseñanza
que es necesario reconquistar la fuerza para no ser la víctima
de las potentes garras de la bestia de la historia. (26)

*The empire of China was a headless corpse. Each settlement
to be conceded, each bail to be paid, was a piece of his body
to be dissected by a foreign nation. Russia seized his right
arm; England grabbed his left arm; his right leg was for
Germany; his left leg was for France. Japan wanted to take
his head but, unable to do so, remained waiting as a dead
man's brother who has inheritance rights. The United States
seized a portion. And even Belgium, in the shadow of her
great sisters in Europe, seized a piece. Italy wanted to take
her piece of the lion; Austria carefully remained waiting, like
Holland, more modest. Portugal, our brother, the discoverer
of China for Europe, having lost his greatness of the past,
walked away from the prey, painfully watching the spectacle
of the beasts of Europe seizing the corpse of the giant, learning from such brutal teaching that it is necessary to regain
strength so as not to be the victim of the powerful claws of
the beast of history.*

The corpse metaphor enables a criticism that is directed both at China
and the West. On the one hand, China has not been capable enough to
integrate the progress and modernity brought by Europe into its own

political and economic institutions. But China still holds a tremendous potential. The organicist metaphor of the present then mutates into a technological metaphor of the future:

> Porque el propósito de Europa al poner su mano hercúlea sobre el cadáver del coloso, no era, mirando las cosas con grandeza, no era el de devorarlo, sino el de galvanizar sus miembros, substituyendo la vida natural que le animó durante los sesenta siglos de su historia por la vida artificial, última fórmula de las maravillosas invenciones del progreso. Porque los hilos del telégrafo y los carriles de la locomotora serán sus nuevos nervios, el oro de los bancos será su nueva sangre, las máquinas de la imprenta serán su nuevo cerebro, y las luces eléctricas sus ojos y el teléfono su voz, cuando los genios de este siglo . . . digan un día al cadáver del coloso, consiguiéndolo: Levántate y anda. (27)

> *Because, if we look at the big picture, the purpose of Europe in putting its Herculean hand on the giant's corpse was not to devour him, but to galvanize his limbs, to replace the natural life that had animated China's history for sixty centuries with artificial life—the ultimate formula for the wonderful inventions of progress. Because the telegraph wires and the locomotive rails will become his new nerves, the gold in the banks will turn into his new blood, the printing machines will be his new brain, and the electric lights will be his eyes and the telephone his voice, when the day will come and the geniuses of this century . . . will successfully say to the giant's corpse: Get up and walk.*

On the other hand, the Western nations should put aside "su política de pequeñas miserias" (their politics of small miseries [i.e., indemnities after the Boxer Uprising]) and undertake, "siquiera por una vez, una política de miras realmente grandes, levantadas" (even for once, a policy of really big, elevated sights [78]). China should be turned into a safe and reliable market. The Western economies must "encontrar en el Imperio chino una salida á sus productos que rebosan en sus aglomerados almacenes" (find in the Chinese empire an outlet for the products that overflow in their crowded warehouses [75–76]). Given China's size and importance, what is at stake is none other than the "porvenir económico del mundo" (the world's economic future [75]). The problem of China is therefore a problem shared by the West.

Antón del Olmet follows his diagnosis with three specific proposals. First, the Western nations need a collective strategy that does not split China into different parts to be distributed among the Western powers: "Esta teoría del reparto de la China para evitar que un día aplaste á Europa, es la antítesis de la otra que sostiene que la China es un cadáver cuyos despojos deben ser repartidos en lotes proporcionales entre las grandes potencias" (The theory that advocates the division of China in order to prevent China from crushing Europe one day is the antithesis of the other theory that maintains that China is a corpse whose remains must be distributed among the great powers in proportional parts [73]). Second, the Western nations must assume their role as executors of modernity, instead of beneficiaries. Progress and modernity are superior forces and Western powers have the duty to intervene in China. While their intervention in China can be doubtful from a legal point of view, it is necessary from a moral perspective, and in fact, it must be done for the sake of "la inmensa mayoría del pueblo chino [que es] infinitamente desdichado" (the vast majority of the Chinese people who are infinitely wretched [46, also 76–77]). Third, Western intervention must be surgical—neither a wide colonial domination nor a radical civilizational change. This implies a certain degree of adaptation. Antón del Olmet notes that when the Jesuits arrived in China "vestidos á la usanza de los chinos" (dressed in the Chinese style), they were welcome. Instead, when Europeans presented themselves with arrogance, "aires de supremacía andando á cañonazos sin rebozo" and a "política de inhabil intrusión" (with airs of supremacy, shooting cannons for no reason, and with a policy of unskillful intrusion [36]), they were refused. Inspired by the successful blended nature of the Chinese Maritime Customs Service, Antón del Olmet proposes a surgical intervention that replaces the official ruling class and puts the army under European control, while keeping China's territorial integrity and legal autonomy (77–78).

Given the spread and vigor of social Darwinism around the world at the turn of the century, Antón del Olmet's argument is not surprising. And El problema de la China successfully integrates Spain's singularity into this framework. To be sure, Spain can only be a witness to such a historical event: "En cuanto á España, desangrada por las últimas guerras y más aún por su interior desconcierto, que fué el origen de todo, sólo podía ser testigo del histórico espectáculo" (As for Spain, bled to death by the last wars and even more so by its interior chaos, which was the origin of everything, it could only witness such historical spectacle [26]). But Spain's weakness singularizes the Spanish perspective and provides a more objective analytical diagnosis. In this way, the singularization of Spain's position in China adjusts to the singularization of the different nations that constitute the West in *El problema de la China*. Unlike the typical accounts of the mid-nineteenth century that conceived of Europe or the West as a unit, and Spain as an unproblematic part of it, *El problema de la China* anticipates the more intense singularization and fragmentation that will take place in future decades when the images of China, as we will see, respond to a different economy of representation.

The last set of questions that need to be asked at this point is: How were Antón del Olmet's ideas received in Spain? Or, more pertinently, how did Antón del Olmet's representation of China fit into the Spanish intellectual debates of the time? What can we infer from the reception of *El problema de la China* in the Spain of 1901?

Rafael María de Labra's preface to *El problema de la China* offers some answers to these questions. Rafael María de Labra (1840–1918) was an illustrious intellectual, well known for his liberal and republican views as well as for his defense of abolitionism. Labra had been one of the founders of the Institución Libre de Enseñanza in 1876, a secular private educational institution inspired by Krausism that played a relevant role in the intellectual environment in Spain.[107] When *El problema de la China* was published, he was the rector of the Institución Libre de Enseñanza and a notorious figure in Spanish intellectual life. Labra's preface is therefore important not only because it may help counterbalance Antón del Olmet's bombastic rhetoric and tendency to self-promotion as a young diplomat with literary aspirations but also because it situates the book—and China—in Spain's contemporary debates and frames the significance of Antón del Olmet's contribution as it was seen at the time.

Labra quickly confirms that China is a hot topic in Spain and that *El problema de la China* is a timely contribution: "Un libro sobre China es en estos momentos de extrema, de insuperable actualidad" (A book on China is nowadays most timely, of extreme timeliness [7]). Labra's informative overview and mature grasp of the complex situation in China at the time also confirms the availability of data and sources on China in Spain. As a piece written by someone who was not an expert on Chinese matters and who lacked any direct experience with the Chinese reality, Labra's preface seems to disprove Antón del Olmet's claim: Spanish intellectuals may have "borrowed someone else's feet to walk," and their knowledge about China may have been indirect, but it was complete, critical, and up to date. Labra also explicitly quotes the foreign sources (French, English, American, and German) that helped him organize such a holistic view—some of which, surprisingly, were not included in Antón del Olmet's exhaustive lists.[108] Labra's preface, then, reinforces the suspicion that Antón del Olmet's insistence on truth functions more as a trope than as an actual reality.

Labra agrees with Antón del Olmet on one thing: China is a problem for the whole world. This is a crucial assumption—not only because it shows the coevalness of China in a world that is now interconnected through capital but also because, as we have seen, it raises questions about Spain's position in such an interconnected network. The same view that recognizes the critical situation in China reveals the weakness of Spain too. It is not surprising, then, that Labra considers *El problema de la China* a "toque de atención" (wake up call [20]): not only because Antón del Olmet's analysis of China is timely and deserves attention but also because it highlights the larger social and moral consequences of modernity and progress—in China *and* in Spain. China is therefore a springboard for criticism: Antón del Olmet's critical view of China raises, in fact, a critical yet ambiguous view of Spain. Defeated by the same processes of progress, modernity, and international competition that are affecting China, Spain looks at China from a subaltern position, subjected to the hegemony of other European centers.

However, Labra's view on China stands on opposite moral grounds from Antón del Olmet's. From his liberal, abolitionist position, Labra digs into certain aspects that remain unexplored in *El problema de la China*. He acknowledges the "difícil situación" (difficult situation) in the East, given the intervention of the Western powers after the Boxer Uprising (14). He mentions aspects of "derecho internacional público" (public international law) and equates the problems in China with issues in Japan and Paraguay. He points out specific ways in which the Chinese have seen their sovereignty under attack: indirectly with financial, religious, or infrastructural interventions and more directly with colonial occupations or the acquisition of territories (16–18). These issues, he remarks, cannot be found in Antón del Olmet's book:

> No entra éste en pormenores ni toma los puntos de vista que acabo de señalar. Está dedicado á apreciar en conjunto la sociedad china *de nuestro tiempo*, á indicar los problemas que surgen de su relación con los Pueblos Occidentales y á

mantener, en el terreno las aplicaciones, el criterio del *con-cierto internacional inexcusable* en la época en que vivimos. (19, my emphasis)

The book does not go into detail or take the points of view that I have just indicated. The book aims at understanding the Chinese society of our time as a whole, at pointing out the problems that arise from China's relationship with the Western peoples, and applying on the ground the criteria of current mandatory international agreements.

The tension between Labra's internationalism and Antón del Olmet's Spencerism reveals a conundrum for Spanish intellectuals at the turn of the twentieth century. What this tension reveals for our purposes is how China, now seen as a coeval reality that is imperative to the Western world to address, remains subjected to and instrumentalized by Spanish internal debates.[109]

In this chapter we have seen how the awareness of a coeval China in the world at the turn of the twentieth century triggered an interest in truth that updated the old interest in an enigmatic China that had prevailed in the ethnographic context of the nineteenth century. The awareness of a coeval China also triggered an awareness of Spain's singularity within the West. The examples discussed previously have shown how difficult it was to develop this new understanding of China from Spain when, besides the dependance on foreign sources for content purposes, there was also an epistemology of China strongly anchored in a particular ethnographic form.

As a constant operation in the process of cross-cultural representation, translation—translated texts but also views and forms in translation—contributed to setting these new horizons while maintaining the old epistemological boundaries. Translation increased the knowledge and information about China available in Spanish society and, at the same time, dissolved the contradictions between new perceptions and old patterns of representation. The coeval and truthful China was a China in translation and *remained* a China in translation.

CHAPTER 3

"My Pride as a White Man Fully Woke Up"

May 18, 1919
Nanjing, China

"I forget they are Chinese a great deal of the time."[1]

American philosopher John Dewey writes this sentence less than three weeks after he and his wife, Alice Chipman, have arrived in China. The sentence is written on a letter to be sent to their children back in the United States. In the letter, Dewey reflects on the peasants the couple has met during their travel from Shanghai to Hangzhou and Nanjing. The sentence could be just a minor, casual remark to be shared with their family back home. But it is not. "I forget they are Chinese a great deal of the time" denotes a way of looking *at* China *from* China that remains quite unusual until the 1920s. The implication of Dewey's remark is that China and the Chinese can also be understood in ways other than difference, exoticism, and sinophobia. Poor Chinese peasants are, first and foremost, poor human beings: "They just seem like dirty, poor miserable people anywhere."[2]

The story of Dewey and China is well known.[3] In the fall of 1918 Dewey was teaching at the University of California, Berkeley, while on sabbatical from Columbia University. Out of intellectual curiosity, Dewey and his wife decided to travel farther west to Japan. The trip was funded by philanthropist Albert C. Barnes and, in exchange, Dewey agreed to write a report on the role of Japan in the future of international relations.[4] A few lectures at Tokyo Imperial University were arranged through acquaintances. Learning that Dewey would be visiting East Asia, Hu Shi—one of Dewey's Chinese students at Columbia between 1915 and 1917—invited him to spend a year in China. Dewey became the first foreign scholar to be formally invited to lecture in China.[5] He seemed to enjoy the experience. He arrived in China right in the middle of the May Fourth Movement, a heated period of social convulsions and claims for political reforms spurred by China's weak position in the international negotiations at the end of World War I. In May 1919, the signature of the Treaty of Versailles spurred student protests and a boycott of Japanese products. Dewey was stimulated by "the social energies being released," and the movement "kept him excited, involved, puzzled, and, at times, frustrated."[6] Dewey even decided to extend his stay in China for a second year.

In China, Dewey was treated like a celebrity. His movements were followed in the press and his lectures were massively attended. The impact of Dewey's theories on China's modernization of education and politics has been widely acknowledged—especially given Dewey's mentorship on Hu Shi, who later became a key cultural and political figure in China.[7] Less attention, however, has been paid to the impact of China on Dewey's thought. Jessica Ching-Sze Wang has recently showed how Dewey's ideas on internationalism, democracy, and the relationship between the state and society were very much influenced by his encounter with China.[8] Even less attention has been paid to Dewey's representations of China themselves. Dewey's observations throughout his two-year stay—written in his letters to his family as well as in articles published in American media—show a new way of looking at China and the Chinese people.

Intellectual and political life in 1919 China was characterized by an amalgamation of discourses and worldviews that could seem confusing, even contradictory: nationalism blended with internationalism, liberalism interacted with Marxism, impulses to follow the Western technological paths coexisted with impulses to preserve traditional Chinese culture. It was a moment in Chinese history that was not easy to depict—especially in real time and without a background in Chinese history. But Dewey's comments on internal politics were always sharp and balanced. The most remarkable aspect of his depictions was his attitude: Dewey followed the complexities and ambivalences he encountered in China with "a deep intellectual interest" and open-mindedness. He was always eager to understand these complexities with curiosity and, especially, on China's own terms—instead of through the prism of Eurocentrism.[9]

To be sure, Dewey's visit was still inscribed in the same old logic that prescribed the stimulation of China's modernization through Western knowledge—assuming that the West held a more advanced technological and intellectual position and that a backward China needed help to "move forward" or "catch up" with modernity. But Dewey's representations nevertheless illustrate a new epistemology: China could be perceived, understood, and represented on different terms or according to different logics. Dewey's representations anticipate the pluralization of views that will fully develop throughout the 1920s and 1930s across the West. Important writers and journalists such as Pearl Buck, Agnes Smedley, and Edgar Snow will project new views of China rooted on new agendas and concerns. These new views will not remain marginal. They will reach much broader parts of society well beyond missionaries and diplomats. The "Hands off China" campaign between 1925 and 1927, for instance, was "the first mass mobilization carried out on behalf of China in Britain," where the left "frequently challenged the popularly held negative stereotypes of China," and in their place "it presented an image of the Chinese as resilient, calm, and dignified in the face of suffering."[10] As a result, images of China gained a wider circulation and the growth of interest in Chinese culture and history was "more widely diffused."[11] Dewey's observations on China, then, were inscribed in a wide and diversified attention for China, which he addressed as an influential figure in American and international politics at the time. In fact, Dewey's letters from China were published in January 1920 while he was still in East Asia. China was present in intellectual, cultural, and social discussions beyond international affairs.

To be sure, the new ways of representing China did not substitute the ways in which China had been represented in the past. The old sinophilia/sinophobia dichotomy remained in operation. The new ways of representing China were rather juxtaposed to, or in interaction with, the old ones. Dewey's views can certainly be contrasted with, for instance, Albert Einstein's xenophobic observations written in his personal travel diaries when he was traveling across Asia.[12] In fact, such an accumulation of representations was not something new. As James St. André has shown, genuine nineteenth-century translations from Chinese into English or French "were, to a certain extent, judged as authentic or inauthentic based on how closely they adhered to the invented style of the eighteenth-century pseudotranslations." Or, in other words, the creation of new Oriental voices always built upon existing views and stereotypical notions concerning the East.[13]

W. Somerset Maugham's *On a Chinese Screen* illustrates this accumulation of views. Originally published in 1922, this travel diary resulted from Maugham's two visits to China in 1919 and 1921, which coincided with Dewey's stay. *On a Chinese Screen* includes a selection of vivid sketches of Chinese people and, mainly, of Westerners in China: missionaries, diplomats, businessmen. On the one hand, Maugham's Orientalist depictions contrast with Dewey's empathetic and analytical observations of a China of the present. Maugham's account is full of "mysteries," "extraordinary stories," and "adventures" that fill the pages with sentences like this: "The Peking cart disappears into the gathering darkness: it seems to carry all the mystery of the East."[14] But, on the other hand, Maugham's writings show signs that even the most Orientalist, essentialist, and condescending visions of the East now include occasional bits of pluralization and criticism. For instance, *On a Chinese Screen* describes the heterogeneous nature of the Western community in China, and Maugham's condescension is also applied to Western expats as their differences, rivalries, and hypocrisies are unveiled. Not surprisingly, the book received only mild reviews in publications such as the *North China Herald*: "Unkind persons like the author of 'On a Chinese Screen,' who returned the kindness of his hosts by writing a book about them of which he ought to be ashamed."[15] *On a Chinese Screen* also includes mixed views when representing a certain topic. Coolies and rickshaw pullers, for instance, are both animalized and the object of admiration. An opium den is both the epitome of "the inscrutable Oriental" and a pleasant location that reminds Maugham "of the little intimate beerhouses of Berlin."[16] The variety of representations is increased by the differences in the expat community: some of the expats have already been living in China for twenty, thirty, or forty years, and their views do not coincide with the views of those who have just arrived.

In sum, in the 1910s and 1920s, the catalog of representations of China became more heterogeneous in an unprecedented way: new agents became involved in representing (i.e., portraying and speaking for) China to Western audiences; new concerns about China turned out to be discussed; new ways of understanding and explaining China's different realities coexisted and brought about new ways in which the West could relate to them; and a wider readership enlarged and multiplied the networks through which all these representations circulated. China became thereby an object of multiple attentions and all these representations of China were put in competition among themselves. The scope, intensity, and interaction of these simultaneous Chinas was new. In the eighteenth and nineteenth centuries, the competition had been a binary one: sinophilia and sinophobia attempted to draw Western readers to their respective poles. At the turn of the twentieth century, representations competed to unveil the "true China," even if the nature of this true China turned out to be not that different from the imagined China of the past. In the new economy for representing China in the 1910s and 1920s, representations were now aimed at gaining the reader's attention through any of the multiple Chinas that had become available across this richer and more nuanced spectrum—which included exoticism and sinophobia, fascination and repulsion, but also, as we have seen in Dewey and Maugham, engagement, puzzlement, humanism, excitement, frustration, open-mindedness, empathy, critical analysis, and intellectual curiosity.

What concerns us primarily here is how the competition for representing these different Chinas interacted with the indirect patterns of representation seen in previous chapters, which were still in operation. To explore this issue, we will focus on the accounts written by Spanish authors who undertook literary travels to the Far East in the 1920s. Vicente Blasco Ibáñez, Federico García Sanchiz, and Luis de Oteyza are examples of early twentieth-century globe-trotters "whose adventures provided a sense of the vast, yet also small, new world of interconnected currents."[17] What were the effects of moving around such a "vast, yet also small, new world" upon the ways China was represented in Spain? How did the new economy for representing China in such an interconnected world affect the ways in which China was imagined and written about in Spain? How was this competition between multiple Chinas played out in a national context that had been imagining China indirectly through the prism provided by other nations? What kind of representations of China emerged from these authors' firsthand experiences when they had still learned about China through mostly secondhand sources originally published in other Western nations?

In this chapter I show how the trialectical structure that had characterized the representations of China in Spain lost its internal coherence for the first time. In the past, the fact that China was being experienced in a local Spanish context after having been conceived through Western languages and discourses had never raised major concerns. The occasional criticisms—such as the ones expressed by Antón del Olmet, as we saw in the previous chapter—never really went beyond limited remarks that were equally engulfed by the effects of indirect mediation. In this chapter I show how the new economy for representing China in the 1920s made the indirect, mediated relationship between China and Spain more visible and how representations became less coherent—not only occasionally but in a more recurrent way. Spanish writers became more self-conscious of their national position as Spaniards describing China—a position that was different from other Western positions. Some Spanish writers even explored this contrast with other Western nations in their works about China. In this context, I argue that the breakdown of trialectical coherence in representing China in the works of the Spanish writers to be discussed was fueled by a strong investment in race and patriotism. This is not surprising as Arthur de Gobineau's scientific racism reached the height of its popularity in the 1910s and 1920s in the West just when "views of the role of race helped construct the language and the understandings of social science and of world history."[18] The racial accounts of China by these acclaimed Spanish authors show the hierarchies and political underpinnings of such language and understanding of the world: as a structure of domination, race situated Spain on the Western side of the West/China colonial binary; as part of a broader notion of Hispanidad—which combined race with values such as patriotism, nationalism, imperialism, and Catholicism—race also re-empowered Spanish identity after the collapse of the Spanish empire. I also argue that, as a result, representations of China produced literary works characterized by weak formal developments. Feeling the verisimilitude of their works seriously challenged by these formal inconsistencies, some writers were even tempted to qualify fiction as the most appropriate genre to describe their own autobiographical experiences in China. Finally, these inconsistencies can be read allegorically too. If imperialist travel narratives have been intimately connected to orderly presentations and allegorical resonances to the traveler's own culture,[19] the disorderly presentations of China we will examine suggest the difficulties in building a strong patriotic discourse in Spain.

CHINA IN TRANSFORMATION

"La China es hoy, así para el turista como para el sociólogo, uno de los países más interesantes del mundo, acaso el más interesante de todos"

(China is today, for the tourist as much as for the sociologist, one of the most interesting countries in the world, perhaps the most interesting of all).[20]

This claim appeared in the December 1911 issue of the monthly journal *Por Esos Mundos* published in Madrid. It was signed by X. Y. Z., a pseudonym of the Mexican poet and essayist Juan Crisóstomo Ruiz de Nervo y Ordaz, also known as Amado Nervo (1870–1919). What made China the world's most interesting country? The answer is to be found in the very same title of the piece: "La China vieja y la nueva: un país en transformación" (New and Old China: A Country in Transformation). Nervo, who had lived in Europe since 1900 and had probably gathered information about China from different sources while in Paris, depicts a China in a moment of transition on the road to progress. Nervo summarizes China's political reforms at the end of the Qing Empire and reflects on China's turn toward modernity. The transformation from the "old China" into a "new civilized China" is characterized by change: changes in politics and institutions, changes in the psychology of the Chinese people, changes in how the West should value China. As a result of all these changes, Nervo argues, China will take a new important role in the world. At this historical juncture, he adds, many contrasts emerge:

A la pureza de lo pintoresco, sucede la extravagancia de los contrastes. En las grandes ciudades, abiertas al comercio con los extranjeros, entre los viejos carricoches indígenas pasan triunfalmente el automóvil y el ferrocarril; junto á los típicos juncos de vela cuadrada suenan las sirenas de los grandes vapores modernos; por las puertas de las vetustas murallas se cruzan con los coletudos celestes figuras europeas; con las miserables habitaciones de campesinos y culíes contrastan las grandes construcciones de las casas de comercio alemanas, inglesas ó americanas; y con la poética soledad de la tumba de Confucio, el bullicio y el humear de chimeneas de los centros industriales.[21]

The purity of the picturesque is followed by the extravagance of contrasts. In the big cities, open to trade with foreigners, the automobile and the railroad triumphantly pass among the old indigenous carriages. Next to the typical reeds of squared sails, there are sounds of sirens from the great modern

*steamboats. Through the gates of the ancient walls, Euro-
pean figures intersect with pigtailed celestials. The miserable
rooms of peasants and coolies contrast with the large buildings of the German, English, or American trading houses.
The poetic solitude of Confucius's tomb contrasts with the
bustle and smoke of chimneys from industrial centers.*

Nervo's depictions of Chinese society, history, and politics are accurate
and balanced. But the article's most interesting aspect lies in its claim:
given the major transformations in progress, the West needs a new way
of looking at China. The West must leave behind clichés, such as the
yellow peril, and must understand China in a more sympathetic way.
Nervo eloquently concludes that "Bastan los ligeros datos apuntados
para comprender que China ha emprendido el camino del progreso y se
dispone á marchar por él rápidamente. Los libretistas de opereta y los
novelistas fantásticos lo sentirán; pero el bienestar de la humanidad no
puede menos de ganar con ello" (The few data pointed out are enough
to understand that China has embarked on the path of progress and
is preparing to march rapidly on it. Operetta librettists and fantastic
novelists will regret it; but the well-being of humanity cannot but gain
from it).[22] Now accepted as a coeval global actor legitimized by Western
progress and modernity, China should not be feared:

> Pero de que esta influencia sea enorme no se sigue que necesa-
> riamente haya de ser funesta. El peligro amarillo es concebido
> por el vulgo como la posibilidad de una poderosa avalancha
> invasora análoga á la de las hordas de Gengis-Khan. Pero
> esto, que sería lógico tratándose de una China bárbara, deja
> de tener visos de verosimilitud atribuido á una China civi-
> lizada. Cualquiera que sea el enigma que el porvenir nos
> guarde, no debe olvidarse que los males de la humanidad no
> han venido nunca de la cultura y de la civilización, sino de
> la barbarie.[23]

> *But this enormous influence does not have to be necessar-
> ily fatal. The common people understand the yellow peril as
> the possibility of a powerful invading avalanche, similar to
> Genghis Khan's hordes. But this, which would be logical in a
> barbaric China, does not appear to be plausible in a civilized
> China. Whatever enigma the future is holding for us, we*

should not forget that the ills of humanity have never come from culture and civilization, but rather from barbarism.

This civilized China became "the world's most interesting country" and appealed not only to "sociologists and tourists" but also to a wide array of social spheres—from business to religion, from science to popular culture. This wider interest turned the representations of China across the West more heterogeneous. Just as the pages of Nervo's article combine photographs that juxtapose images of the new and old China, the different representations of China across the West during the 1910s and 1920s diversified. Contrasting images existed side by side.[24]

Such diversification has been explained by many historical, social, and ideological causes. Most notably, important technological advances increased even more the speed of travel and communication that had already been significantly improved at the end of the nineteenth century. Nervo himself reminds readers that "en 1911 han llegado á 8.697 los kilómetros de longitud de las líneas de telégrafo, por las cuales se transmitieron en 1909 la cantidad de 807.841 despachos" (in 1911 telegraph lines reached 8,697 kilometers in length, through which 807,841 dispatches had been transmitted in 1909).[25] Radio, telegraph, and transpacific transportation systems and communications kept improving until the 1930s and 1940s. And, as Richard Jean So has shown, the rise of a new era in media technology brought about a new way of looking at the East and a new framework for intellectual and cultural relations between China and the West.[26] All these technological developments made it possible to represent China from a distance with a remarkable degree of immediacy and accuracy. Moreover, a mushrooming of foreign missionary schools, hospitals, and other social services were set in China, particularly after the American Congress forgave the unused balance of the Boxer indemnity in 1908 under the condition that it was used for educational activities. Mobility of Westerners to China and Chinese to the West also played an important role in the diversification of understandings and representations of China—particularly as new agents became involved in these exchanges around the interwar period, considered the golden age of travel writing.[27] Major Chinese artists and intellectuals spent years in Europe: intellectual Liang Qichao (1919–1920), painter Pan Yuliang (1921–1928) and writers Lao She (1924–1929) and, later, Qian Zhongshu (1935–1938) are but a few examples of a general trend. Prominent Western scholars, writers, and activists visited China, some of them for rather long periods of time: besides John

Dewey (1919–1921) and W. Somerset Maugham (1919–1920), already mentioned, other important figures who gave lecture tours or spent significant time in China included Bertrand Russell (1920–1921), Albert Einstein (1922), and Margaret Sanger (1922). China (and Asia, more generally) was seen as an opportunity to revitalize Western culture given the spiritual crisis that followed World War I and intellectuals' pessimism toward Western civilization. The popularity of Rabindranath Tagore's visits to Europe and the United States can be explained by this generalized spiritual search.[28] In addition, about 140,000 Chinese workers had been recruited by the British and French governments between 1916 and 1918 to offer nonmilitary support in factories and trenches during World War I. Their bleak working conditions were protested by French and British labor unions, and the YMCA offered recreational and educational activities to these Chinese workers.[29] Needless to say, the spread of communism and the interest of the left in creating a global network also brought about new concerns for—and new images of—China around the world.[30]

All these encounters between China and the West differed from the encounters represented in conventional, ethnographic travel writings by diplomats and missionaries that had characterized the representations of China in previous decades. However, without the understanding of a China *in transformation*, these new encounters would most likely have remained polarized and limited to the same topics and concerns that had characterized the visions of China in previous decades. China was now represented in a more varied and plural way not only because of the important changes in technology and the new agents who mediated these new interactions but also—and especially—because there was a new understanding of China that enabled that representational diversity. Understanding China as an organic reality in transformation was crucial to habilitate the coexistence—and the ambivalence—of multiple Chinas in the West.

China's transition from empire to republic provided the strongest historical crystallization of this transformation. The abdication of the Qing dynasty and the proclamation of the Republic of China in 1911 and 1912 had an enormous impact in the West. As China was publicly acclaimed and welcomed into the world of democracy by Western societies, the proclamation of the republic was promptly announced in 1911 by Western media. The political instability that later caused the failure of the republican project was also closely reported on a regular basis. Nervo's article also shows this monitoring and how the weekly or monthly publications could not keep up with the ongoing political developments in China:

> Al entrar en prensa este artículo, las últimas noticias publicadas por los telegramas de la prensa diaria han hablado del fracaso de las negociaciones de paz entre imperialistas y revolucionarios, y hasta del establecimiento de un gobierno republicano en China. Pero en estos despachos había bastante confusión. Es muy posible que al llegar estas líneas á manos del lector, haya publicado la misma prensa diaria noticias de última hora más precisas.[31]

> *As this article went into production, the latest news published by telegrams in the daily press have reported the failure of peace negotiations between imperialists and revolutionaries, and even the failure of the establishment of a republican government in China. But there was quite a bit of confusion in these dispatches. It is quite possible that when these lines reach the reader, the same daily press will have already published more precise breaking news.*

In Spain, parallel to the close media attention to these political developments, China gained unprecedented attention in many other spheres. Unlike previous works on China that had only enjoyed a limited circulation in literary and intellectual circles, some of the texts on China from this period became very popular. The works by Blasco Ibáñez, García Sanchiz, and Oteyza that will be examined in this chapter, for instance, reached wide readerships—in Spain and even abroad, especially in the case of Blasco Ibáñez and Oteyza.[32] These works coexisted with works by other notable writers who integrated China in their own literary projects—from avant-gardist Ramón Gómez de la Serna in *Los dos marineros* and *Caprichos* (The Two Sailors, 1924; Caprices, 1925) to realist Pío Baroja in *Yan-Si-Pao*, *Los pilotos de altura*, and *La estrella del capitán Chimista* (Yan-Si-Pao, 1928; The Pilots of High Altitude, 1929; The Star of Captain Chimista, 1930), and even to Federico García Lorca, who, following Rubén Darío's integration of Oriental culture in the Spanish language tradition during the last decades of the twentieth century,[33] turned to Chinese images in a sustained way throughout his career and even declared that "el chino bueno está más cerca de mi que el español malo" (the good Chinaman is closer to me than the bad Spaniard).[34] Besides this array of literary works, more diversified interest in China also implied a growing body of essays and nonfiction works trying to make China accessible to different readerships. Some of these essays remained within missionary circles,[35] or within the limited boundaries of specific topics—from pisciculture to braided straws, from furniture to soy beans.[36] But many of these essays became widely available and read: from overarching introductions to Chinese religion or philosophy, such as Richard Wilhelm's introductions to Confucianism and Daoism,[37] to works explaining the leftist "awakening" of China.[38] Finally, China was also a regular presence in popular culture: from memoirs such as Princess Der Ling's *China: Dos años en la Ciudad Prohibida* (China: Two Years in the Forbidden City, 1913) to fantasies about mythical demon hunters such as *Chung-kuei, domador de demonios* (Chung-kuei, the Demon Tamer, 1929) to comedies such as John Colton's *Shanghai* (Shanghai, 1930).[39]

In sum, enabled by an understanding of a China in transformation, representations of China in Spain became more heterogeneous and circulated more widely in the 1910s and 1920s. While these representations permeated across different social spheres and integrated China more tightly in Spain's culture, they were still subjected to a secondhand condition: China was represented in Spain either through translations or in works originally written in Spanish but that continued to rely heavily on foreign sources.

José Ortega y Gasset's review of Bertrand Russell's *The Problem of China* exemplifies this combination of Spanish singularity and foreign dependence. The review was published in one of the first issues of *Revista de Occidente* in September 1923. Ortega reviewed Russell's original work, published the year before, which remained untranslated in Spanish.

The Problem of China followed Russell's visit to China in 1920 and 1921 to teach at Peking University. *The Problem of China* is built upon the premise that there is nothing inherently inferior in Chinese culture and that the West may not have an adequate understanding of the complexity of China: "A European lately arrived in China, if he is of a receptive and reflective disposition, finds himself confronted with a number of very puzzling questions, for many of which the problems of Western Europe will not have prepared him."[40] This lack of knowledge and inadequate attitude, Russell argues, should be challenged. China's magnitude and potential urge the West to develop a more critical understanding of China:

Chinese problems, even if they affected no one outside China, would be of vast importance, since the Chinese are estimated to constitute about a quarter of the human race. In fact, however, all the world will be vitally affected by the development of Chinese affairs, which may well prove a decisive factor, for good or evil, during the next two centuries. This makes it important, to Europe and America almost as much as to Asia, that there should be an intelligent understanding of the questions raised by China, even if, as yet, definite answers are difficult to give.[41]

Russell's claim for a new, more integrative understanding of China in the world is sustained by the view of China in transformation. As "the culture of China is changing rapidly, and undoubtedly rapid change is needed,"[42] polarized views of China coexist in his text. While he praises some aspects of the Chinese character such as a "instinctive happiness" or "intellectual integrity," he also points to avarice, cowardice, and callousness as China's chief defects.[43] *The Problem of China* turns this heterogeneous imagery into a more integrative view of the world. China's transformation should lead to a productive fusion with the West, one that builds upon this variety and avoids both a complete Westernization and an anti-foreign conservatism. By modernizing without losing its essential positive qualities, China's transformation can help the world overcome the challenges of industrialism and modernity that led to the disaster of World War I. Russell sees in China the ethical qualities that "the modern world most desperately needs," such as pacific temper instead of frantic militarism.[44]

The Great War showed that something is wrong with our civilization; experience of Russia and China has made me believe that those countries can help to show us what it is that is wrong. The Chinese have discovered, and have practised for many centuries, a way of life which, if it could be adopted by all the world, would make all the world happy. We Europeans have not. Our way of life demands strife, exploitation, restless change, discontent and destruction. Efficiency directed to destruction can only end in annihilation, and it is to this consummation that our civilization is tending, if it cannot learn some of that wisdom for which it despises the East.[45]

Russell's conception of China as a "beacon of hope in a troubled world" was highly influential on the left in the interwar years. As Tom Buchanan argues, "The image of a civilized, peaceable people cruelly attacked by a brutal neighbour wielding the weapons of modernity, which underpinned the left's profound sympathy for China in the face of Japanese aggression during the 1930s, owed much to Russell."[46]

Ortega's review of *The Problem of China* is written from the position of a nation that has not suffered the effects of World War I. Ortega rejects Russell's pacifism and his view of a potential world emerging from a productive fusion between China and the West. Instead, he sees China and the West as two incommensurable poles that not only remain in opposition but also are bound to clash with dramatic consequences: "la realidad histórica más profunda de nuestros días, en parangón con la cual todo el resto es sólo anécdota, consiste en la iniciación de un gigantesco enfrentamiento entre Occidente y Oriente" (the beginning of a gigantic confrontation between West and East is the deepest historical reality of our days; anything else compared to it is barely an anecdote).[47] In fact, for Ortega this opposition is nothing but an acceleration and amplification of a situation that has existed since the period between the first and the seventh centuries, when the Germans saved a Europe that was about to be conquered by the East: "La nueva lid que ahora comienza promete ser de dimensiones mucho mayores; en rigor, el primer hecho verdaderamente global, pese a las ilusiones de mundialidad que la última guerra se hizo" (The new battle that now begins promises to be of much larger dimensions; it will be, strictly speaking, the first truly global event, despite the illusions of globality raised by the last war).[48]

Given Spain's neutrality in World War I, it seems only cynical that Ortega criticizes Russell's pacifism and defends war as "un mal que emerge trágicamente de la energía occidental para el bien" (an evil that tragically emerges from Western energy for goodness' sake).[49] Ortega's arrogance dismisses Russell's claim as sentimental:

> Hoy por hoy, la lucha entre Oriente y Occidente tiene todo el aire de un enamoramiento. Europa, conmovida por la más honda crisis espiritual que nunca ha sufrido, acaba de descubrir sentimentalmente el Asia y atraviesa una etapa de entusiasmo. A su vez, el Oriente, sobre todo el fondo más hondo de Oriente, China, descubre a Europa y cae en parejo arrobo. Los mejores occidentales del presente quisieran ser

un poco chinos, y los más agudos chinos gentes de Londres, Berlín o París.[50]

Today, the struggle between East and West very much looks like falling in love. Europe, touched by the deepest spiritual crisis it has ever suffered, has just sentimentally discovered Asia and is going through a period of enthusiasm. In turn, the Orient, especially the deepest bottom of the Orient, China, discovers Europe and falls into equal enchantment. The best Westerners of the present would rather be a little Chinese; and the sharpest Chinese people would rather be from London, Berlin, or Paris.

Ortega refuses to admit any reassessment of values between East and West. He simplifies Russell's attempts to illustrate the complex interrelations between civil society, education, and political development in China. The result is a polarized, xenophobic image of China that Ortega qualifies as a "pueblo equívoco, casi extrahumano, que hace todo al revés que nosotros" (equivocal, almost extrahuman people, who do everything the other way around).[51]

Setting aside the origins for Ortega's arrogance toward Russell's political—yet utopian—proposal, what is most significant for our purposes is that Ortega remains uncritically captive of the representations of China traced by Russell. Ortega's text never offers any serious counterexample that—besides discredit, simplification, or mockery—critically questions the representations offered by *The Problem of China*. Ortega remains locked within the representational boundaries traced by his British colleague. In the next sections we will explore further the paradoxical combination between this new economy of representation of China in Spain and the old secondhand patterns for representing it.

CHINA CALLING

"China nos llama" (China is calling us).

Journalist José María Romero Salas (1853–1929) sent this exhortation to fellow Spaniards during his travel to China in 1920. His letters first appeared in Manila, published by *El Mercantil*, and were later collected as a book also published in Manila in 1921.[52] While the primary readership for Romero Salas's thoughts was the remaining Spanish community in the Philippines, his exhortation was aimed at Spanish institutions—still understanding Spain as a metropolis with the potential to recover its past strength more than two decades after the colonial collapse. Why was China calling for Spain? What was in China to be found by Spain?

To be sure, the image of China as an economic marketplace avid for Western products was shared across Europe and North America. The image would later become famously condensed in the title of Carl Crow's best seller, *Four Hundred Million Customers*, published in 1937.[53] China as a market was also a consolidated image in Spain at the time when Romero Salas visited Shanghai. In fact, the potential of China as a market had been the main reason for Fernando de Antón del Olmet's critical views already in 1900. The potential of China as a market was also the main claim underlying *El comercio en el Extremo Oriente* (Trade in East Asia), an accurate account of China's trade published in 1918 with a limited distribution written by Father Gaudencio Castrillo (1878–1945). Supported by plenty of data taken— and painstakingly quoted—from publications such as *The China Year Book*, *La Politique de Péking*, and *L'Echo de Chine*, Castrillo argued that China needed foreign investment and advised the Spanish administration to take advantage of that opportunity.[54] For Romero Salas, however, China's attraction was beyond the market. For him, China was a golden opportunity to revitalize Spanish identity: "He venido a China, país ideal para todas las expansiones de la actividad *y del pensamiento*, con la firme resolución de inquirir por qué procedimientos y por qué vías puede España tener acceso en este inmenso estadio, ahito de explotación y hambriento de amor y de ayuda" (I have come to China, an ideal country for all sorts of expansions of activity *and thought*, with the firm resolution to learn about which procedures and by what means Spain could have access to this immense arena, which is filled with exploitation and hungry for love and help).[55] Unlike the spiritual revitalization of Western civilization sought by Western intellectuals such as Bertrand Russell, Romero Salas's interest in China reveals the latent mourning for Spain's imperial defeat. His visit had a specific mission: to flag Spanishness and raise national pride. Given the Spanish legacy in the Philippines, Romero Salas believed that China was an ideal place for that mission: "Si el capital español de Manila . . . extendiese a China uno de sus brazos; qué negocio espiritual y qué material negocio le esperaban!" (If the Spanish resources in Manila . . . extended one of their arms to China; what a spiritual business and what a material business would be waiting!).[56] Even the minor yet well-established Spanish community in Shanghai could contribute to the cause and act as a bridge for major commercial and ideological developments.[57]

"China nos llama" is therefore a call for patriotic action. For Romero Salas, to strengthen the Spanish presence and reputation (in China) is only a question of will. He claims that the usual excuses for the weak Spanish presence in China (historical fatalism, China's isolationism, or Chinese hostility) should be rejected. Like Antón del Olmet had declared almost a decade ago, it all depends on Spain's determination. Yet, unlike previous exhortations, Romero Salas's vehement appeal is explicitly sustained by a set of nationally-loaded concepts. In his letters, the Spanish colony in Shanghai is associated with values such as "hidalguía" (nobility), "honradez" (honesty), "heroicidad" (heroism), or even with traditional weapons such as "adarga" (a hard leather shield of Moorish origin and used by Christian soldiers) or "tizona" (El Cid's sword).[58] Within such semantic landscape, will and patriotism get inevitably connected to "raza española" (Spanish race).[59]

It is important to clarify that for Romero Salas, as for the writers we will examine, "race" is part of the broad idea of Hispanidad (Hispanicity), a macro-concept that gathers notions such as race, patriotism, nation, state, empire, or Catholicism.[60] This "strong patriotic-cultural" connotation is certainly inscribed within the racial view of the world that was fully consolidated at the time and that, as James St. André has shown, also affected the perception of China in the West.[61] However, this patriotic-cultural connotation is different from the ethnic connotation of race that characterized, for instance, Nazi Germany.[62] The racialized depictions of China found in authors such as Romero Salas, Vicente Blasco Ibáñez, and Luis de Oteyza in the 1920s anticipate the combination of race, patriotism, and Hispanidad that would turn essential in the notions of Hispanidad developed by Ramiro de Maeztu (1874–1936) and Manuel García Morente (1886–1942) in the 1930s or in the influential model of travel narratives developed by José María Pemán (1897–1981) in the 1940s. In other words, all these influential works that contributed to the ideological reconfiguration of "Spain" during the first years of Franco's dictatorship were built on existing mechanisms of racial othering to be used for an imaginary spiritual and imperialist renaissance—just like the ones we will examine in this chapter.[63]

"China nos llama" was a claim that Vicente Blasco Ibáñez and Federico García Sanchiz shared with Romero Salas in their almost simultaneous visits to China in the mid-1920s. In fact, García Sanchiz himself invented a term that synthesized Romero Salas's mission: *españolear*, to brandish Spain's flag and ideals across the world. Blasco Ibáñez and García Sanchiz's writings on China also test Romero Salas's patriotic exhortation on literary terrain. *La vuelta al mundo de un novelista* (A Novelist's Tour of the World, 1924) and *La ciudad milagrosa* (The Miracle City, 1926) show the formal effects upon literary texts of such a nationalistic investment. Both works also show how the investment in Spanish patriotism in China was inevitably mediated by Western discourses and realities. While Blasco Ibáñez's travelogue maintains the old China/West opposition through a strong investment in race that blends national differences within a homogeneous West, García Sanchiz's account offers a more critical portrayal of Chinese reality through a singular Spanish narrative that breaks up national differences within a heterogeneous West. Despite their differences, however, the "China" that comes out as a synthesis between the physical China encountered by both authors, the textual China conceived mainly through English and French discourses, and the processed China targeted at a patriotic reception in Spain cannot sustain a coherent narrative throughout the pages of both works. The competition that characterized the new economy for representing China in Spain did nothing but exacerbate such inconsistencies: each author tried to singularize his own particular views of China, which were competing with other travelers' accounts and, as a result, turned more distorted and extravagant.[64] In the next section we will see how these inconsistencies were taken to extreme, even hyperbolic levels—always enabled by the position of China as the passive object of representation.

When Vicente Blasco Ibáñez visited China in the winter between 1923 and 1924, he was already one of the most internationally well-known Spanish authors. In Spain, he was much more than an acclaimed writer: he was an extremely popular figure who had been involved in the political insurrections in favor of republicanism since the mid-1890s and who had funded initiatives such as the newspaper *El Pueblo* in 1894 and the publishing house Prometeo, which produced books and novels at widely accessible prices. A polemical activist, he was a member of the Spanish Parliament between 1898 and 1905. After his political career, Blasco Ibáñez turned to literature and journalism, touring around different countries and becoming an internationally best-selling author. During the dictatorship of Primo de Rivera (1923–1930), he stayed in France and published articles denouncing Primo's regime. The English translation of *Los cuatro jinetes del Apocalipsis* (The Four Horsemen of the Apocalypse) became a best seller in 1919, especially in the United States, and some of his novels were turned into Hollywood movies. It was following this success and at that mature point in his career that Blasco Ibáñez first set foot in China.

The visit was part of a trip around the world on the ocean liner *RMS Franconia*. Blasco Ibáñez arrived in New York in November 1923 to depart on the journey to the West and disembark back in Monaco, close to Menton, where he was living at the time, in March 1924. The trip resulted in his book *La vuelta al mundo de un novelista*, in which he offers an account of the different places he visited. The China section of the book has thirteen chapters that follow the trajectory of Blasco Ibáñez's journey in that country: from Mukden (present-day Shenyang), he travels south to Beijing (where he visits temples, the Forbidden City, the Summer Palace, and the Great Wall), farther south to Shanghai, and finally to Hong Kong, Canton, and Macau.[65]

Throughout the China chapters, Blasco Ibáñez's account experiences a gradual transformation that reveals the complexity of representing China from a Spanish perspective. The first chapters make a strong effort to find cross-cultural common ground between China and the West, mainly by remarking on some positive aspects of Chinese society. For instance, Blasco Ibáñez praises the order and security of Chinese cities, which are much safer than many European cities (59). He also downplays gastronomic differences with expressions such as: "Nosotros también saboreamos manjares y bebemos líquidos que hubiesen dado náuseas a nuestros bisabuelos y tal vez a nuestros abuelos" (We also savor delicacies and drink liquids that would have nauseated our great-grandparents and perhaps our grandparents [73–74]) and "El pueblo chino ha cometido crueldades, como todos los pueblos de la tierra, pero muchas menos que las imaginadas por la ignorancia occidental" (The Chinese people have committed cruelties, like all the peoples of the earth, but far less than those imagined by Western ignorance [111]). And he justifies political confusion and anarchy as states that have manifested themselves all around the world at some point in history (166). Blasco Ibáñez also criticizes Christian missionaries and excuses the Chinese opposition they encountered "porque se han inmiscuido muchas veces en los asuntos políticos del país, protegiendo a terribles malhechores convertidos a sus creencias para escapar a la justicia" (because they have interfered many times in the political affairs of the country, protecting terrible criminals who have converted to Christian beliefs only to escape justice [93]). China, as a result, is often portrayed in these first chapters as a vigorous nation, with the potential to modernize and develop itself (163–68).

However, these instances of common ground between cultures are not easy to hold on to. Blasco Ibáñez's frame of reference remains unquestionably Western, and his assumption of Western superiority, strongly based on racial binaries, grows throughout the text and ends up monopolizing the narrative. During the trip, Blasco Ibáñez mingles with the rest of the passengers of the *Franconia*, and the narration sees this collective as a homogeneous Western group, which is to be contrasted with China and the Chinese. There is almost no mention of the nationality of the passengers in a way that would differentiate their experiences in China or their understanding of Chinese society. Occasional references to specific nationalities within the group (Americans, for instance) do appear, but they remain anecdotal curiosities, usually connected to humorous but inoffensive characterizations. Minor national singularizations also appear when criticizing incidents such as the Opium War: Blasco Ibáñez talks about "naciones europeas" (European nations [106]) or "tropas europeas" (European troops [107]) in a way that suggests that these were conflicts harmful to China but in which Spain was not involved. And he certainly denounces the "rapacidad de los invasores" (invaders' rapacity) and the looting of Beijing (107–110). However, while the long historical surveys he includes in the China chapters would have allowed him plenty of occasions to develop a narrative singularizing the different agents within Western collective, including Spain, Blasco Ibáñez does not demonstrate here any of his well-known capacity for sharp observation and critical punch.

Similarly, the reality of China is described in such a textual and dichotomous way opposed to this homogeneous West that Blasco Ibáñez has trouble fully engaging with the lives of the Chinese people he encounters—so much so that Blasco Ibáñez's account cannot reconcile his predetermined image of China with the reality he is actually witnessing. For him, the China he has read about remains more relevant. This textual China has become so strongly anchored in his imagination that he rejects the evidence gained from what he is actually experiencing firsthand day after day. In spite of all the economic and social transformations he is describing, for instance, China maintains "el prestigio misterioso y el novelesco interés que envolvió siempre su nombre" (the mysterious prestige and the romantic interest that were always enveloped in its name [49]). This denial creates nearly surreal moments.

Blasco Ibáñez very much doubts he is in Beijing because what he is seeing is far removed from what lies in his imagination: a city so remote that it is impossible to visit (48–49). To reassure himself that he is truly where he believes himself to be, Blasco Ibáñez decides to stay at the Wagons-Lits, the oldest hotel and the one that appeared in the texts he had read. In this way he is "más de veras en China" (more in China for real [59]). Blasco Ibáñez is most comfortable when he remains on the textual level and offers historical contextualization to his daily experiences. His comments are as accurate as could be expected in a nonspecialized book, and they draw upon unquoted sources: the summary of the Qing ascent to power is short but informative (19–20); the conflicts with Japan in Manchuria are well contextualized both in terms of international relations and internal dynamics (32–36); the syncretism and the coexistence of various religious practices in China are adequately addressed (79–96); and the history of the Great Wall is quite rigorous (137).

Between a Western frame of reference, a dichotomous representation, and a textual China, race emerges as a discourse that gradually colonizes Blasco Ibáñez's narration. As the chapters unfold, references to whiteness and race become more abundant. This racial prism determines the way in which the Chinese reality is experienced. This racial prism contributes to solidify the division between China and the Western nations—including Spain. Even more: as in a battle for discursive supremacy, the increasing references to race conform a monolithic view of China that ends up degrading the Chinese people. In the last chapter we thus encounter passages such as "¿Qué importa unos chinos menos? ¡Hay tantos!" (Who cares about a few Chinese less? There are so many! [175]) and "¡Hay tantos chinos . . . ! La fecundidad de la raza lucha con las cóleras del Océano, con las inundaciones homicidas de los ríos, con las epidemias, con los temblores del suelo, y acaba por triunfar, considerando un episodio ordinario la pérdida de algunos centenares de miles de seres" (There are so many Chinese . . . ! The fecundity of this race struggles with the rages of the ocean, with the homicidal floods of the rivers, with epidemics, with earthquakes. And this race ends up successful. The loss of some hundreds of thousands of beings is considered only an ordinary episode [195]). The progressive racialization of Blasco Ibáñez's account culminates in a final outburst of plain xenophobia and animalization (203–4, 223–247).

To be sure, this xenophobic eruption casts doubt on the culturalist discourse about the importance of Chinese history and the splendor of the Chinese past, which supported the argument for having confidence in the future of the Chinese nation in transformation. The xenophobic eruption destroys the potential for cross-cultural understanding and, worse still, leads to thinking about war: "Para que el mundo de los blancos se entere de la existencia e importancia del Pacífico, será necesaria una gran guerra. Así se dio cuenta por primera vez de que existía el Japón" (A great war will be necessary for the white world to become aware of the existence and importance of the Pacific. This is how the white world first realized that Japan existed [206]). However, besides the eclipse of cross-cultural respect, what is even more relevant for our purposes is how the gradual racialized drive could not sustain the mature, critical vision of China and the Chinese other that Blasco Ibáñez himself had set up to develop in the first chapters of his account. *La vuelta al mundo de un novelista* is incapable of offering a consistent image of China throughout its pages.

Only a few months later, a younger and determined Federico García Sanchiz wrote what he labeled none other than "el primer libro que sobre la totalidad de Shanghai se publica en el mundo" (the first book about Shanghai as a whole that is published in the world).[66] The competition between different accounts that was in place under the new economy for representing China in the 1920s can probably explain the grandiloquence of such a statement—an open attack on the writings on China recently published by Blasco Ibáñez. García Sanchiz was then trying to gain notoriety at the beginning of his career as a journalist, writer, and *charlista*. After the outbreak of the Spanish Civil War in 1936, he would support the nationalist side and would later become one of the most representative writers of fascist literature.[67]

García Sanchiz traveled to China as part of a journey that also took him to Japan, the Philippines, and Singapore. He saw himself as an "intellectual ambassador."[68] His goal in Manila, for instance, was to establish closer links between Spanish and Filipino intellectuals and unite these peoples under a new phase of Spanish history in which Spain would awaken from stagnation and become again "invincible."[69] Coined by himself, the term *españolear* summarized his project: "Los siglos XIX y XX crearon y afirmaron la anti-España. Salí yo a correr tierras y, al observar la insidia con que se nos combate y convencido de que muchas de nuestras ideas y actitudes clásicas son de un valor universal y permanente, me consagré a su predicación con el fervor de un misionero, y en ello sigo" (The nineteenth and twentieth centuries created and consolidated the anti-Spain. I went out to run around the world and, observing the insidiousness with which we are fought and convinced as I am that many of our classic ideas and attitudes are of a universal and permanent value, I devoted myself to the preaching of these ideas and attitudes with the fervor of a missionary, and I am still on it).[70] The assertion of Spanish nationalism provides the framework for understanding the ways in which China is represented in *La ciudad milagrosa*. While Blasco Ibáñez had stressed Spain's position in China through a racial, homogeneous conception of the West that erased any trace of a distinctive Spanish positionality, García Sanchiz stresses Spain's position through the singularity of his account and a heterogeneous conception of the West in China.

García Sanchiz arrived in China in April 1925. Having reencountered Julio Palencia, a childhood friend who at the time was the Spanish consul in Shanghai, García Sanchiz stayed in the city for longer than he had planned. It was probably all the information gathered under Palencia's hospitality that explains García Sanchiz's more comprehensive, critical understanding of China. *La ciudad milagrosa* is an attempt to rise above not only the occasional short contributions that García Sanchiz wrote for the journal *La Esfera* but also the kind of homogenizing portrayals of China that were exemplified by Blasco Ibáñez's work. It is through a singularizing view that he aspires to contribute to international discourses on China too: "Como escritor español, he querido ofrecer a mi país las primicias del estudio de un tema internacional, universal, más que ninguno del momento. Mucho, y a veces de calidad, se ha escrito acerca de Shanghai, pero siempre de pasada, o desde especiales puntos de vista" (As a Spanish writer, I wanted to offer to my country the first results of a study about an international, universal subject—more international and universal than any other subject right now. Much has been written about Shanghai, sometimes of great quality, but always in passing, or from special points of view [10]).

Unlike the prominence of a textual China in Blasco Ibáñez's account, *La ciudad milagrosa* offers a collection of vignettes about Shanghai in 1925 that stress the China perceived by García Sanchiz during his visit, even if that creates more chaotic and unorthodox depictions. *La ciudad milagrosa* opens with a brief introduction, still written from the steamer, that sets up the tone and argument of the book: "Admirable vida la de Shanghai. A cada paso, una genialidad, un absurdo, un milagro, aunque del diablo" (How admirable the life of Shanghai. At every step, a stroke of genius, an absurdity, a miracle—even if it comes from the devil [16]). The book's main section, "Shanghai, la ciudad milagrosa" (Shanghai, the Miracle City), has seventy-four entries of unequal length (from a couple of pages to more than twenty) that explore this city of prodigies, paying attention to all sorts of settings, characters, atmospheres, and anecdotes. A final section, "La selva" (The Jungle), is a report of the strike and social turmoil following the famous 1925 anti-imperialist workers' demonstrations culminating in the May Thirtieth Incident. The book's paratext also attempts to display the originality claimed by García Sanchiz's text: a cover finely illustrated by modernist artist Rafael de Penagos shows a Chinese driver pulling a rickshaw with a (Western) woman in it, the book's title and the author's name appear written in Chinese calligraphy on the opening pages (*Fanhua zhi Shanghai* and *Shengjieshi*)—a display of authenticity with the indication that they were written in Chinese especially for this edition.

García Sanchiz depicts an assembly of different nations with different positions, characteristics, and interests in China. Casual distinctions abound, such as "ingleses, americanos, belgas, noruegos, holandeses, griegos, españoles, ninguno sin su *smoking* o la chaquetilla blanca de gala" (English, American, Belgian, Norwegian, Dutch, Greek, Spanish, none of them without their tuxedo or their white formal dresses [87]). But deeper disparities with larger implications appear regularly as well. Westerners in Shanghai, for instance, live in separate quarters of the city, which denotes cultural incommensurability even among groups from different Western nations (23). Even in a place such as the cemetery, where all Westerners are buried in the same common soil with no separate sections for different nations, the narrator stresses their differences by specifying the family names inscribed on the tombs (59). Heterogeneity also characterizes the different religious groups and their enterprises: Spanish padres combine evangelization with mah-jongg games; British and American missionaries add a political and commercial purpose to their crusade; and French priests produce statues for converts and Asian "antiques" for export (149). Perhaps the most significant example of such heterogeneity is the different attitudes of the Western nations with regard to the anti-imperialist workers' riots of May 30, 1925, which are described in the final section of the book. By insisting on this variety among Westerners living in Shanghai as a point of departure, the weak position of Spain in China turns out to be only one minor component within this complex set of nations. Such emphasis on variety also embraces the contradictions and intricacies derived from the Western presence in China: "La vida compleja e intensísima de Shanghai es como una tromba en cuyo vértice estuviesen todas las pasiones, todas las inquietudes, todos los problemas que hoy torturan el Mundo: el oro, la raza, la sensualidad, la política, el comercio, la ambición, el colonialismo, la guerra . . ." (The complex and intense life of Shanghai is like a deluge holding at its apex all the passions, all the worries, all the problems that are torturing the world today: gold, race, sensuality, politics, trade, ambition, colonialism, war . . .).[71] Shanghai is a "miracle city" because it embraces the totality of all of these things. And this chaotic heterogeneous totality epitomizes the modern world.

This new, more heterogeneous framework allows García Sanchiz's observations to be more critical, even if that implies leaving aside the textual Orientalist stereotypes internalized by the Spanish reader. For instance, he targets colonial domination and often refers to how colonialism has brought corruption and immorality both to colonizers and the colonized (232), and how Western domination has made China lose its original charm. Colonialism and the West have even destroyed the Orientalist and textual China that had been so revered: "La invasión de los occidentales, las claudicaciones de los nativos, la misma naturaleza, adulterada, acabaron por disipar el originario embrujamiento de estas tierras, creando esa realidad absurda que en las cancillerías y en los mercados se conoce por el Extremo Oriente" (Westerners invading, natives surrendering, nature itself, adulterated as it is, all this ended up vanishing this land's original charm. All this created the absurd reality that is known as the Far East in chancelleries and markets [56]). García Sanchiz's criticism also targets social inequalities. This is most visible in the last section of the book, "La selva," which deals with the anti-imperialist workers' riots of the May Thirtieth Incident. During these protests, "Shanghai se transformó en una selva donde se persigue a los indígenas" (Shanghai became a jungle where indigenous people are persecuted [257]). García Sanchiz gives an ample explanation of the direct causes of the incident (258), as well as a more contextual analysis, including the role played by Western-educated young Chinese (261–62) and by the Bolsheviks as ultimate instigators (267). The incident is not a casual coda to the book, but rather an event of great relevance, as it encapsulates all the contradictions described in the previous chapters. The May Thirtieth protests symbolize the eruption of a social problem that has its roots in colonial slavery: non-white peoples have served the white race under the passive consent of religion and the Bible (270). Most interestingly, García Sanchiz's account of the May Thirtieth protests shows each nation's reaction (271–72), none of which address the actual problem: England insists on the infallibility of the British; France suggests a disproportionate zeal on the part of the British army; Japan desires war and actually welcomes the conflict; and America "con su ideología democrática, y sus miras comerciales y previsoras en la cuestión del Pacífico, manifiesta su simpatía hacia los chinos" (with its democratic ideology, and with commercial and farsighted aims on the Pacific question, expresses its sympathy for the Chinese [271]). Spain—the land of "Seneca's grandchildren"—is also harshly criticized for its indifference (272).

To be sure, García Sanchiz was not the only voice who criticized the inequalities caused by imperialism in China at the time. Following writings such as Lenin's 1917 essay against imperialism and the role that colonies should play in the communist movement, criticisms abounded in British Marxism or in Manabendra Nath Roy's book about his experience with communism in China, which would be translated into Spanish in 1932.[72] However, García Sanchiz's critical view on imperialism in China is built from outside the dichotomy of colonizer/colonized. What we find in *La ciudad milagrosa* is a concern for class that emerges from a non-Marxist—or, in fact, protofascist—intellectual and that also allows the inequalities within the West itself to be seen. García Sanchiz combines the denunciation of blatant elements of colonial aggression such as slavery (68) with a critique of subtler modes of subjugation within the West itself: for instance, the case of the American-influenced "new woman," who symbolizes the new kind of colonialism imposed by capitalism. There is no proletariat among Westerners in Shanghai and women in Shanghai face the hardships of life just as men do in the rest of the world. Americans are to be blamed for "un procedimiento de colonizar con sus mujeres" (a way of colonizing with their women [82]).

While *La ciudad milagrosa* makes a great effort in portraying the heterogeneity of the Western presence in China, Chinese people are still seen en masse—not in explicitly racialized terms, as in Blasco Ibáñez's text, but still as a homogeneous group fundamentally characterized by their subalternity. More importantly, the view of Shanghai as a heterogeneous, multinational city is emphasized by a formal structure that also affects the way China is represented. García Sanchiz's impressionistic portrayal relies on a set of modernist techniques such as fragmentation, montage, and discordant rhythm. These techniques are used to portray the dramatic combination of characters and nationalities, policemen and criminals, order and chaos, and good and evil that cast Shanghai as a miraculous "Grand Guignol" (48). Painted through these techniques, Shanghai appears as a sensational monster that becomes almost fictitious for the reader. And García Sanchiz actually marks it as such: interestingly, he insists on labeling *La ciudad milagrosa* a *novel*. He wants to make it clear that it is neither an essay nor a collection of travel notes—literature by and for tourists—which he dismisses as genres too frivolous for such an ambitious, original project (9).

For García Sanchiz, fiction turns out to be more adequate for representing the complexity of China. While defending fiction as the most appropriate genre to capture a complex reality experienced firsthand might seem paradoxical, the claim is understandable when we consider how "factual" or "textual" China was rigidly carved into the readers' imaginations at the time—to the extent that it had lost its moorings in reality, as demonstrated in Blasco Ibáñez's writing. Fiction then becomes the genre that allows one to transcend readers' expectations, portray a more nuanced view of China, and reflect critically on its relationship with the West. García Sanchiz claims that behind the "voluptuosidades de la visión artística" (voluptuousness of artistic vision), the reader will find "una *denuncia*, que no carece de oportunidad en este día en que la mirada del mundo se fija en el *Far East*" (a *complaint*, which is not untimely today when the world's gaze is fixed on the *Far East* [9–10, my emphasis]). Even if this critical punch is eroded by its formal extravagances, *La ciudad milagrosa* competes effectively in the new economy of representations of China by reclaiming fiction as a realistic genre to depict China anew.

EL DIABLO BLANCO

Almost a synthesis of the works examined in the previous section, Luis de Oteyza's *El diablo blanco* (The White Devil) is a vivid example of how the tension between competition and patriotism, race and Spanishness, and fiction and realism in the representations of China in Spain could be stretched to hyperbolic levels in the mid- and late 1920s. As a novel originated in Oteyza's travelogues *De España al Japón* (From Spain to Japan) and *En el remoto Cipango* (In the Remote Cipango), both published in 1927, *El diablo blanco* is also a particularly useful example to see how the porous boundaries between fiction and nonfiction already problematized by García Sanchiz worked in a popular adventure novel.

Luis de Oteyza's biography shares some aspects with Blasco Ibáñez's and García Sanchiz's trajectories. His career in journalism started at a young age, and he worked for different publications like *El Liberal*, *El Imparcial*, and *La Libertad*. As a public figure, he was also a "polemista" and became involved in political affairs for the liberal and republican causes. He was elected diputado a Cortes by the Huelva district in 1923 but Primo de Rivera's coup d'état put a stop to his career as a politician. He was forced to step down as director of *La Libertad* in 1925 and became more engaged with the "nuevas batallas del periodismo moderno, diarismo reporteril y viajero . . . que estaba haciendo furor en la España insurgente de comienzos de siglo" (new struggles of modern journalism, of travel diaries and reports . . . that was raging in insurgent Spain at the beginning of the century).[73] In 1922 Oteyza became internationally famous as the first European reporter to interview Abd el-Krim (the political and military leader who fought against the Spanish colonial occupation in the Rif) and published the report as *Abd-el-Krim y los prisioneros* (Abd el-Krim and the Prisoners). He then traveled to the Philippines and worked on pieces that combined journalism, *dietarismo*, and fiction, such as *De España al Japón*, *En el remoto Cipango*, *La edificante aventura de Garín* (Garín's Edifying Adventure, 1927), and *Al Senegal en avión* (Flying to Senegal, 1928). *El diablo blanco* was published in 1928 and became his most successful novel.[74]

El diablo blanco is narrated in the first-person voice by Pedro García Gómez, a gray man who works as an accountant for Bofill & Vendrell, a small Spanish textile company based in Barcelona. García could very well be one of Pío Baroja's characters: a passive man, quite alienated from the world that lays outside his daily routines. García takes care of his daily chores with just the necessary amount of energy required. But his life changes dramatically when Bofill & Vendrell encounters a difficult situation. The company, which manufactures underwear and strongly relies on exports to China, discovers that Li-Hong, the Chinese agent who places the orders, has disappeared. Facing a potential collapse, the owners decide to send García to China to sort things out: find Li-Hong, resume the business activities, and save Bofill & Vendrell from bankruptcy. Against his will, García travels to China and gets involved in all sorts of adventures. The search for Li-Hong works almost as a MacGuffin that enables the depiction of places, people, and customs. In this mixture of travel writing and adventure fiction, García experiences a dramatic transformation: he turns into an intrepid and cruel bandit; he becomes the White Devil, feared by everybody and famous around the world; and he has a torrid affair with Fo-Ling, a fearsome woman bandit. When everything seems to indicate that García will continue on in China, he eventually finds Li-Hong and unexpectedly decides to go back to Spain to reunite with his family and resume his old tedious routine as a gray accountant for Bofill & Vendrell.

El diablo blanco became a highly successful novel in Spain and abroad. It was originally published as a book by Editorial Pueyo in 1928. *La Libertad*, the journal Oteyza had directed, advertised the novel prominently during January 1929. It was later published by installments in several Spanish newspapers and magazines such as *El Heraldo de Madrid* (March 1929) and *Mundo Gráfico* (August 1931). Several editions followed (at least five by 1934) and several translations were also announced.[75] The novel was also turned into a book for American students learning Spanish.[76]

El diablo blanco's success testifies to the keen interest in China in Spain during the late 1920s and reveals many of the views, interests, and obsessions related to China at the time.[77] However, it has only received minor critical attention. Critics have mainly provided a biographical reading of the novel. In this reading, Oteyza's novel has been understood as a story that partially overlaps with Oteyza's biography:

> En el simple vaivén del mundo cotidiano, en la grisura del puesto burocrático, en la vida menuda y cansina del apartamento, la sensibilidad despierta del creador ha descubierto que la sola condición de estar vivo en medio del presente, hace del ciudadano sin relieves, masificado en la rutina y el aburrimiento, una figura excepcional, un paladín anónimo, dotado de cualidades superiores. He allí al protagonista urbano del siglo xx, que Pío Baroja anticipó en sus novelas y que Luis de Oteyza nos presenta, vivo y al natural, vestido con rasgos peculiares de ironía y sarcasmo. ¿Quién es el héroe, después de todo, sino un mínimo, indefenso y trivial componente de la especie humana? . . . Pedro es como Luis, si se quiere. Es uno más.[78]

> *In the simple fluctuations of the everyday world, in the grayness of the bureaucratic job, in the small and tiresome life of the apartment, Oteyza's enlightened sensibility has discovered that, in the midst of the present situation, only by being alive the citizen—without any kind of special feature, sunk in routine and boredom—is in fact an exceptional figure, an anonymous paladin, endowed with superior qualities. Here*

is the urban protagonist of the twentieth century, anticipated
in Pío Baroja's novels and which Luis de Oteyza presents
to us, alive and natural, dressed in the singular qualities of
irony and sarcasm. What is the hero, after all, but a mini-
mal, helpless, and trivial component of the human species?
. . . Pedro is like Luis, if you like. He is one among many
others.

In fact, the identification goes even beyond García and Oteyza. Any
reader of the novel could be García in China: "Y es que cualquiera
de los infinitos Pedros Garcías que pasean por el parque y van al cine,
guarda en su interior un anhelo confuso que en un segundo lo va a con-
ducir de un cuerpo entero a la sábana blanca, para colocarlo de una vez
en el mismo lugar donde Douglas Fairbanks realiza cualquiera de sus
inverosímiles hazañas" (And so any of the infinite Pedro Garcías who
walk around the park and go to the movies, keeps within him a confused longing that in a second will take him on the screen and place him
right where Douglas Fairbanks performs any of his unlikely feats).[79]

Given the ways in which China is represented in Oteyza's novel,
these interpretations remain rather limited. The significance of *El diablo blanco* transcends the mere biographical dimension and reveals the
discourses and mechanisms of representation that not only determined
Spain's imagined China in the 1920s but also illustrate the relationship between Spain and the world at the time. García's metamorphosis,
as we will see, depends both on a racialized vision of China and on
a strong competition with other Westerners. García's heroism also depends on the destruction of the coherence that had characterized the
trialectical representations of China in Spain. While Blasco Ibáñez or
García Sanchiz had already pushed the limits of this trialectical tension,
El diablo blanco resolves this tension in a hyperbolical way. García's
first-person, half-confessional, and half-journalistic account makes a
long list of weaknesses and miseries found in China. García's aim is not
to denounce them but rather to emerge from them as a superior hero.
García's radical transformation from a gray accountant to a fearless
hero makes use of a racialized, animalized, and feminized China, on
the one hand, and of a competitive patriotism between Spain and other
Western nations established in China, on the other.

El diablo blanco begins as a conventional work of travel writing.[80]
Indeed, the itinerary followed by García in the first pages of the novel
is not much different from the itineraries followed by Oteyza himself

and by many other writers who had traveled to China in the previous decades. Many passages follow the usual conventions of the genre. The chapters in which García travels on the ship (chapters 4 to 6) would almost be interchangeable with travel accounts written by Enrique Gaspar or Vicente Blasco Ibáñez. Once in China, García's narration remains also quite stereotypical, seasoned with conventional historical asides and folklore depictions: he summarizes the Boxer Uprising and the Chinese civil wars (74, 107–8); he adds sensationalist and costumbrista depictions that range from food and drinks to Chinese torture and abandoned girls (181, 109, 144); and he almost lectures about places such as Macau (127) and the history of some missions (144). García's reactions to race are also similar to the ones found in previous works: he qualifies Asians as ugly (71), considers the sampan population filthy (72); and pays close attention to the rickshaws, which leads to the animalization of the Chinese people: "esos cochecillos a los que, en vez de ir enganchado un caballo o un burro, va un hombre. La bestia humana de tiro no dejó de asombrarme. Y es que nunca supuse que el hombre hiciera de animal tan francamente" (those small carriages that, instead of being hooked to a horse or a donkey, are hooked to a man. That working human beast did not cease to amaze me. I never imagined that a man could play an animal so realistically [71]). Set under the same binary racial division at play in Blasco Ibáñez's *La vuelta al mundo de un novelista*, García is perceived in China under the inclusive category of "European" or "white devil."

As chapters develop, *El diablo blanco* combines the conventions of travel writing with a set of features typically associated with the action novel. García's heroism gradually unravels as he discovers he has a real talent for adaptation and survival. Despite his early fears for abandoning his steady routine and modest social environment, he integrates well among the group of high-class European and American seasoned travelers and flirts with several women (68–69). Surprisingly, language is never an issue for his socializing. While we learn he is fluent in French and English thanks to his reading habits, we never get any proof of his language skills—except for the implicit fact that no misunderstandings arise. In contrast, most of the Chinese who try to speak Spanish in later chapters will be repeatedly ridiculed.

García's transformation grows exponentially: from humble Spaniard clerk to sociable European tourist to universal fearless hero. China, a chaotic place where everything is possible (92, 93), pushes García into this new identity:

Ardía en deseos de afrentar de una vez a los chinos con los que tenía que entenderme. Y si entre ellos los había que pertenecían a la ancestralmente terrible clase de piratas, ¡pues mejor! (123)

No; no tenía miedo. Se encendía en mí más y más el afán de la lucha, que, con incipiente ardor, me llevó en Hong-Kong a embarcarme lo más pronto posible. . . . No tenía miedo, no; tenía saña homicida. En tal furioso estado navegaba hacia la costa, sobre la que iba a arrojarme con salto de tigre. (126)

I burned with desire to fight once and for all with the Chinese I had to deal with. And if among them there was any who belonged to the ancient terrible stock of pirates, then even better!

No; I was not scared. The desire to fight was burning in me. The new fervor made me embark as soon as possible in Hong Kong. . . . I was not scared, no; I was in a murderous rage. That was the furious state in which I sailed toward the coast, on which I was going to throw myself like a tiger.

Parallel to García's transformation, violence becomes more present in the novel. As García moves to the interior of China in search for Li-Hong accompanied by a group of Chinese converts, depictions turn harsh and bloody (134–39). When the group is attacked by Chinese bandits, García becomes a fierce warrior: he gives orders, gallops his horse around, and shows an unexpected determination. Similarly, García's metamorphosis in China depends on the racialization of the reality he encounters. It is also a transformation that goes in crescendo. The more his racism intensifies, the more his nature becomes violent, and the more he becomes a hero. In the first chapters his depictions conform to the ethnographic accounts of travel writers and align him with other Westerners (118, 128). But as he becomes a cruel and famous hero, he proclaims stronger, more explicit xenophobic assertions:

Entonces comprendí las diferencias raciales, específicas, que de los chinos me separaban. No eran seres de la especie humana. Podía matárseles como a perros, y, con matárseles, se les hacía un favor. *Mi orgullo de hombre blanco se despertó entero.* ¿Orgullo infernal? ¡Bien! Si los chinos eran hombres, sentaba yo plaza de diablo . . . (129, my emphasis)

*Then I understood the specific racial differences that sep-
arated me from the Chinese. They were not beings of the
human species. They could be killed like dogs, and by killing
them you were doing them a favor. My pride as a white man
fully woke up. A hellish pride? All right! If the Chinese were
men, I would then enlist as a devil . . .*

García's metamorphosis culminates with his affair with Fo-Ling, an ag-
gressive leader of a group of bandits who support the Canton government in the South of China and fight against the republic in the North
(124–25). The encounter with Fo-Ling awakens García's sexual desire:

Me miró con un brillo en los ojos, que no era luz de curio-
sidad sino lumbre de deseo. Y de su mirada saltó una chis-
pa que inflamó mi sangre y abrasó mi carne, ya dispuesto
a arder. Sin duda en la subsconsciencia, era aquello lo que
me inspiró el afán de seguir buscando a Li-Hong: disfrazada
ansia loca de poseer a Fo-Ling. El instinto sexual se exacer-
ba con los riesgos fatales. Es como una defensa de la especie. . . . Gocé infinitamente allí; en el lugar mismo donde
estuve a punto de sufrir un horrible tormento . . . ¡Deleite
inaudito! (162)

*She looked at me with a gleam in her eyes, which was not a
light of curiosity but the heat of desire. And from her gaze a
spark jumped and inflamed my blood and burned my flesh,
which was already about to burn. There is no doubt that, in
my subconscious, that was what inspired in me the desire to
keep looking for Li-Hong: the disguised, mad desire to possess Fo-Ling. The sexual instinct is exacerbated with fatal
risks. It is like a way to preserve the species. . . . I enjoyed infinitely right there; in the very place where I had been about
to suffer a horrible torment . . . Unimaginable pleasure!*

Having a relationship with a Chinese woman incites García's darkest
instincts and intensifies his violent and racist behavior. Depictions of
García's cruelty become frequent, gory, and even grotesque. He kills one
man cold-bloodedly to give credibility to his new leadership in Fo-Ling's
gang. After the assault of a fortified town, he orders to disembowel all
enemies and punish those of his own soldiers who hesitate to follow his

orders (164–65). He kills a baby and delivers half of the corpse to the baby's father as a punishment for having tricked him (167–70). García becomes "el diablo, el más diablo de todos. El único diablo" (the devil, the most devil of all. The only devil [166]). His cruelty in China is made known internationally—even back in Spain: "Entre los horrores del caos chinesco, cablegrafiados por las Agencias de información a todos los periódicos de Europa y América, tuvieron preferente acogida, para emocionar a los lectores sensibles, muchas de las acciones de 'El Diablo Blanco.' Cuando regresé a Barcelona, en un número atrasado de *La Vanguardia* todavía alcancé a ver . . ." (Among the horrors of the Chinese chaos, cabled by press agencies to all the newspapers in Europe and America, many of the scenes in "El Diablo Blanco" were selected to get sensitive readers excited. When I returned to Barcelona, I still managed to see them in a back issue of *La Vanguardia* . . . [166]).

How can we make sense of García's grotesque metamorphosis? How can we explain the excruciating attitude against the China and the Chinese that grows in Oteyza's novel? To be sure, we could take *El diablo blanco* as a hyperbolic example of popular fiction or even as a parody originated in Oteyza's idiosyncratic humor. Yet, it seems important to address what made such grotesque depictions worthy of being read and praised by Spanish readers. I want to point out two aspects that contributed to the structure of feeling that made Oteyza's extravagance possible and socially acceptable. First, China. García rejects any personal responsibility for his own evil transformation and rather blames China and the Chinese (167). Fo-Ling in particular is accused of having stirred in him such a sadistic drive: "Como las destructoras lavas en el cráter de un volcán, surgían mis crueldades del fondo de ígneo abismo. . . . Fo-Ling era el espíritu de la lujuria torturante y mortífera" (Like the destructive lava from a volcano's crater, my cruelties arose from the bottom of an igneous abyss. . . . Fo-Ling was the spirit of a torturing, deadly lust [170]). As a Chinese and a woman, Fo-Ling is considered an androgynous embodiment of evil (171).

Second, the differentiation between Spain and other Western nations in China. When García arrives in Shanghai at the beginning of the novel, he quickly notices the diversity of the city's population:

> Pero si existen algunas ciudades mayores, no existe ninguna tan complicada. ¿Por los chinos? ¡Oh, no! Cierto que los chinos resultan bastante complicadores. Sin embargo, en la complicación de Shanghai los chinos son lo de menos. Lo de-

más es que con los chinos se mezclan allí todas las razas del planeta, y hasta puede que de otros astros. . . . Los guardias del sector donde los ingleses dominan son indios, y los del dominado por los franceses, anamitas. Marinos de todas las escuadras y soldados de todos los ejércitos, con los uniformes de sus naciones respectivas. Un ciudadano con *chaquet*, pantalón de corte y sombrero frégoli, junto a un explorador con guerrera de *dril*, bandas en las piernas y *salacot*; un japonesito envuelto en media docena de kimonos, al lado de un negrazo medio desnudo, y un árabe imponente bajo la arrogancia de su turbante, cruzándose con un coreano que hacía reír sosteniendo una chistera de pala en la coronilla, estuvieron un momento ante mis ojos dilatados por el asombro. Babel, ¿no? (77)

Some cities may be larger, but none is so complicated. Because of the Chinese? No way! It is true that the Chinese complicate things. However, the Chinese are the least responsible for the complication in Shanghai. The thing is that in Shanghai the Chinese get mixed with all the races from the Earth and maybe even from other planets. . . . The British concession is guarded by Indians. The French concession is guarded by Annamites. Officers of all fleets and soldiers of all armies, all wearing the uniforms of their respective nations. A man in a dinner jacket, elegant trousers, and fedora, right next to an explorer in battle dress and pith helmet. A short Japanese man wrapped in half a dozen kimonos, right next to a big black man almost naked. An imposing Arab under the arrogance of his turban running into an amusing Korean who is holding a top hat on his crown. I saw them all for a moment or two, with my eyes dilated by amazement. Babel, right?

Within this Babel, Spain remains insignificant and invisible—quite literally: García has trouble finding the Spanish consulate (78). When he finally gets there, the consulate turns out to be a shabby, dirty office in an unremarkable location. The consul is gone and the atmosphere suggests lousy management. But as the action evolves in the following chapters, García's transformation will also imply an inversion of Spain's insignificance—at the cost of the novel's formal consistency.

Incongruities increase as the novel approaches its finale. After García has joined Fo-Ling's gang, he finds out that Li-Hong has been kidnapped by another gang and is waiting for a ransom to be paid. García then befriends two Europeans who belong to the gang that keeps Li-Hong captive and plans a scheme to set him free. Initially, for García the encounter with Delacroix (French) and Van Ander (Dutch) means a racial reunion: "Tanto mi rostro como los de ellos, destacaban, sobre el tono amarillento de las telas kakis, de un modo que los rostros de los chinos no lograban destacar ni con mucho. . . . De la raza blanca me vieron y de la raza blanca les vi" (My face and their faces stood out from the yellowish shade of the khaki fabrics. Our faces stood out in a way that was impossible to replicate by the Chinese faces. . . . For them I stood out as a man of the white race and for me they stood out as men of the white race [176]). But differences quickly arise as Delacroix and Van Ander trigger García's patriotic pride (177). Moreover, they find out that both gangs will join an army that is planning to attack Shanghai, where there is an international settlement with Dutch and Spanish warships and soldiers (178). Having to attack their fellow countrymen becomes a major concern for García and Van Ander, and patriotism emerges as the leading force in the plot. While the attack never happens because the Northern army withdraws at the very last minute (180), a new thread has already taken over the novel's final chapters: García's full transformation depends not only on race, as a white man among the Chinese, but also on patriotism, as a respected Spaniard. The plot's resolution acts almost as a synthesis of these two aspects. When Delacroix and Van Ander find out that García is actually the White Devil, they recognize him as their "superior" (179, 182). But García kills them both and frees Li-Hong. Then another artificial twist stresses García's patriotism even more: Li-Hong had been held captive with a fellow hostage, Mister Harris, an American. García takes Harris back to Shanghai, where they meet Harris's sister, Betty, who considers García an "héroe salvador" (saving hero [195]). In an overplayed reaction hastily sketched in a few lines, Betty falls madly in love with him:

> Betty Harris, la encantadora joven americana—bella y pura—que me abrazó agradecida cuando nos encontramos, me había abrazado apasionada al despedirme. Quiso antes retenerme en China. . . . Y acabó por confesarme que si deseaba dilatar mi permanencia junto a ella, era pensando llegar a hacérseme tan necesaria que quisiera yo siguiésemos unidos toda la vida. (207)

*Betty Harris, the charming young American woman—
beautiful and pure—who hugged me gratefully when we had
met, hugged me passionately as I said goodbye. She had tried
to keep me in China. . . . And she ended up confessing that
she wanted to keep me by her side because she wanted to
become so necessary for me that I would like us to remain
together for the rest of our lives.*

Having gained such symbolic capital, García then unexpectedly decides
to return home. This is another clumsy final development, as only a
few pages before García had confessed he was living a "superior life"
in China: "Nada me importaba de la fábrica de Barcelona, ni de toda
Barcelona, ni de España entera. Coronel de un ejército chino en cam-
paña, amante rendido de la ardorosa Fo-Ling, la lucha y el placer me
embargaban. Vivía una nueva vida, mil veces superior a la antigua, y de
la vida antigua no quería ni acordarme en la nueva" (I didn't care at all
about my company in Barcelona, about anything in Barcelona, about
anything in Spain. I was a colonel of a Chinese army in campaign, I
was a lover surrendered to the ardent Fo-Ling. I was seized by fight and
pleasure. I lived a new life, a thousand times superior to my previous
one. In my new life I did not even want to remember my old life [196]).
But back in Shanghai it is a racial re-encounter that, again, brings about
change: "Ver por las calles hombres y mujeres sobre todo mujeres de la
raza blanca despertó en mí sensaciones agradabilísimas. Estaba en un
mundo que era el mío, tras de haber vivido en otro. ¡En otro mundo
extraño, exótico, absurdo! . . . Era la civilización en que me eduqué,
que se me presentaba reviviendo mis necesidades" (Seeing in the streets
men and women of the white race, especially women, aroused in me extremely pleasant feelings. After having lived in another world, I was in a
world that was my world. It was another strange, exotic, absurd world!
. . . The civilization in which I was educated was presenting itself and
reviving my needs [198]). This racial reencounter now has a new sym-
bolism. García goes back to his old self as a Spaniard reassured by his
own superiority among the white race. It is only then that he misses "mi
vida antigua: la pacífica, la ordenada, la monótona. Aquella vida que,
embargado por el combatir y el gozar, juzgara despreciable. Ansié de
pronto, con ansia infinita, con ansia irresistible, ir otra vez a la oficina
de la fábrica para ocupar mi puesto en el viejo pupitre" (my old life: the
peaceful, orderly, monotonous life. The life that, seized by combat and
pleasure, I had deemed worthless. Now I suddenly yearned—an infinite
yearning, an irresistible yearning—to go back to the company's office

and take my place at the old desk again [206]). At the end of *El diablo blanco* we leave García back in Barcelona, where he has resumed his old life with his wife and daughter and his job as a gray accountant.

While García's final decision seems to shape the plot in a coherent way by turning full circle, it cannot hide an awkward denouement: Fo-Ling and Li-Hong are suddenly forgotten; García's dark adventures get redeemed by his killing two Europeans, saving an American and seducing the American's sister; and, even more striking, the racist and misogynist drive that had fueled García's adventures becomes almost like a dream: "Como pienso que mis andanzas y mis aventuras, *más que vividas, las soñé* . . . [. . .] todo lo demás y todos los otros, son ya para mí *fantasmagorías de ensoñación que se esfuman* . . . No; no tengo que añorar" (As I think that all my wanderings and all my adventures were *more like dreams instead of real experiences* . . . [. . .] everything else and everyone else are all now *phantasmagorias of reverie that disappear* . . . No, I don't have anything to long for [211, my emphasis]). Captured by a combination of xenophobia and Spanish singularity, *El diablo blanco* cannot offer a coherent outcome that accommodates the Chinese, Spanish, and Western dimensions that had shaped its own story.

El diablo blanco not only synthesizes the tension between racial and patriotic concerns in China expressed in Blasco Ibáñez's *La vuelta al mundo de un novelista* and García Sanchiz's *La ciudad milagrosa*. It also reveals in a much more blatant way the formal and political challenges of representing China from Spain in the 1920s. All together, these works illustrate how the coherence that had characterized the trialectical representations of China in Spain could be compromised when more weight was put on the Spanish side of the historical equation. These works offer allegorical responses to the China call examined in previous sections. On the one hand, China was an opportunity for Spain indeed. And if such a gray man as García could turn into a hero in China, who couldn't? On the other hand, Spain's potential to adapt and survive in China had its limitations as it was inevitably dependent on, and confronted with, other Western nations in China. The formal inconsistencies shared by these three works illustrate the complex coexistence between these two responses. And, more generally, they illustrate the complex coexistence between the multiple ways of representing a China perceived to be in transformation in the 1910s and 1920s.

Perhaps even most significantly, *La vuelta al mundo de un novelista*, *La ciudad milagrosa*, and *El diablo blanco* also illustrate the malleability of China as an object trapped inside this new economy of representation. Blasco Ibáñez's increasingly xenophobic portrayals, García Sanchiz's critical views, and Oteyza's incongruous twists and turns can all accommodate a ductile, passive image of China in the 1920s. China can be a ground for racial transformation; a competitive terrain where Spain can fight and win over other European nations; and a hyperbolic reality turned into a dream that can most cynically be abandoned. It is probably not a coincidence that writers such as Federico García Sanchiz and Luis de Oteyza considered fiction a suitable genre to encapsulate all these contradictory drives. These works from the mid-1920s anticipate the intensification of these multiple overlapping representations of China that will take place in the next decade. Let us turn to it.

CHAPTER 4

"As It Has Not Been Made Known by Chinese Writers Themselves"

April 12, 1931
  Hollywood, California, United States

In April 1931 Fox Film released the fourth movie of the series that would keep the corporation afloat in the 1930s: *Charlie Chan Carries On*.[1] In the three previous films of the series, the role of Charlie Chan had been played by the Japanese American actor George Kuwa, the Japanese actor Sōjin Kamiyama, and the Korean American actor E. L. Park.[2] In *Charlie Chan Carries On* the role of Charlie Chan is played for the first time by the Swedish American actor Warner Oland, who will continue to play the Honolulu police detective in sixteen films between 1931 and 1937. Ironically, Oland had played the role of Charlie Chan's antagonist, Fu Manchu, in *The Mysterious Dr. Fu Manchu* (1929), *Paramount on Parade* (1930), and *The Return of Dr. Fu Manchu* (1930). And, in fact, only five months after the release of *Charlie Chan Carries On*, Oland would appear again as Fu Manchu in *Daughter of the Dragon* (September 1931).

Can we think of two characters who are more contradictory than Fu Manchu and Charlie Chan? Fu Manchu: the archetype of the evil villain, the embodiment of the yellow peril. Charlie Chan: the epitome of the benevolent hero, the personification of the clever and honorable detective. The coexistence of Fu Manchu and Charlie Chan as embodiments of China in the public imagination exemplifies the diverse, even contradictory ways of representing China in the 1930s. The new economy for representing China that was developed in the 1920s saturated the Western public sphere with multiple images of China in the following decade. The signifier "China" occupied all kinds of positions across the scale of signifieds. Is it just a coincidence that such an antagonistic pair—Fu Manchu and Charlie Chan—was played by the same Western person? Had China and the Chinese become so mutable that they could always be embodied by Warner Oland?

Sax Rohmer's novels, upon which the films were based, started developing the yellow peril trope in the 1910s. *The Mystery of Dr. Fu Manchu* was serialized from October 1912 to June 1913. It was followed by *The Yellow Claw* (1915), *The Devil Doctor* (1916), and *The Si-Fan Mysteries* (1917). Their success was remarkable in a Britain that "buzzed with Sinophobia" and where "respectable middle-class magazines, tabloids and comics, alike, spread stories of ruthless Chinese ambitions to destroy the West."[3] In the 1930s Rohmer returned to the Fu Manchu saga: *The Daughter of Fu Manchu* (1931) was soon followed by *The Mask of Fu Manchu* (1932), *The Bride of Fu Manchu* (1933), *The Trail of Fu Manchu* (1934), *President Fu Manchu* (1936), and *The Drums of Fu Manchu* (1939).

Fu Manchu's popularity transcended literature. The density of Fu Manchu references across popular culture is striking. In drama, many plays included representations of Chinese people that were based on Rohmer's archetypal character. Fu Manchu on stage was so popular that in March 1929 there were at least five plays in London's West End that included representations of Chinese people in "a vicious and objectionable form," according to the complaints by the chargé d'affaires at the Chinese legation in London.[4] In film, the silent *The Yellow Claw* (1921) was followed by silent film serials such as *The Mystery of Dr. Fu Manchu* (1923) and *The Further Mysteries of Dr. Fu Manchu* (1924), and by *Mr. Wu* (1927), which delt with the yellow peril topic but was not based on Fu Manchu himself. In 1929 the production of films about Fu Manchu moved to Hollywood. Warner Oland starred in *The Mysterious Dr. Fu Manchu* (1929), *The Return of Dr. Fu Manchu* (1930), and *Daughter of the Dragon* (1931). Boris Karloff took over the role in *The Mask of Fu Manchu* (1932). In radio, three adaptations of Fu Manchu were dramatized in *The Collier Hour* program between 1929 and 1931. In 1931 and 1932 the NBC Blue Network, which broadcasted nationally across the United States, and CBS, on its local broadcasts in Chicago, turned Fu Manchu's works such as *The Daughter of Fu Manchu* into different serials.[5] Between December 1936 and November 1937 Radio Luxembourg, an important English-language commercial radio station in Europe, broadcast fifty-two fifteen-minute episodes of *Dr. Fu Manchu*, based on the first three books. Sax Rohmer himself wrote the script for the first half of the series and supervised the scripting of the second half. The entire series was rebroadcast on Radio Lyons between March 1937 and March 1938.[6] In 1939 the BBC prepared a show also written by Rohmer that was aired in Australia.[7] In 1939, *The Shadow of Fu Manchu*, an adaptation of Rohmer's first novels in the form of 156 fifteen-minute programs, was broadcast in various parts of the United States. In comics, Leo O'Mealia adapted the first Fu Manchu novels and published them as comic strips between 1931 and 1933.[8] Detective Comics had a Fu Manchu–style character, Ching Lung, in its first issue in March 1937. Fu Manchu later appeared in Detective Comics between July 1938 and June 1939.

Charlie Chan was born a bit later. Fu Manchu's antagonist came to light as a literary character in 1925 and remained a popular figure during the 1930s in novels and, particularly, in movies. The origin of the character is uncertain. Earl Derr Biggers, who originated the character of Charlie Chan in his novels, seems to have been inspired by Chang Apana (a Chinese American police officer who served in the Honolulu police force) and declared that he had created Charlie Chan to counterbalance the evil stereotype of Fu Manchu and present "a correct portrayal of the race."[9] Yet Biggers first introduced Charlie Chan only at the very end of *The House Without a Key* and later gave Chan a minor role in the next two novels of the series. Biggers received many letters about potential sequels to *The House Without a Key*, "with most of the inquiries curious about the character of the Chinese detective. . . . The character was found to be fascinating by the majority of the readership."[10] It was then when Biggers decided to give Chan a more prominent role in later novels such as *Charlie Chan Carries On*.[11]

The House Without a Key appeared first in installments in the *Saturday Evening Post* starting on September 24, 1925. It was quickly published as a book and followed by five other novels by 1932: *The Chinese Parrot* (1926), *Behind That Curtain* (1928), *The Black Camel* (1929), *Charlie Chan Carries On* (1930), and *Keeper of the Keys* (1932).[12] But, as in the case of Fu Manchu, Charlie Chan's popularity was mainly reached through films. The sixteen films in which Warner Oland starred between 1931 and 1937 turned the series into a successful product, with a total of forty-seven Charlie Chan movies released between 1926 and 1949.[13] Charlie Chan could also be found in radio series on the NBC Blue Network, Mutual, and ABC between 1932 and 1948, as well as in a comic strip drawn by Alfred Andriola and distributed by the Mc-Naught Syndicate between 1938 and 1942.[14]

Such a sequence of titles evokes the saturation of China images across the Western public sphere in the 1930s. Omnipresent and influential as they were, Fu Manchu and Charlie Chan (as well as other Asian characters and sequels inspired by them, including James Lee Wong and Mr. Moto) were only a small part of the representations of China available along the arc that goes from the yellow peril to the wise Oriental. To be sure, many of these views had existed to some degree in previous periods. However, in the late 1920s and, particularly, in the 1930s their coexistence was unique. As works by Hua Hsu and Richard Jean So have shown, the 1930s saw new advances in technology, an increased cross-cultural mobility, and the emergence of new forms of expertise and authority, which fully consolidated the new framework for intellectual and cultural relations between China and the West that had begun in previous decades.[15] Moreover, the relations between China and the West also became embedded in the cultural and economic networks that characterized mass consumerism, "a mass-production and mass-marketing system that imagines an abundance of goods within a culture that emphasizes purchasing, desire, glamour, and flexible, consumption-driven identities."[16]

What primarily concerns us in this chapter are the effects of this combination of saturation, diversity, and consumerism that characterized the representations of China and the Chinese in the 1930s. How did this combination turn out? How did the new economy for representing China that emerged in the 1920s evolve in the following decade? And what happened to the China represented under saturation, diversity, and consumerism in cultural contexts where China had traditionally been represented indirectly? Were these conditions—saturation, diversity, consumerism—merely replicated there? Did this new context bring about any kind of adaptation?

In this chapter I show some of the effects produced under these new conditions in relation to representing China. I show how the images of China adjusted to different local contexts in Spain without fully losing their dependence on pivotal English and French sources. I also show how China became embodied by Western agents to an unprecedented degree. Figures such as Pearl Buck and André Malraux played a crucial role in representing China for Western and Spanish readers. Their double position as both Western subjects and representative of the Chinese was crucial in legitimizing their new views and sensibilities toward China.

Let us briefly go back to *Charlie Chan Carries On* and Warner Oland, as they illustrate two aspects that will be further developed in the following sections. First, in 1931, just as *Charlie Chan Carries On* premiered in theaters across the United States and Britain, a Spanish-language version of the movie was released in Spain. *Charlie Chan Carries On* and *Eran trece* (They Were Thirteen) had been filmed in parallel with two different casts: each scene was shot first in English and later in Spanish.[17] Warner Oland's role as Charlie Chan in the former was played by the Spanish actor Manuel Arbó in the latter. Despite the different cast and some minor changes in names and songs, both films followed the same script, which is based on the American version.[18] The example illustrates how the transculturated images of China did adjust to the Spanish context but only to a minor degree, as they were still very much subjected to a non-Spanish original frame.

Second, Warner Oland visited China in 1936. Charlie Chan films had been a success in cities like Shanghai and would inspire Chinese imitations in the late 1930s and 1940s. Audiences included intellectuals like Lu Xun, for whom "going to a showing of any detective movie, like those of Charlie Chan, was practically a must . . . because this Chinese role was presented in such a positive way, and he found the stories used as plot material enjoyable."[19] Oland arrived in Shanghai on March 22 and was welcomed as a star.[20] Interestingly, Oland's identity was conflated with Charlie Chan's identity:

> The typical headline on the story was, "Great Chinese Detective Arrives in Shanghai," the reports all referring to him as "Mr. Chan." Oland held a press conference at 5 pm the day of his arrival, during which he tirelessly maintained his Charlie Chan persona while answering reporters' questions, even at one point referring to the goal of his China trip, not without humor, as being to "my ancestors." He expressed this again a few days later at a welcome banquet held for him by various Shanghai society and community leaders. He wore the familiar clothing the Chan character usually wore in the movies, stood up when the audience applauded him enthusiastically, and emotionally declared, "visiting the land

of my ancestors makes me so happy." At that moment, Warner Oland and Charlie Chan had merged into one, becoming in the eyes of those present, one and the same Chinese
person.[21]

The confusion between Oland as Chan not only illustrates how a Western figure like Oland could embody a Chinese identity (even in China
and for the Chinese!), but also how the representations of China could
frivolously adjust to different contexts: Oland was widely identified
with Charlie Chan—but not with Fu Manchu. In other words, "China"
was a signifier very much open to a wide range of signifieds—that could
be assigned and recognized quite arbitrarily.

In this chapter I explore further the importance of these adjustments
and embodiments in the representations of China in Spain. To do so, I
focus on the Catalan context as a particularly useful site to probe into
these concerns and questions and show how the adaptation of China
to different localities could take place even within a national context
and across different national languages. The ways in which China was
represented in the Catalan language illustrate with particular eloquence
how China was used to singularize a project of modernity that differed
from the projects in which China was represented in Spanish language,
which we have seen in previous chapters. In the 1920s and 1930s Catalan intellectuals and writers were particularly active in incorporating
China in their own elitist projects, often aimed at distancing themselves
from Spanish literary circles. While this was a singular project of Catalan modernity, the archive of representations of China that was available to Catalan intellectuals and writers was not much different from
the archive of representations of China that was available in the rest of
Spain. To put it simply, in the first decades of the twentieth century a
library in Barcelona held the same references on China as a library in,
say, Madrid: similar books, journals, and magazines, written in the same
languages, by similar writers. Yet the fact that, starting in the 1920s,
Catalan intellectuals used the same catalog of representations in such
a different, emancipatory way is a vivid example of how malleable the
image of China was, even within the same nation-state. Moreover, the
ways in which China was represented in the Catalan language also illustrate how the connection with China continued to be mediated by European discourses and voices. Influential Catalan poets and intellectuals
were keen to incorporate China into their works but were even more
eager to flaunt their English and French sources.

As a result, in this chapter I argue that in the 1930s "China" turned into an empty signifier with a ductile signified. Just as the mixture of cultural attributes produced by mass consumerism brought about a consumer code-switching that, instead of assimilation or hybridity, implied a going "back and forth, strategically producing an assemblage, at any given time, of different cultural and political signification,"[22] the signifier "China" supported the code-switching between the different Chinas coexisting in the West and the ways in which Western society had related to them in the previous decades. In other words, I argue that "China" accommodated multiple, often contradictory demands arising from different historical contingencies—even in neighboring cultural and linguistic contexts such as Spain and Catalonia. I argue, in short, that as images of China saturated the public sphere, "China" could be used by anyone and could mean pretty much anything.

MULTIPLE CHINAS, NEW SENSIBILITIES

When French sinologist Paul Pelliot visited the 1929 International Exhibition of Barcelona to give a talk on archeology in Western China, he was impressed by the abundance, quality, and condition of the books on China that were on sale in secondhand bookstores around the city.[23] He expressed his astonishment to his host, Catalan art critic Feliu Elias (1878–1948, aka Joan Sacs). It would be impossible, he declared, to find books like those in cities like Paris, London, or Berlin. Such a wealth of materials had remained unnoticed for Catalan intellectuals until a French sinologist remarked its importance. And, having become conscious of such wealth, Elias was, in fact, even more impressed than Pelliot:

> A la casa Palau el senyor Pelliot no trobà res del qual cercava, però tingué la sorpresa de desenterrar-hi *una obra francesa* en deu grossos volums concernent les missions arqueològiques franceses de l'Extrem Orient durant els començaments del segle XIX, obra completa, en perfecte estat de conservació, amb l'enquadernació original, etcètera, etcètera. . . . Aquella alegría, però, no era res en comparació de la que l'esperava a can Babra. En aquesta casa l'alegria fou seguida d'estupefacció i després de desconhort. Perquè és tan quantiós el tresor bibliogràfic que ens revelà el llibreter, que el senyor Pelliot se sentí descoratjat: no hi havia prou diner per adquirir aquells

llibres, àdhuc manuscrits raríssims i valuosíssims des de tots els punts de vista. . . . A casa Babra el senyor Pelliot descobrí els llibres concernents a l'Extrem Orient que arreu es consideren introbables . . . *àdhuc d'autors francesos que a França són recercats sense esperança.*[24]

In Casa Palau, Mr. Pelliot did not find anything he was looking for, but he was surprised to unearth a French work *in ten large volumes concerning the French archaeological missions in the Far East during the early nineteenth century, a complete work in perfect condition, with its original binding, and so on and so forth. . . . That joy, however, was nothing compared to what awaited him at Casa Babra. In this shop the joy was followed by astonishment and then bewilderment. Because the bibliographic treasure revealed to us by the bookseller was so large that Mr. Pelliot was disheartened: there was not enough money to acquire those books, even very rare manuscripts, extremely valuable from all points of view. . . . At Casa Babra, Mr. Pelliot discovered books about the Far East that are considered untraceable anywhere else* . . . even books by French authors who are hopelessly sought after in France.

The variety and number of images of China in Spain and Catalonia were as remarkable as in other locations across Europe. In the 1930s, moreover, a complex mosaic of representations of China was formed. The sinophobic yellow peril and the sinophilic exoticism now coexisted with many other views: compassion and sympathy, empathy and admiration, geopolitical interest and commercial attraction. Fu Manchu and Charlie Chan entertainment movies were premiered next to more historically grounded films such as *Shanghai Express* (1932), *The Bitter Tea of General Yen* (1933), and *The General Died at Dawn* (1936). The exoticism of Puccini's opera *Turandot* (1924) overlapped with popular expressions of Oriental wisdom and paraphernalia in art exhibitions, circuses, and magician's shows, each proclaiming itself "as the most spectacular of its day and as the model for others."[25] The stereotypical travel writings on China were juxtaposed with new travelers' accounts that portrayed China under new concerns. Pearl Buck and André Malraux, among others, developed further the new sensibilities for understanding China that were opened up by figures such as John Dewey and

Bertrand Russell in the previous decade. These new sensibilities did not remain within the intellectual sphere but became popularized too. Edgar Snow's *Red Star over China*, published in 1937, quickly sold 23,500 copies in the United States and 100,000 copies in Britain and was translated into six languages.[26] A radical critique of the limited ways in which China had traditionally been understood by Westerners and a claim for a more empathic relation between East and West could be found in popular cartoons such as Hergé's *Le Lotus bleu*, for example.[27] At that time, moreover, Chinese writers and public figures began to participate more actively in the generation and circulation of these new images of China: Lin Yutang's *My Country and My People*, originally published in 1936, had seven reprints by 1938, received rave reviews in numerous media, and positioned Lin "to be 'Mr. China' for a wide English-speaking audience;"[28] Soong Mei-ling was an influential Chinese icon in the United States, especially during the war between China and Japan from 1937 to 1945.[29] On top of all these developments, the spread of communism and revolutionary ideals that had stimulated a new interest for China in the 1920s intensified in the 1930s, when China's conflict with Japan was regarded as a global war against fascism.

In Spain and Catalonia specifically, representations of China increased and diversified with particular intensity. Many Chinas coexisted in Spain and Catalonia at the time. The number of books on China that were published between the late 1920s and the 1930s increased almost by 20 percent compared to the previous decade.[30] Writing about China was not a privilege restricted to diplomats, missionaries, and journalists. Firsthand impressions of China were also penned by unconventional writers like Elisenda Casas, an eight-year girl who was traveling in China with her family and shared her experiences in her school's magazine, or industrialists and dilettantes such as Juan Marín Balmas and Ricardo Martorell Téllez-Girón, who accompanied their chronicles with photographs.[31] In fact, knowledge about China was so available and could be so precise that, as we will see, writers who had never set foot in China were able to write compelling depictions of Chinese locations and characters. But the interest in China transcended literary and intellectual circles too. While libraries and scientific societies continued hosting the talks and activities that diplomats such as Juan Mencarini and Eduard Toda had started in the first decades of the twentieth century, China was now a frequent presence in Catalan and Spanish media and popular culture as well. China could take several columns on the international page of newspapers, with long reports on intricate political developments that had no direct connection to Spain.[32] China was the object of several art exhibitions.[33] The Spanish premiere of Puccini's *Turandot* took place in Barcelona's Liceu in 1928. Catalan theater companies also showed a sustained interest in China, and plays that represented China under different guises, comical or exotic, were premiered at playhouses such as Teatre Tívoli, Teatre Romea, and Teatre Còmic del Paral·lel.[34] The troupes of Chinese artists that had started touring around Spain in the 1910s now became a regular attraction in cities and towns.[35] Catalan folklore associations added Chinese dancing giant figures to their repertoires.[36] These popular images of the exotic China even transculturated into kitsch examples, such as the stage decoration of performances at cabaret Wu-Li-Chang in Barcelona, and Vicente Hong, a Chinese toreador who fascinated audiences across Spain.[37]

The 1929 International Exhibition of Barcelona captures the abundance, availability, and contradictions of the representations of China in Catalonia in the late 1920s and 1930s. The China (Hong Kong) section was hosted inside the Pueblo Oriental, which included other countries such as India, Persia, Egypt, and Morocco. Pueblo Oriental was advertised as "la atracción más original de la Exposición" (the most original attraction of the Exhibition), a place where "Vd. puede vivir las verdaderas maravillas del MÁGICO ORIENTE" and "con todo el personal nativo . . . trabajando, en sus respectivas artes y vestidos con sus típicos trajes" (you can experience the true wonders of the MAGICAL EAST and with all the native staff . . . working on their craftwork and dressed in their typical costumes).[38] Next to this exotic China, representations of a fearful China or a compassionate China were on display. While in the Palacio de las Misiones China was considered the biggest of "pueblos infieles" (infidel people), Catalan schoolgirls were kindly dressed as Chinese and Japanese in a "multiracial" parade that celebrated the Palacio's opening.[39]

The exoticist enthusiasm of the Exhibition's official advertisement contrasts with journalist chronicles:

> Dentro se ven algunos trajes exóticos de los vendedores que exhiben su conocida mercancía en departamentos de excesiva sencillez. Al verlos recordamos que en un extremo de la plaza de la Fuente Mágica, delante del pabellón de la ciudad de Barcelona, hay un quiosco oriental en el que se venden análogas mercancías, y que es de mucho más bello y agradable aspecto, sin que cueste nada su contemplación y su visita.[40]

Inside you can see some exotic costumes from vendors who display their well-known merchandise in excessively simple stalls. When you see them, they remind you that at one end of the Plaza de la Fuente Mágica, in front of the pavilion of the city of Barcelona, there is an Oriental kiosk where similar merchandise is sold. The kiosk is much more beautiful and pleasant and you can contemplate it and visit it for free.

In other words: the singular, exotic China that had been so treasured in 1888 was now available—and consumable—all around the city. As Chinese goods and images were easily available outside the China section, and even outside the world's fair, the exotic displays in the China section inside the fair became kitsch and inauthentic.

Such abundance devolved into a paradoxical presence: China could be the most common, ordinary reality in a modern world that incessantly advertised the singularity of the Chinese exotic. This paradox was insightfully expressed in *L'home que es va perdre* (The Man Who Got Lost), Francesc Trabal's avant-garde debut novel published in 1929.[41] Francesc Trabal (1899–1957) and his friends Joan Oliver (1899–1986) and Armand Obiols (1904–1971) had an ambitious project: a literary and intellectual revolution against a Catalan cultural scene that, at the time, was stagnated in a long-lasting fight between a romantic Modernisme and a more rationalist Noucentisme. Trabal and his peers proposed a more cosmopolitan approach to modernity, largely inspired by surrealism and connected to Dadaism and the transgressive movements of the European avant-gardes.

L'home que es va perdre illustrates their irreverent project. The novel tells the story of Lluís Frederic Picàbia, a young man from a well-to-do family in Catalonia, who loses his fiancée, Sílvia, after she breaks up with him. Picàbia leaves his family and a promising future in his family's business and decides to travel around the world. One day Picàbia loses a golden cigarette case that Sílvia had offered him as a present when they were still engaged. He then begins an obsessive project of losing and finding things—his existential quest turns into an absurd project. He starts with daily objects: he loses umbrellas, suitcases, photo cameras, just to be able to find them again. But the project quickly turns into a dadaistic business. With his associate, Costa, Picàbia turns the project into a surreal venture that makes the front pages of the media around the world: they lose and find elephants, buildings, thousands of cars. Their most ambitious operation is to make five thousand Chinese orphans disappear only to be found later in Mexico. The company eventually goes bankrupt, and Picàbia moves to Sweden, where he meets Sílvia again—only to lose her once more. Devastated, Picàbia decides to lose himself and disappears from the world.

China plays an essential role in Trabal's parody at its most hyperbolic moment. The predetermined images of China as a foreign, exotic, different land get turned upside down as the action in the chapters set in China takes place quite naturally. While the action in the chapters set in Catalonia is full of fantastic, extraordinary events, the action in the chapters set in China is removed from any kind of exoticism. Echoing the use of art to break with certainties by authors such as Francis Picabia, Blaise Cendrars, and Guillaume Apollinaire,[42] *L'home que es va perdre* makes use of China to break with fixed meanings: contrary to all the works that wanted to show a "real" China through clichés and stereotypes, Trabal depicts a "fictional" China through a realistic portrait. For Trabal—and for his iconoclast peers—China was part of the common currency that connected modern cultures around the world.[43]

One of the most important developments within the multiple, contradictory Chinas that overlapped in the late 1920s and early 1930s in Spain and Catalonia is the consolidation of new sensibilities toward China and the Chinese. These new sensibilities emerged out of the new economy for representing China that developed in the 1910s and that we saw in the previous chapter. Having more Chinas, more diverse and more available in different spheres, also implied having Chinas that appealed to emotions that differed from fearful sinophobia or intellectual sinophilia. Reports on the Chinese immigrants in Barcelona, for instance, could refer to the yellow peril only ironically, as in Joan Alavedra's humanist depiction of Chinese immigrants in 1930, which would have been impossible decades earlier.[44] Similarly, Ramon Pei's series of articles published in *Mirador* in 1933 described his travel to China focusing on the poor and lower classes: refugees, prostitutes, and workers.[45] In a later article Pei even adopted the first-person voice to convey the feelings of a rickshaw puller.[46]

The successful Spanish and Catalan reception of Sheng Cheng's memoirs *Ma mère* (My Mother) and *Ma mère et moi* (My Mother and I) was also framed within this new range of sensibilities.[47] Sheng Cheng (1899–1996) participated in the Work-Study Movement and lived in France for ten years. He was involved in left-wing politics during the 1920s and was a founder of the French Communist Party. His involvement in leftist political agitation gained him access to "the café society of artists in Paris" and public notoriety.[48] Unlike Chen Jitong, who had played the role of cross-cultural mediator while reinforcing the binary separation between China and Europe, Sheng Cheng's works were motivated by a universalism that tried to awake an empathic, sentimental reaction in French readers. In *Ma mère* and *Ma mère et moi* Sheng provides an autobiographical account of his mother's experience as an embodiment of China's past and present. Both works were highly successful in France and across Europe.[49]

Sheng's involvement in leftist political agitation also probably explains why *Ma mère* was "graced" with a preface written by Paul Valéry.[50] Valéry's preface was impassioned. He expressed his "moral indignation against the carnage of war and its destruction of the spirit of humanism, an outrage which he turned into a veritable crusade in the 1930s."[51] Valéry empathized with the universal humanism embodied by Sheng's mother. He claimed that her example—and Sheng's work—should promote a "cultural, intellectual, and political cooperation amidst a climate of growing international socialist movements."[52] In other words, Sheng, his mother, and his family should generate sympathy and affection in European readers, and these feelings should contribute to "a unified world," combining the best attributes of East and West and avoiding both tradition and progress as extreme polarities.[53]

Reviews of the Spanish translations of Sheng's works show how this new kind of engagement with China came along with a vocabulary conveying new emotions: "emoción, ternura, pasión" (emotion, tenderness, passion); "un libro admirable, repetimos, acerca del cual con sólo dejar correr la pluma se harían comentarios, por diez veces la extensión que permite esta nota" (an admirable book, I insist; if I let the pen run, comments would extend ten times the length allowed in this note); "se desvela a nuestros ojos la intimidad de una raza y de unas costumbres lejanas" (the intimacy of a race and of distant customs is revealed to our eyes).[54] Sheng's visit to Barcelona and the talk he gave at the Ritz Hotel on April 10, 1935, were described with a similar sentimental investment.[55]

Boosted by the agency of international figures like Buck and Malraux, as we will soon see, these new concerns for China in Spain and Catalonia gained momentum in the 1930s. The combination of sentimental and internationalist views on China made the perception of political affinities between China and Catalonia more visible during the late 1930s. The publication of essays and articles representing China and Asia from the perspective offered by communism and anarcho-syndicalism preceded the coexistence of the Spanish Civil War (1936–1939) and the Second Sino-Japanese War (1937–1945).[56] These new sensibilities then inspired a feeling of antifascist brotherhood between certain social and political groups both in China and Spain—especially in republican territories such as Catalonia. The simultaneous conflicts in Spain and China were understood in both locations as well as internationally as "an overarching global struggle by democratic (or at least progressive) governments against fascism and xenophobic ultranationalism."[57]

A piece written by journalist Jaime Menéndez illustrates this new bond between the two peoples. Menéndez described the "relación íntima entre las dos invasiones: la germanoitaliana, que resiste con gallardía y arrojo el pueblo español, y la japonesa, que va aplastando el pueblo chino" (intimate relationship between the two invasions: the German-Italian, which the Spanish people are resisting with gallantry and fearlessness, and the Japanese, which is crushing the Chinese people). Based on French sources, Menéndez surveys the history of China in the decades that led to the Japanese invasion of 1937.[58] The bonds became even tighter when about a hundred Chinese volunteers joined the units of the International Brigades to fight against fascism in the Spanish Civil War.[59] Solidarity was mutual and worked both ways: the republican resistance holding the city of Madrid was taken as a model for Chinese troops in the Battle of Wuhan between June and October 1938; and Wuhan came to be known as the "Madrid of the East." Essays on the Spanish situation were published by important Chinese writers like Ba Jin. Mao Zedong referred several times to the Spanish context as a model of resistance.[60] Young Chinese students who were studying in Europe visited Spain before going back to China to join the Chinese resistance against Japan.[61] Menéndez's piece, published in *Estampa*, also includes Sun Peiyuan's (aka Mai Xin) poem "Baowei Madeli" (Let's Defend Madrid!), both the original Chinese version and the translation into Spanish, which became a popular piece among Chinese troops and inspired the poem "Baowei da Wuhan" (Let's Defend Wuhan!).[62]

EMBODYING CHINA

Another important phenomenon that came out of the multiplicity of Chinas coexisting in Spain and Catalonia during the late 1920s and 1930s was a more explicit recognition of the indirect nature of many of these representations. From the late 1920s onward, the number of works related to China that explicitly declared themselves to be translations from English or French sources increased.[63] To be sure, works on China that tried to pass as originals or that did not mention the origin of their information about China continued to exist. But in the 1930s it became more common to display the origin of these representations of China. The fascination for the Western mediators with China became even more remarkable than the fascination for China itself.

Take George Bernard Shaw's visit to China in 1933, for example. Shaw was at the time a famous figure in Catalonia. His popularity can be explained not only by his literary merits and awards, such as the 1925 Nobel Prize in Literature, but also by his eccentricities. Shaw's extravagant declarations appeared regularly in journals and newspapers of different political slant published in Barcelona such as *La Vanguardia*, *La Humanitat*, *La Veu de Catalunya*, *La Publicitat*, *L'Esquella de la Torratxa*, *El Diluvio*, and *Flama*. Shaw's travel around the world in 1933 was therefore closely followed by the media.[64] On February 22, for instance, a portrait of the Irish author appeared on page 3 of *La Humanitat* under the headline: "Bernard Shaw, a Xina: divendres volarà damunt la Gran Muralla" (Bernard Shaw in China: Will Fly Over the Great Wall on Friday).[65] The piece reported on Shaw's visit to China and his interview with General Zhang Xueliang while summarizing the current development of the conflict between China and Japan and the danger involving Japan's expansionist ambitions. But both the headline and a major part of the piece focused on Shaw himself. Shaw's flying over the Great Wall seemed just as relevant as the fate of China's resistance against Japan's militarism.

The coverage of Shaw's visit to China clearly shows the link established between Shaw's experiences in China and the political situation in the Sino-Japanese conflict. Shaw became a privileged "medium" to interpret the evolution of the conflict between China and Japan, even if he never played the role of mediator in the sense that literary studies, translation studies, or transfer studies have attached to cross-cultural mediation.[66] Shaw never translated any Chinese works, did not have any project for cross-cultural understanding between China and Europe, and did not have a network nor an agenda for connecting Chinese and European intellectuals. But Shaw was an instrumental agent for bringing in some China content to the Catalan readers. He acted as a textual and "visual" facilitator: *La Vanguardia* opened its April 2, 1933, issue with a photograph of "el famoso escritor irlandés, Mr. George Bernard Shaw, con un grupo de estudiantes chinos que le saludaron a su llegada a la ciudad" (the famous Irish writer, Mr. George Bernard Shaw, with a group of Chinese students who greeted him upon his arrival in the city),[67] which was later mentioned in other media as well.[68]

Needless to say, the circuit for reporting on Shaw's travels and the ongoing Sino-Japanese conflict remained indirect—information about Shaw arrived in Catalonia through foreign press releases. Most of the pieces were released by Fabra news, a Spanish news agency that had an agreement with Havas to release in Spain the international news previously released by this French agency. As a result, the texts depicting Shaw's experiences in the East published by the different Catalan media were very similar, almost identical. Shaw's meeting with General Araki in Tokyo, for instance, is reported almost with the same wording in publications such as *La Vanguardia, La Humanitat, La Publicitat, La Veu de Catalunya*, and *El Diluvio*.[69] Likewise, Shaw's controversial exhortation to Hong Kong students to embrace communism is reported verbatim in *La Vanguardia* and *La Humanitat*.[70] In other words, representations of China continued to rely upon translations of sources written in English or French, and events in China continued to be followed on the basis of foreign press releases, either direct (Reuters, United Press, Havas) or indirect (Fabra based on Havas). However, in the 1930s these foreign mediations acquired visibility, acceptance—even reverence. These foreign mediations not only reaffirmed their agency, but almost took the space of China itself in the readers' attention: for Catalan readers, Shaw was in China and *Shaw was China*.

The reception of Sheng Cheng's works in Catalonia illustrates how the new sensibilities toward China were intertwined with a fascination for the foreign mediators who revealed a new kind of China that had remained hidden. *Ma mère* and *Ma mère et moi* were reviewed and advertised in Barcelona not only by stressing their humanist, sentimental values but also by pointing out their great success in France and their being originally written in French. The French originals were also sold (and advertised) in Barcelona bookstores, where Sheng Cheng signed copies during his visit in 1935.[71] Paul Valéry's preface to *Ma mère* was of course widely highlighted as well.

In this context of an increasing reverence for foreign mediation while images of China saturated the public sphere in Catalonia and Spain, Pearl Buck and André Malraux were crucial figures for consolidating the diverse views of China that were opened within the new epistemology that had emerged in the 1910s. Buck and Malraux legitimized a more humane vision of China and the Chinese based on gender and class. These views were also promoted by other figures in the West such as Lin Yutang or American sinophiles such as Henry Luce, not so popular in Catalonia and Spain, who "strove to arouse sympathy for China among the general American population" and claimed that China "was becoming more democratic under the leadership of the Nationalist government."[72]

Pearl Buck was probably the most crucial figure in the Western understanding of China in the twentieth century. Buck's early novels, written from China, had a tremendous success around the world. *East Wind: West Wind* (1930) and, especially, *The Good Earth* (1931) became immediate best sellers and remained on best-seller lists during the 1930s.[73] Thanks to her fiction and nonfiction writings, Buck became a public advocate for cross-cultural understanding. Her humanized vision of the Chinese was decisive in the important awards she received—notably the Pulitzer Prize in 1932 and the Nobel Prize in Literature in 1938.[74]

The Good Earth was "a kind of talisman of cross-cultural imagination" that has continued to influence the Western public up to the present day.[75] Buck popularized a "sentimental" mode of representing China, which was developed by women writers from North America and Great Britain.[76] Between the end of World War I and 1949 most of the best sellers on China published in the English-speaking market were written by women.[77] Works such as Louise Jordan Miln's *Mr. Wu* (1918), Dorothea Hosie's *Two Gentleman of China* (1924), Alice Tisdale Hobart's *Oil for the Lamps of China* (1933), Nora Waln's *The House of Exile* (1933), and Emily Hahn's *The Soong Sisters* (1941) featured contemporary China in a way that "demanded on the part of the reader a level of identification and emotional engagement with Chinese individuals, and Chinese women in particular, that was unprecedented."[78] Many of their books were later adapted for the screen and became popular movies too.

Following the success of Buck's works in the mid-1930s, some of these works were translated into Spanish in the late 1930s and 1940s.[79] But it was Buck who capitalized on the attention of Spanish and Catalan readers. In fact, while *The Good Earth* was translated into Spanish in 1935 and other translations followed in the 1940s,[80] Catalan intellectuals were already paying close attention to Buck's works either in the English original or in French translations. J. V. Foix (1893–1987), one of the most important Catalan poets and intellectuals at the time, reviewed *La Première Femme de Yuan* (the 1936 French translation of the collection *The First Wife and Other Stories*, originally published in 1933) almost ten years before the work was published in Spanish.[81] Catalan reviewers stressed how Buck revealed "una Xina incògnita, pintoresca sí, *però molt més humana* que la que altres escriptors han fet conèixer" (an unknown China, certainly picturesque, *but much more humane* than the China revealed by other writers).[82] Foix, who referred to Buck as a half-American and half-Chinese novelist, also praised the sober style with which Buck depicted generational conflicts and the revolution. Foix stressed Buck's engagement with these topics. But, above all, Buck was praised for how she embodied China herself. Buck was not only a "witness" of China's history but also China "en cos i ànima" (in body and soul).[83] It could be argued that this new mode of representation of China (gendered, half-Western, and half-Chinese) was also the basis for Marcela de Juan's prestige in Spain in later decades.[84]

This new sensibility shifted the understanding of China to its "real" place as a modern location, away from exoticism and fantasy, which should be now considered exhausted topics. While the China represented from the West had become more exotic—and more artificial—than the China depicted by Chinese themselves, Buck was revealing the real modern China.[85] For critics like Ramon Vinyes, Buck and Malraux were highly valuable as facilitators of these new views on China, which could be connected to universal concerns with communism and the lower classes. For Vinyes, this potential made Buck more authentic, even more Chinese than Chinese themselves: writers like Buck "ens fan conèixer l'actual Xina com no ens la fan conèixer els seus escriptors mateixos" (make the real China known as it has not been made known by Chinese writers themselves).[86]

André Malraux's novels were also discussed in Catalonia even before they were published in Catalan or Spanish language. *Les Conquérants* (The Conquerors) was reviewed right after its original publication in French in 1928, before the Spanish translation was published in 1931.[87] The novel left a deep impression on Catalan intellectuals, who were moved by the experience of Chinese idealists. Jaume Miravitlles, for instance, praised *Les Conquérants* as "el llibre més impressionant que he llegit en la meva vida" (the most impressive book I have read in my life).[88] *La Condition humaine* (Man's Fate) was equally successful and widely reviewed in Catalan media right after its original publication in 1933—the Spanish and Catalan translations would remain unpublished in Spain until the late 1960s and 1970s.[89] Reviews frequently mention that *La Condition humaine* was awarded the Goncourt Prize in 1933, and some pieces even survey the reception of Malraux's works in the

Anglophone market, with references to Aldous Huxley and Edmund Wilson.[90]

Just as Buck popularized a new sentimental mode for approaching China, Malraux's works nurtured a new mode of representation that connected Chinese history and society with universal existential concerns. This connection humanized China in the Buck sense but also enabled a depiction of the Chinese characterized by more psychological depth. Comparatist and literary critic Ramon Esquerra (1909–1938) isolated this new approach to China as Malraux's most valuable contribution.[91] Esquerra's influential reviews praised how Malraux was capable of going beyond the superficial differences between Chinese and Western historical developments to unveil aspects that may lay deeper but that can be shared across the world. Malraux's works became the meeting point for universal feelings such as idealism and nihilism, ethics and passion, tragedy and pain—all explicitly related to the contemporary world or contemporary life.[92] Through Malraux's authorship, then, China gets legitimized as a site for universal literary and intellectual concerns.[93]

To be sure, the ideas about China developed by Catalan reviewers cannot be dissociated from Malraux's biographical experience. Reviewers often remark that Malraux had "un *coneixement íntim* del conflicte de forces en la Xina moderna" (an *intimate knowledge* of the conflict between different forces in modern China), that he "feu coneixença amb nacionalistes, revolucionaris i terroristes xinesos," that he "fou *testimoni visual* d'alguns dels conflictes revolucionaris més sagnants del 1925 al 1927," or that he "estigué en el fort dels combats" (met Chinese nationalists, revolutionaries, and terrorists; was a *visual witness* to some of the bloodiest revolutionary conflicts from 1925 to 1927; was right in the middle of the fighting).[94] In other words, it is Malraux's firsthand experience as a Frenchman in China that empowers China's secondhand reception in Catalonia.

Given the prestige acquired by Western embodiments of China like Buck and Malraux, it is not surprising that, as we saw in the introduction, in 1931 Mario Verdaguer decided to impersonate both a foreign author (T. S. H. Thompson) and a Spanish translator (Fabián Casares) to publish an essay on Chinese culture and society that he had composed on the basis of foreign sources. Covering his identity behind pseudonyms was not an unusual practice for Verdaguer, especially when he edited or translated works without great literary quality.[95] However, in the case of *El enigma del despertar de China* (The Enigma of China's

Awakening) this practice was not applied to a book with a particularly commercial orientation. *El enigma del despertar de China* is a rather dull compilation of articles, manifestos, talks, and literary pieces originally published in China and that Verdaguer most surely rewrote on the basis of French translations.[96] In any case, Verdaguer's artifice influenced the circulation of the book outside Spain. *El enigma del despertar de China* was quoted in research articles in Argentina and Brazil, which took Thompson as a real person "who around 1934 had traveled to China." Even if somewhat trivially, then, the chain of indirectness persisted and a secondhand China in Spain turned into a thirdhand China in South America.[97]

Given the combination between, on the one hand, the increasing availability and heterogeneity of the representations of China in Catalonia and, on the other, the explicit reverence for foreign mediators who developed new sensibilities toward China, let us now examine two texts that illustrate the effects of such combination in both the intellectual and the popular culture spheres. Joan Sacs's essay "Àsia" (Asia) and Joan Crespi i Martí's novel *La ciutat de la por* (The City of Fear) show with particular eloquence the impact of Western mediation, the possibilities and limitations of Catalan agency within this cultural hegemony, and above all, the malleability of the images of China within these politics. Both texts reveal how code-switching—or the freedom to move fluidly among different, even contradictory, images of and assumptions about China—satisfied all the different demands imposed upon the representations of China in the late 1920s and early 1930s.[98] Code-switching facilitated a productive cohabitation of these different images of China, even within the same work. Code-switching empowered Catalan writers and intellectuals with a certain agency to generate their own images of China. At the same time, code-switching kept China a passive object.

"ÀSIA"

If we browse the Catalan canon of the first half of the twentieth century, chances are that we will find a poet who engaged actively with Chinese (or Japanese) poetry in one way or another. Figures such as Josep Carner (1884–1970), Josep Maria de Sagarra (1894–1961), Carles Riba (1893–1959), and Marià Manent (1898–1988) acted as translators, imitators, or critics of East Asian lyrics. Why did these Catalan poets approach Chinese poetry? And what do their poems and reflections tell us about the representations of China by Catalan intellectual elites in the 1930s? The former question has partially been answered.[99] The latter remains to be explored.

It is commonly accepted that Catalan poets were interested in Chinese poetry because Chinese lyrics were a tool for renewing their cultural credentials. The Catalan literary tradition had mainly valued the splendor of the medieval period, and twentieth-century Catalan poets looked for ways to update and expand their cultural capital through what they considered a universal affiliation. They approached Chinese poems beyond the simple fascination with chinoiserie, but rather as pieces of international currency.[100] In other words, the Catalan translations of classical Chinese poems were part of a modernization through Europeanization. For Catalan high culture, Chinese poetry was a gate toward cosmopolitanism and universality.[101]

A lesser-mentioned but also important reason that explains the interest that Catalan poets showed for Chinese poetry is the ductility of China as the object of that interest. Catalan translators of Chinese poetry belonged to different cultural cliques, and their interest in China was part of different projects. Chinese poetry was such a distant reference that it allowed each Catalan poet to appropriate it and reelaborate it in his own way and according to his own agenda. Each poet found in China whatever he was looking for.[102] Apel·les Mestres (1854–1936) published *Poesia xinesa* (Chinese Poetry) in 1925 as a reaction against the classicism and formalism that characterized the hegemonic Noucentisme. Marià Manent criticized Mestres's approach. In his own versions of Chinese poems Manent showed precisely the opposite: a formalist engagement with Chinese classics. Manent's collections *L'aire daurat* (The Golden Air, 1928) or *Com un núvol lleuger* (Like a Light Cloud, 1968) were grounded on his empathy for the scenery, moderation, and subtlety of Chinese lyrics. Josep Carner also valued the harmony of classical Chinese poetry. But, as he reveals in the "introductory confession" to "La passejada pels brodats de seda" (The Walk Through the Silk Embroidery, 1932), which would later become the important collection *Lluna i llanterna* (Moon and Lantern, 1935), he mostly valued the possibility of expressing himself through the otherness provided by Chinese voices.[103]

All these Catalan poets openly acknowledged the secondhand nature of their approach to Chinese lyrics. Josep Maria de Sagarra's programmatic essay on Chinese poetry published in 1923 already offered a justification:

Avui dia, sembla que, entre la gent que s'interessa per les qüestions literàries, la poesia de l'Extrem Orient és un motiu apassionant per als ulls més delicats i les orelles més fines. Ha passat una mica la mode dels "haikais" i de les falsificacions ridícules, però, en canvi, els estudis honrats de famosos xinòlegs, la recerca de la pura expressió dels grans lírics de l'imperi celestial són coses d'un valor inapreciable pels gustadors de sensibilitats noves i d'emoció condensada.[104]

Today, it seems that, among those who are interested in literary issues, the poetry of the Far East is an exciting subject for the finest ears and the most delicate eyes. The fashion for "haikais" and for ridiculous forgeries has almost passed. But, instead, the honest studies written by famous sinologists, the search for pure expression by the great lyricists of the Celestial Empire are highly valued by the tasters of new sensibilities and condensed emotion.

To be sure, "the finest ears and the most delicate eyes" are references to what is going on in the European cultural and intellectual centers. Sagarra wants to speak as a "europeu modern i de sensibilitat exigent" (modern European, with a demanding sensibility) and places himself "sense impostació i sense complexos a un corrent coetani i a un rapte poètic compartit amb els francesos, germànics i anglesos" (unabashedly and without imposture within a contemporary current and a poetic spell shared with his French, German, and English peers).[105] The Catalan project of becoming part of the modern European cultural scene is connected to the indirect ways of translating China. Sagarra exhibits the dependence on "honest studies written by famous sinologists" as well as on English and French sources. He mentions translations by Marquis d'Hervey de Saint-Denys, Arthur Waley, Madame Judith Gautier, and George Soulié de Morant that remain a reference for other Catalan poets in later years. These references will be joined by other translations that can be located along the chain that goes from the sinological versions of James Legge and Herbert Giles to the more popular versions by translators such as Helen Waddell, Charles Budd, Launcelot A. Cranmer-Byng, W. J. B. Fletcher, Amy Lowell, and Ezra Pound's *Cathay*.[106]

At this point in this book, this kind of reliance on English and French sources should not be surprising, but it is still quite striking how these

Catalan poets displayed their foreign sources in such an unabashed, exuberant way. By this I do not (only) mean that they apologized for having rendered Chinese poems indirectly and that they preferred to call their versions "interpretations" rather than translations, for instance. I particularly mean that their reliance upon English and French sources was indeed explicitly acknowledged again and again—even flaunted. Marià Manent provided long and detailed lists of the sources used for his "interpretations."[107] Carner confessed that he had followed "algunes antologies angleses i franceses de poesia celeste" (some English and French anthologies of celestial poetry) and mentioned the "vels i infidelitats successives en diferents idiomes" (successive veils and infidelities in different languages), given that some poems "han passat del xinès al llatí, del llatí a una o dues llengües més abans de deixar-se caure a les meves mans" (have moved from Chinese to Latin, from Latin to one or two more languages before falling into my hands).[108]

The reverence for the English and French translations contrasts with the indifference for the essence of the Chinese originals. Carner, for instance, confesses that "les esperances d'haver conservat alguna essència originària són de les més vagues" (the hopes of having preserved some of their original essence are very vague).[109] In other words, while the traces of the English and French intermediary versions were left visible enough to be appreciated by the reader, the historical traces of the original Chinese poems were erased—even if many of the English and French intermediary versions included notes and information about the biographical, geographical, or cultural context of the original pieces.[110] For these poets, China was nothing but a springboard to get closer to Europe and to carry out their own formal and aesthetic projects. China was very much present on their pages, but at the same time, China was ultimately irrelevant.

Other than flaunting their English and French sources and including some brief remarks on their practices in the prefaces of their works, poets like Carner or Manent did not leave any elaborate reflection on these issues. Joan Sacs's "Àsia" is therefore a valuable exception. Sacs's essay allows us to see how this contradictory conception of a frequent yet insignificant China was theorized. We have met Sacs before in this chapter, under his real name, Feliu Elias. We left him impressed by Paul Pelliot's praise of the wealth of books on China available in Barcelona bookstores. Sacs was in fact an influential figure in Catalan culture between the 1910s and 1930s. He was a renowned painter, illustrator, and caricaturist, as well as an influential critic and regular contributor to

artistic and cultural journals and magazines. Sacs was initially involved
in the development of Noucentisme, which turned the ideals of order
and civility into a hegemonic movement in the 1920s. In fact, back in
1914 Eugeni d'Ors (1881–1954), founder of Noucentisme and the leading Catalan intellectual at the time, already traced striking similarities
between the political project that *noucentistes* were trying to promote
in Catalonia and the reforms being carried out in China after the fall of
the Qing Empire. D'Ors published six consecutive op-ed columns in *La
Veu de Catalunya* about these political similarities.[111] He was fascinated
by Zhang Zhidong's proposal for reforming education and morality as
prior steps for reforming the laws and the political structure of China,
which had many programmatic similarities with Noucentisme.[112] Yet
the connections between China and Catalonia via France that d'Ors
had sketched through Albert Maybon did not develop in the political
field. These connections developed a few years later in the aesthetic and
cultural field.

In fact, Joan Sacs was probably the Catalan intellectual who elaborated the
connections initially traced by d'Ors in a more recurrent and systematic way. Sacs's interest in China, and in Asia in general, was sustained
during the 1920s and early 1930s, when he published several works
related to China from different angles.[113] Written in 1927, "Àsia" appeared in *La Nova Revista*, a cosmopolitan cultural monthly magazine
with a particular attention to the arts, which included frequent references to Asia. Between 1927 and 1929 *La Nova Revista* released thirty-
two issues and almost half of them incorporated contents about Asia or
mentioned Chinese or Japanese topics. References were not extempo-
raneous, but part of the magazine's scope and mission. Joan Sacs had a
section entitled "Orient i Extrem-Orient" (East and Far East), which appeared in six issues (2, 3, 6, 11, 16, 19). A long article by Josep Maria de
Sagarra on Chinese poetry was published in issue 5, and Josep Lleonart
published a series of short fiction pieces entitled "Notes xineses" (Chinese Notes).[114] As part of its project *La Nova Revista* even announced a
book series on Chinese and Japanese literature, which would start with
Marià Manent's translation of an anthology of Chinese poetry and then
continue with a biography of Matsuo Bashō and a book by Saint-John
Perse.[115]

In fact, the process through which Asian content was incorporated
in *La Nova Revista* did not differ much from the practices described in
previous chapters. Sacs himself reveals in detail the secondhand nature
of their references to China:

El reportatge que avui oferim als lectors de *La Nova Revista* és, pel que fa a la Caldea, resum de reportatges de *The Sphere* i de l'*Illustrated London News*, particularment d'aquest darrer periòdic, de data 18 d'abril i 22 d'agost de 1925, de 20 de març de 1926, de l'1 de juny i de 17 de desembre de 1927 i 23 de febrer de l'any que som, reportatges del Sr. Leonard Wooley, director de la missió organitzada pel British Museum i el Museu de la Universitat de Pensylvània [sic] per a fer excavacions en terres de la Baixa Caldea. Pel que fa a les excavacions de l'Índia resumim tres altres informacions publicades en *The Times* de 26 de febrer de 1926, del 4 i 5 de gener d'enguany, pel Sr. John Marshall, director general d'arqueologia a l'Índia. De les recents excavacions d'Ur no sabem pas que n'hi hagi cap llibre ni que se'n prepari cap. De les excavacions de l'Índia sí que se'n prepara un, obra que s'anuncia important, amb caràcter monogràfic, redactada pel propi Sr. J. Marshall, la qual ha de sortir durant l'estiu proper.[116]

The article about Chaldea that we offer today to our readers of La Nova Revista *is a summary of reports from the* Sphere *and the* Illustrated London News, *particularly from the latter, originally published on April 18, 1925; April 22, 1925; March 20, 1926; June 1, 1927; December 17, 1927; and February 23, 1928. These reports were written by Mr. Leonard Wooley, director of the joint expedition of the British Museum and the Museum of the University of Pennsylvania to conduct excavations in Lower Chaldea. As for the information on the excavations in India, we summarize three other pieces published in the* Times *on February 26, 1926, and January 4 and 5, 1928, by Mr. John Marshall, director general of the archaeological survey of India. We do not know whether there are any books, published or in preparation, about the recent excavations in Ur. As for the excavations in India, we do know there is one book in preparation, which will be an important one: a monograph written by Mr. J. Marshall, which is due out next summer.*

Sacs exhibits these sources to show his updated knowledge of the current developments in the scholarship on Asian matters being carried out in Western centers. The symbolic capital increased if there were personal connections involved: "L'anunci d'aquesta col·lecció ha transcendit a les més altes i competents esferes de l'orientalisme. L'il·lustre i volgudíssim M. Ch. Vignier ens ha fet indicar, mitjançant el nostre benemèrit amic Pere Inglada, alguns documents gràfics per a la decoració dels llibres i àlbums que tenim en projecte" (The announcement of this book series has become known by the highest and most competent spheres of Orientalism. The illustrious and beloved M. Ch. Vignier has pointed us, through our worthy friend Pere Inglada, to some graphic documents to be used in the design of the books and albums we have in preparation).[117]

"Àsia" develops different arguments that back up this symbolic economy.[118] Sacs's essay is grounded on a contradiction that was not perceived as such at the time. On the one hand, Sacs claims the need to understand the East in a nondichotomic way. Instead of perpetuating the division between East and West, both contexts should be understood as parts of a unicity of cultures. This view was aligned with the new epistemologies of China developed in the 1910s and 1920s. On the other hand, Sacs also claims that the main reason for this nondichotomic approach is to better appreciate the value of Western culture. Let us see how Sacs reconciles such contradictory statements.

Sacs takes as a point of departure a false cliché: the lack of knowledge about the East throughout Western history. According to him, such ignorance can be attributed to provincialism and colonialism, which have impeded a better understanding of the Asian other (69). Using pronouns in a way that equates Catalans with Europeans or Westerners, Sacs adds that such ignorance was understandable in the past as "we" were not sufficiently prepared for a proper understanding of Asia and Asia remained closed in itself due to "la seva passiva indiferència, la seva duríssima voluntat de no voler fer-se interessant als homes de raça blanca" (its passive indifference, its extremely hard will to remain uninteresting for men of white race [69]). But things have now changed and history has revealed Asia to "us" (69). For Sacs, Asia is valuable because it can be both the opposite and the supplement to the West. Asia can help eliminate the "insuficiència del nostre humanisme greco-romà, la bàrbara ceguera del nostre contentament humanístic" (insufficiency of our Greco-Roman humanism, the barbaric blindness of our humanistic contentment [69]). Humanism without Asia is incomplete.

By moving the question of cross-cultural understanding to the terrain of humanism, Sacs takes the discussion to a comfortable site for Noucentisme. Sacs and other Catalan *noucentistes* considered humanism as a long project of hard intellectual labor that should be mirrored in European centers. Sacs's most interesting confession follows: "Tenim, doncs, obligació d'eixir de la condició d'aerolit i d'orbitar-nos en l'orientalisme europeu; devem, almenys, esforçar-nos a posar-nos al corrent de la sinopsi oriental que la més docta Europa i l'Amèrica del Nord estan treballosament elaborant des de fa tants anys" (We must therefore leave our aerolite condition and put ourselves into orbit around European Orientalism. We should at least strive to bring ourselves up to date on the Oriental synopsis that the clever Europe and North America have been laboriously elaborating for so many years [70]). In other words, the main goal for Catalan intellectuals (the "we" now implied) is neither understanding Asia better nor developing a more serious approach to Asian cultures but rather getting closer to Europe. Catalan intellectuals must take advantage "repapadament i gratuïtament" (comfortably and for free) of the efforts that other countries have spent to understand the Orient. For Sacs, to become modern is not to learn about Asia; to become modern is to read publications like *Journal asiatique*.

To be sure, a critical humanism that pays attention to Asia only through "the cleverest Europe and North America" can only be led by a Catalan intellectual elite. Mere exoticism is despicable, as it is based on facile contemplation. Sacs argues that Asia is not a place for difference or prejudices but rather a place for a real intellectual endeavor. Mystery, lust, superstition, extravagance, or mysticism are nothing but phantasmagorias that deny Asia's complexity and, therefore, deny the effort required to understand Asia. As a complex reality that needs a long process of learning to be properly understood (73), Asia turns out to be as complex as the West. The focus on intellectual elitism and diligent study makes Asia and the West commensurable, even on moral grounds:

> Hom no pot dir si un bandit xinès trinxà un missioner anglès en cent mil bocins perquè cada anglès abusà abans de cent mil xinesos, o bé si els anglesos s'imposaren severament i ràpidament als xinesos perquè l'Emperador de la Xina empalava els missioners europeus que anaven a l'Imperi celest només que a salvar les ànimes de les descarriades ovelles grogues. (74)

> *One cannot tell whether a Chinese bandit tore an English missionary into a hundred thousand pieces because each Englishman had previously abused a hundred thousand Chinese;*

or whether the English defeated the Chinese severely and
fast because the emperor of China had previously impaled
the European missionaries who had gone to the Celestial
Empire only to save the souls of the stray yellow sheep.

Having set humanism as the cornerstone of his argument, Sacs warns that the abundance of representations of Asia that circulate across Catalan society does not imply a deeper knowledge about the East. In fact, the saturation of representations without critical knowledge can produce

> estralls espantosos entre els desconeixedors. Aquests, *sense preparació, sense facultat ponderativa*, s'han deixat emportar de l'entusiasme més superficial; s'han engrescat abusivament amb infra-valors d'aquell art sobtadament revelat únicament a la vista llur, mentre que d'altra banda la veritable valor i significació de l'art oriental passà i s'aturà davant de llur retina, sense aconseguir ésser contemplada, talment com si no existís. (74, my emphasis)

> *frightful damages among the ignorant. These ignorant peo-*
> *ple,* unprepared and unable to think critically, *have been*
> *carried away by the most superficial enthusiasm; they have*
> *been overexcited with the low values of a kind of art that*
> *has suddenly been revealed only for themselves, while on the*
> *other hand the true value and significance of Oriental art*
> *passed in front of their eyes and stopped there without get-*
> *ting any kind of attention, as if it did not exist.*

Superficial enthusiasm and "Orientalist emotionalism" can carry "terrible consequences," which Sacs describes as a major disease for all the arts:

> La música, l'arquitectura, la pintura, l'escultura, totes les arts modernes, estan infectades, mortalment enverinades, per un sens fi de falsíssimes estimacions d'orientalisme. És una vergonya de les més humiliants per a les generacions modernes o per al sector que s'ha llançat a la babalà, cegament, a un fàcil deduccionisme d'aquest *superficial* i *peresós* emocionalisme orientalista. El balanç que les gèneres venidores faran

d'aquest xarlatanesc sector d'esteticisme serà més que sever.
El balanç que en faran els economistes serà ruïnós, perquè el
temps perdut serà reconegut incalculable. (74, my emphasis)

*Music, architecture, painting, sculpture, all modern arts,
are infected, mortally poisoned, by an endless number of
Orientalist false estimates. It is one of the most humiliat-
ing shames for modern generations or for those who have
blindly thrown themselves into easy interpretations about
this superficial and lazy Orientalist emotionalism. The evaluation that the coming generations will make of this charlatanic aestheticism will be more than severe. The evaluation
that economists will make of it will be disastrous, because
the value of the time that has been lost will be incalculable.*

The availability of Asia is therefore both an opportunity and a danger.
It is the role of the intellectual elites, then, to prevent the latter and promote the former. It is also their responsibility: the worst that could happen is that Orientalism (understood as a superficial fascination for the
exotic East without any intellectual effort) moved beyond the populace
and reached also artists, writers, and intellectuals: "És terrible de cons-
tatar que aquests estralls no s'aturin en aquest sector de la literatura
curanderesca, que aquest desconeixement nociu de l'Orient, que aquest
orientalisme per a senyores arribi a seduir talents refinats de veritables
literats, pintors i escultors" (It is terrible to confirm that these damages
do not remain within this field of charlatanic literature, that this harmful ignorance of the Orient, that this Orientalism for ladies, gets to the
point of even seducing the refined talent of true writers, painters, and
sculptors [74–75]).

Sacs ends "Àsia" by closing the circle. A deep, demanding knowledge of Asia is part of a broader, ambitious humanist project that
aims at rediscovering "amb claror més intel·ligent que mai la valor de
l'Hel·lenisme i de Roma, del Goticisme i de la Renaixença" (with the
most intelligent light the value of Hellenism and Rome, of Gothicism
and the Renaixença [75]). It is by studying the East that we can better understand the West—and the reasons why we prefer Western art
over Eastern art, for instance. To get to know Asia from a universalist
assumption means to cultivate an intellectual process that, in the end,
protects "primordialment la permanència d'aquestes valors occidentals
que a desgrat de tot el negatiu que porten amassat són les conquestes

més grans i més belles" (above all the permanence of these Western values, which in spite of all their negative aspects, are the greatest and most beautiful conquests [75]).

Sacs's "Àsia" illustrates the contradictory ways in which China was represented in Catalonia at the time. The impulse to understand China properly and the mature proposals for cross-cultural commensurability between China and the West coexisted with underlying assumptions that considered Asia and China as part of an intellectual journey that should reinforce the value of the West. Sacs code-switches naturally between extremely mature reflections about cross-cultural understanding and very classical Eurocentric assumptions. His piece, in sum, illustrates how China was presented as contradictory and ductile for Catalan intelligentsia. A similar malleable China could be found in Catalan popular culture.

LA CIUTAT DE LA POR

Joan Crespi i Martí's *La ciutat de la por* captures with incomparable lucidity the contradictory ways in which China was imagined in Catalonia in the late 1920s and early 1930s. This novel, moreover, provides an explicit reflection on many ideas and problems discussed throughout this book. *La ciutat de la por* is therefore an appropriate final stage in our itinerary.

La ciutat de la por was published in January 1930. It was, in fact, a posthumous publication. On December 26, 1929, the Catalan literary community was shocked upon receiving the news that Joan Crespi i Martí, a young and unknown author, had died only two days after having been awarded the second prize in the prestigious award Les Ales Esteses for a novel entitled *La ciutat de la por*.[119] Other than this sad mention, we don't have much information about Crespi i Martí himself. He wrote outside the established canonical circles, and references mainly tell us that he was a poor young man who died too early just when he had a promising career ahead. The novel was well received by reviewers, who stressed its unusual combination of literary ambition and popular appeal.[120]

The novel narrates the story of Albert Garriga, a young man who abandons his position as the director of a textile factory in Catalonia and travels to the China he has read about since his childhood. In China Albert will discover the city of Canton through the guidance of Mr.

Lawrence, a mysterious Englishman who seems to know everything about the place. Thanks to Lawrence's mediation Albert will gradually realize how the West has caused the loss of the traditional, exotic China that he had fantasized about since his childhood days.

It is probably safe to presume that Crespi i Martí wrote *La ciutat de la por* without having ever set foot in China. In spite of that, his novel displays a wealth of colorful and accurate accounts of China and the Chinese. To be sure, the availability of information about China in Catalonia made it possible for someone like Crespi i Martí to depict Canton with such a degree of realism. In fact, it is as if the books enthusiastically read by the novel's main character during his childhood (the titles of which are never mentioned) were the sources used by the author himself. Some of these sources probably included photographs, which made it even easier for a writer like Crespi i Martí to gather information and recreate locations and atmospheres.[121]

But *La ciutat de la por* goes beyond a simple import of local color. The similarities between *La ciutat de la por* and Jules Verne's *Les Tribulations d'un Chinois en Chine* (Tribulations of a Chinaman in China, 1879) illustrate the adoption of a certain frame of representation too. Both works share a starting point: a main character who is in a deep existential crisis. And both works develop the plot in a similar way: a (secret) intervention of a wise friend will enable the main character to regain the joy of life through a series of adventures that will become the actual leitmotif of the novel.

Verne's works had been instrumental in the success of adventure fiction in Catalonia since the late nineteenth century. Verne's novels arrived in Catalonia through Spanish translations and became classics during the first decades of the twentieth century, when many of these Spanish translations were republished several times.[122] Starting in the late 1920s, Catalan translations of *Le Tour du monde en quatre-vingts jours* (*La volta al món en vuitanta dies*, 1926; Around the World in Eighty Days), *Michel Strogoff* (*Miquel Strogoff*, 1930; Michael Strogoff: The Courier of the Czar), and *L'Île mysterieuse* (*L'illa misteriosa*, 1937; The Mysterious Island) increased Verne's popularity even more. Verne's works inspired many works and genres, from parodies to operettas, even if his name was absent from the cover of his books, as was typically the case with pulp fiction.[123] Verne's influence on Catalan writers of the early twentieth century can easily be found in important popular works.[124] Similarly, Verne's *Les Tribulations d'un Chinois en Chine* contributed to the increasing volume of images of China circulating in Catalonia at the time. The influence of *Les Tribulations* over the extremely popular Catalan novel *Aventures den Bolavà en el país dels xinos* (Bolavà's Adventures in the Chinese Country, 1912) by Josep Maria Folch i Torres cannot be overstated.[125] Folch i Torres, who was at the time the most widely read author in Catalan popular fiction, recreated Verne's novel through a main character with similar pursuits and an equally similar plot that combined technology and adventures. Folch i Torres also added a comical dimension to Verne's fascination for China's mysterious exoticism. The metaphor of the yellow peril, for instance, became nothing but a caricature in *Aventures den Bolavà en el país dels xinos*.[126]

Crespi i Martí adopted a similar Vernian frame as well, but he developed the action with great originality. *La ciutat de la por* depicts China both as an attainable reality of the present, full of details that are described with almost photographic accuracy, and as an unattainable fantasy of the past, a land of mystery, action, and terror that is described according to the conventions of adventure fiction. *La ciutat de la por* is a remarkable novel because of the creative way in which it combines, on the one hand, the interplay between these two Chinas and, on the other hand, a set of historical, social, and existential reflections. Albert's cross-cultural journey highlights the dilemmas of a young Catalan bourgeois who seeks in China what he has lost when, as an adult, he must assume the responsibilities at his father's factory. Crespi i Martí accommodates all these multiple demands in an overarching plot that makes them coexist and shine in their own way.

La ciutat de la por opens with a powerful image: a magnificent European figure stands on a "desgavellat i llantiós" (shabby and filthy) Chinese raft (7–9). We are told that he is arriving in Canton "pres d'una violenta emoció" (overwhelmed by a violent excitement [11]). The man in ecstasy is Albert Garriga, the son of a Catalan textile industrialist who travels to China to experience firsthand the thrills from his childhood readings. As a child he had been a free spirit, very fond of books and novels. He used to remain in his bedroom and fantasize "seduït per la lectura apassionada dels enigmes de qualque mansió xinesa o bé dels horrors i suplicis que el bàrbar d'un mandarí causava als seus súbdits" (seduced by the passionate reading of the enigmas of Chinese mansions or the horrors and tortures that a barbarian mandarin inflicted upon his subjects [16]). A quixotic, voluptuous Orientalism remained his passion and, after he became a lawyer, Albert traveled to Paris where he was finally able to realize one of his ambitions: to learn some Chinese language. Albert's father died and our young man inherited the family fortune that came along with "un compromís i una responsabilitat excessivament pesants per al seu tarannà lliure" (a commitment and responsibility too heavy for his free spirit [17]). Now a man in an adult world, Albert is forced to lead the life of an adult. In despair, he decides to leave for Canton, the most "authentic" city in China, to recover "el més dolç record de la infantesa" (the sweetest souvenir from his childhood [17]).

Albert's expectations increase during the journey. His thoughts become more intense, "saturat tot ell per l'orientalisme elevat a l'enèsima potència" (filled with the most extreme Orientalism [19]). We are convinced of his engagement when, during the last stage of his journey, he repudiates the luxurious steamer as too comfortable and too Western and decides to embark on a miserable raft that is about to break up (20). Just when his imagined China is about to encounter the real China, Albert pictures himself as a hero: "Per fi l'Orient encisador i enigmàtic anava a revelar-se; per fi seria l'heroi d'alguna aventura misteriosa; entorn d'ell gravitaria l'acció d'un drama xinès, obscur i tràgic, curull de terrors i sadollat de perills" (At last the fascinating and enigmatic Orient will be revealed to him; at last he would become the hero of a mysterious adventure; the action of a Chinese drama would gravitate around him, tragic and obscure, full of terrors and filled with dangers [19]).

Albert's first days in Canton burst with emotions. He is finally in China, and we share his excitement through long depictions of Canton. But his excitement soon begins to wane: he realizes that the real China does not have the charm of the China he read about when he was a child. At this point, he meets Mr. Lawrence, a mysterious Englishman who knows everything about Canton. Through Lawrence, Albert finds the reason for his disenchantment: it is the impact of Western modernity that has caused the loss of the traditional China—with its Oriental mysticism, its exotic charm (31). Albert's discontent is such that he even becomes sympathetic toward Chinese nationalism: "Cal treure tota aquesta brolla inútil del terrer patri. Cap necessitat tenim de venir a embrutar l'Orient amb les nostres coses" (All these useless weeds must be removed from this land. We don't have any need to come and pollute the Orient with our things [31]).

Right in the middle of this existential cul-de-sac, Albert gets caught up in a frantic adventure. He witnesses the kidnapping of a young Chinese woman—the daughter of a good friend of Lawrence's. Albert tries to find out her whereabouts and gets gradually involved in a series of fights and chases. All this action reconciles him with the quintessential China of his childhood readings: the girl seems to have been kidnapped by a triad with a cruel leader; he meets with an informant inside an opium den; he experiences torture while imprisoned in a rat-infested jail; and he finally escapes through dark, secret corridors. Albert is now vibrant and optimistic (98), full of energy again. All his rancor has vanished. But when he has finally escaped from his evil rivals as a marvelous super-hero, he discovers that all these actions were part of a scheme devised by Lawrence. Wishing to combat Albert's disillusionment, the Englishman had decided to recreate for him the original and exotic Canton of the past (and the books), which is the Canton where Lawrence had met his lover, who had died the previous year. For Lawrence, to recuperate the old Canton for Albert was also a way of bringing Helen back to life through the old city.

Through this formal disposition of a story within a story and the tropes of China as a reality and China as a fantasy, *La ciutat de la por* conveys a plurality of representations that illustrate some of the con-tradictory visions of China that circulated in Catalonia at the time. On the one hand, we find China as a reality that is perfectly attainable. Al-bert shows how it is actually possible to understand China and Chinese people—despite its remote location and their different culture and even if sometimes that knowledge has to be acquired through a European connection like Paris, where Chinese language learning seems to be more systematized (16). Contrary to similar novels of the same period, with pages and chapters describing the time spent on the steamboat to China, here the actual journey receives less attention. Getting to China is not difficult at all: we move from Barcelona to Hong Kong in merely a couple of pages (18–20), and, during the final stage of the journey to Canton, Albert is even able to choose the mode of transportation—a simple raft instead of the sumptuous steamer (20).

There are plenty of details about life in Canton that make it possible for the reader to perceive China as a tangible reality too. A street, for in-stance, is described with a very concrete texture: "Els carrers són bruts, empedrats de grosses i mal escairades llambordes, mal fixades i cobertes d'una molsa, fina i negrosa, de pou. Pels intersticis, de vegades, l'aigua infecta de les clavegueres sobreix, i pel damunt s'escapa un líquid cor-romput. Les cases són negres i ruïnoses, i la humitat hi regalima per les parets" (The streets are dirty, paved with large irregular stones, badly laid and covered in a thin, dark moss, as if from a well. Sometimes, around the gaps, the pestilential water from the sewers overflows and a putrid liquid spills over. The houses are black and run-down. Dampness drips down the walls [22]). Elsewhere, we are told about a temple in almost photographic relief:

> L'arquitectura del temple és austera i construïda amb marbre blanc, ja brut per l'acció del temps. La seva teulada és de majòlica blava, amb uns dracs rampants, de coure oxidat, que davallen per les cornises. Encara es troba en bon estat, a despit de les ruïnes que l'envolten. És bell i sòlid; trencant la monotonia, unes arcades grotesques i uns passadissos aparedats de paper d'arròs i de nombroses inscripcions i ofrenes. . . . És per una graderia de pedra gastada i coberta de molsa relliscosa que baixen fins al riu. Ací la terra forma com un promontori damunt l'aigua; limitant-la hi ha una barana de fusta podrida, que, en alguns llocs, ja ha caigut. Dintre la susdita placeta hi ha, en semicercle, uns pedrissos de pedra tallada, amb inscripcions i figures quasi completament esborrades pel lent desgast. (46–48)

> *The temple's architecture is austere, built with white marble now dirtied by the action of time. The roof is made of blue majolica, with rampant dragons of weathered copper going down the ledges. It is still in good shape, despite the ruins that surround it. It is beautiful, solid. The monotony is broken by grotesque arches and long corridors with rice paper walls and full of inscriptions and offerings. . . . They go down to the river by a ruined flight of stone steps covered with moss. Here the land makes a kind of promontory above the water. There is a banister made of rotten wood that has fallen off in certain places. Inside a little square there is a semicircle of stone benches with inscriptions and figures almost completely worn away.*

And even exotic practices such as opium smoking are described with attention to every minor detail:

> L'Albert escollí un lloc i s'hi estirà. Un petit minyó agenollat al seu costat preparava la droga. Prop d'ell tenia un plat, en el qual hi havia un fanalet de vidre, diverses agulles d'argent i unes capses d'idèntic metall. Amb l'ajut d'una de les agulles, prenia de les capses una porció d'una pasta fosca

i la duia a la flama del llumet, fent-la girar de manera que tota ella hi fos exposada; després la introduïa al fornell de la pipa. Aquest fornell era de vori, lleugerament corbat, i tenia l'aparença d'una copa tapada amb un forat petit al centre. Per aquesta obertura era establerta la comunicació entre el fornell i el llarg tub d'aspiració, acabat per una punta d'ambre. (82)

Albert chose a space and lay down. Kneeling at his side, a young child was preparing the drug. Next to him there was a plate with a small lantern made of glass, a few silver needles, and some boxes made of silver too. With the help of one of these needles the child was taking a small quantity of a dark paste from one of the boxes and was holding it to the flame of the lantern, turning it around. He then introduced the paste into the bowl of the pipe. It was an ivory bowl, slightly curved, looking like a covered glass with a hole in the middle. Through that hole the bowl connected to a long stem with an amber mouthpiece.

China's accessibility is most notably expressed through an unproblematic perception of communication. There is no place in the novel where we have the impression that Albert has trouble communicating with Chinese people—it is not even clear in which language characters talk to one another (103 or 124, for example). The feeling of linguistic alienation, so characteristically expressed by many travelers since González de Mendoza's accounts in the sixteenth century, is surprisingly absent in *La ciutat de la por*. There are very few mentions of the Chinese written script, but only to remark that characters can be easily translated (71). The only instance in which Albert cannot communicate with a Chinese person is because the old man is deaf and Albert carries neither paper nor pencil to communicate in writing (115–16). Closeness to language relates to a feeling of familiarity with some Chinese people, such as Tsu-Liang and his daughter Xe-Lao (54), and with the city of Canton itself. Under Lawrence's guidance, Albert quickly becomes acquainted with the city and wanders around confidently.

On the other hand, in *La ciutat de la por* we find China as an unreachable fantasy as well. Besides the obvious distance projected by the fantastic exoticism of Albert's adventures, inaccessibility is mainly created through a temporal dislocation: juxtaposed to the available China of the present lies the distant China of the past that resembles the one from the books Albert read as a child. Meeting Lawrence reinforces that distance, as both men are trapped in a China that is not the China they cherish. They remain alienated from the present, although in a different way: while for Albert the real China lies in the fictional dreams of a teenager, for Lawrence the real China remains in his love story with Helen. Both men are trapped in their own pasts and fantasies.

The plot stresses the impossibility of turning the fantasy of Albert's childhood into a reality of the present. Lawrence and his Chinese friends recreate that fantasy for Albert. China becomes for a while the impossible land of mysterious pursuit along dark labyrinths, obscure opium dens, secret societies, and secret traps that turn China into a familiar defamiliarized image, where Chinese people are stigmatized in a Fu Manchu characterization: "Penseu que cada xinès amaga un espia o un assassí" (Remember that every Chinese person hides a spy or an assassin [74]). Re-entering his own utopia of the past feels like a hallucination: "un món fet de somnis i de deliris torbadors, d'al·lucinacions joliues, de perfums i de fantasies exòtiques" (a world made of dreams and disturbing delusions, of beautiful hallucinations, of exotic perfumes and fantasies [82]). Being inside his own fantasy is so shocking that Albert even has doubts about what he is experiencing: "El cap li voltava, no sabia si somiava o si realment estava despert. Potser totes aquestes aventures que li semblaven reals no eren sinó l'efecte del son de l'opi que havia ingerit. Somiava o estava despert? Era ell qui vivia aquests misteris o era el seu cervell sobreexcitat que es complaïa a turmentar-lo? (His head was spinning, he didn't know whether he was dreaming or truly awake. Maybe all these adventures that looked so real were nothing but the effect of the opium he had taken. Was he dreaming or was he awake? Was he experiencing all these mysteries or was it his overexcited brain that was trying to torture him? [94]). In a place of contradiction and uncertainty, the fear in *La ciutat de la por* defines not only Albert's unexpected experiences in Fu Manchu's Canton but also the mutability of a place that seems to remain remote and close, imaginary and real at the same time.

What makes *La ciutat de la por* a remarkable novel is not only how it combines the tropes of China as reality and China as fantasy that we have been encountering, under one form or another, throughout the chapters of this book, but also how it moves beyond a simple catalog of representations. *La ciutat de la por* provides an insightful explanation for these antagonisms and connects them with the philosophical discussions being held at the time around the West. This blending is done without erasing the popular appeal of the adventure novel.

At this point, Lawrence emerges as an extremely critical voice. The West, he proclaims, has broken the purity of China and "el blanc, en introduir-se pel Celest Imperi, ha destruït la major part de l'exotisme d'aquest país d'insomni" (the white man, after getting into the Celestial Empire, has destroyed the exoticism of this land of dreams [132]). Western modernity has caused the loss of the authentic, quintessential China that has now been left behind on the timeline of history. Lawrence's reflection goes beyond the specific frame of China, as exoticism has disappeared everywhere and progress and brutality have evolved hand in hand all around the world (132–35). The scale of the problem is no less than global:

> La civilització, amb el seu formidable impuls, no respecta res, i, al seu pas, els països de somni i de fantasia desapareixen. . . . Tot el món ha seguit i seguirà aquest camí invariable d'ambició. Els vells països llegendaris: Egipte, Aràbia, Palestina, l'Índia, el Japó, tots els països que atreien amb llurs múltiples encants l'atenció dels fantasiosos i dels romàntics. (132)

> *Civilization, with its formidable impetus, does not respect anything. As it makes its way, lands of dreams and fantasy disappear. . . . The whole world has followed and will follow this unchanging path of ambition. The old legendary countries—Egypt, Arabia, Palestine, India, Japan—all the countries that used their multiple charms to attract the attention of all the romantics and those who fantasized.*

To be sure, Lawrence's critical reflection on modernity echoes Oswald Spengler's *Der Untergang des Abendlandes* (The Decline of the West). The impact of Spengler's work on Spanish and Catalan intellectuals during the second half of the 1920s was remarkable yet slightly different in each context. Translated in 1923 under the impulse of José Ortega y Gasset, *Der Untergang des Abendlandes* was published as *La decadencia de Occidente* in Biblioteca de Ideas del Siglo xx, a series edited by Ortega at the time. Like many Spanish intellectuals, Ortega had an ambivalent relationship with Spengler's ideas. On the one hand, he considered Spengler's work "sin disputa, la peripecia intelectual más estruendosa de los últimos años" (without dispute, the most thunderous intellectual event in recent years).[127] Ortega's main source of disagreement was Spengler's pessimism about the end of Western culture: Spengler's work (originally published in two volumes in 1918 and 1922) argued that civilizations followed a biological cycle and that Western civilization had entered into a final, declining phase. Ortega, instead, agreed that war had certainly destroyed culture, but also argued that war had improved science at the same time—and it was impossible to conceive of science as something separate from culture. As he argued in the review of Russell's *The Problem of China*, Ortega did not share the idea of a Europe in fatal decadence. For him, Spengler was only overreacting to the present economic difficulties of European nations. Europe had suffered even deeper crises in the past, and it had always reemerged stronger and revitalized.

On the other hand, Ortega was unable to think outside the paradigm that Spengler had set and prompted the translation to be published in Biblioteca de Ideas del Siglo xx. Spurred by Ortega's intervention, the discussion of Spengler's ideas had an enormous impact on the different trends of Spanish political culture.[128] Qualified as the best book of the past few years, whose impact was similar to Einstein's impact on science,[129] the reception of Spenglerian universal morphology in Spain was more intense and complete than in any other European country, due to the fact that this discussion inserted Spain into a transnational discourse at a European level while retaining a certain Spanish specificity.[130]

In Catalonia, Spengler's ideas were also influential, yet in an additional, overlapping dimension. Important intellectuals such as Gaziel (1887–1964, pen name of Agustí Calvet) connected Spengler's work with a critique toward the development of the modern city—and, by extension, modern civilization. Instead of the Spanish skepticism for Spengler's diagnosis, Catalan intellectuals found more in common with Spengler's project. Gaziel proudly declared that he was the first Catalan to use Spengler's ideas to analyze Catalan society, which he compared to a flashlight to be directed at Catalonia—and the resulting image offered, according to him, a sinister impression.[131] As we have seen in previous sections, for Gaziel, Spengler's reflections were a way of connecting Catalonia and the European intelligentsia.

Following the Catalan reception of Spengler's work, the merit of *La ciutat de la por* lies in introducing a Spenglerian reflection inside a pulp novel aimed at a wide readership. As was the case with Oteyza's *El diablo blanco*, *La ciutat de la por* combines entertainment action with critical reflections on modernity, progress, and the human condition. Both works add a "escepticismo radical sobre la capacidad de mejoramiento de la condición humana y sobre los pretendidos avances de ese progreso" (radical skepticism about the capacity to improve the human condition and the so-called advances in this progress), which were typical of the anxieties at the end of the interwar period.[132] However, instead of the frivolous resolution of *El diablo blanco*, Crespi i Martí's novel takes this criticism more seriously: Albert and Lawrence end up abandoning China, and we are left with a sound critique of the dark side of progress and Western civilization.

La ciutat de la por summarizes some of the arguments claimed in this chapter and, more generally, in this book as a whole. First, *La ciutat de la por* illustrates the flexibility of "China" as a signifier and how code-switching allowed for engagement with the different Chinas available in Catalan and Spanish society. In the 1930s imagining China as a reachable reality was as plausible as imagining China as an unreachable fantasy of a sublime world. While both visions could not be reconciled, free movement within this assemblage was possible after all—even on the pages of one single novel, where the China that has disappeared still "existeix, actualment, entre les pàgines dels llibres dels antics viatgers i dels novel·listes" (exists today among the pages of old books by travelers and novelists) who, as Crespi i Martí ironically claims, are "poc escrupulosos" and "no dubten, encara, d'emprar aquest gastat tòpic del misteri groc" (not very scrupulous and still use without doubt that worn-out cliché of the yellow mystery [134]).

Second, *La ciutat de la por* concludes with a poignant critique of Western civilization and colonial expansion, which is articulated through the voice of an Englishman. Lawrence was the character who really knew about Canton. Lawrence orchestrated the plot. Lawrence offers now a final critical reflection. Having both the factual knowledge about China and the conceptual vision of China, the Englishman is the demiurge who monopolizes the narrative. His position in the formal structure of the novel is in striking contrast with the position given to Chinese characters—mostly passive and without any real voice—and to Albert, who is also a piece moving at Lawrence's rhythm. Just as Western modernity has colonized China, Lawrence's narration also colonizes the explanation of China's predicament derived from such colonization.

Finally, at the end of the novel we find out that our narrator has been unreliable. *La ciutat de la por* opens with a *captatio* announcing that all the adventures that will follow are real as they had actually taken place. This is a "true story" (15), we are told. While this lie could either be a conscious trick to capture readers' attention or a slip due to Crespi i Martí's inexperience as a writer, the fact is that reading Albert's farce in Canton as a true event keeps the readers as ignorant as Albert himself and secures the narration under Lawrence's command. Albert's voiceless position symbolizes the limits of Catalan—and Spanish—agency in understanding China. Equally voiceless, the readers of La ciutat de la por cannot read China without the authority of a foreign mediator.

The Lure of Translation

"Have you ever heard of Peking?"

This question opens *Pekin* (Peking), a short, witty one-act monologue written by the multitalented Catalan intellectual Apel·les Mestres at the turn of the twentieth century.[1] *Pekin* is probably the most lucid anticipation of what would happen to the images of China in the West during the first decades of the twentieth century. *Pekin* predicts how the images of China would saturate the public sphere and how, ironically, such popular knowledge of China would turn "China" into an empty reference ready to be filled with diverse, often contradictory meanings. *Pekin* epitomizes all we have seen in the previous chapters.

Pekin is a very funny monologue too. Mestres eloquently plays with "China's" emptiness. As a true modern-day stand-up comic, the monologuist, "un senyor que sembla que ha viatjat molt" (a gentleman who looks like a seasoned traveler), makes repeated allusions to China but, in fact, never reveals much about any of the aspects he mentions:

> No els diré res del camí perquè és com tots els camins si fa no fa: aquí camps, aquí muntanyes; ara un riu, ara un poble; avui una calor que uf! Demà una fresqueta que brrr! Ademés, que pot anar-s'hi per mar o per terra.
>
> . . . Doncs bé: fem el supòsit que ja hem arribat a Pekin. El primer que s'els presenta és el gran portal de la ciutat; primera sorpresa. Quin portal! Vostès es figuraran que ve a ser

per l'estil de l'arc del triomf del Saló de Sant Joan; què té de ser, sants cristians, què té de ser! S'hi assembla com un ou a una castanya. Es tan diferent, que . . . vaja . . . com els diré jo? Res, és completament diferent de l'arc del Saó de Sant Joan.

Passen el portal i ja són a dintre. El primer que troben és un carrer . . . però quin carrer! Vostès, que no s'han mogut mai de Barcelona, diran: "Bé, sí, un carrer com el carrer Nou o el carrer de la Princesa" eh? Doncs, res d'això! No s'hi sembla de res, però de res m'entenen? No es figurin per xo, que les cases són al mig i que la via passa pels costat, per exemple; no, no tant! La via passa pel mig i les cases són arrenglerades a cada costa . . . però quines cases! (29–30)

I will not tell you much about the road because it is pretty much like all the roads. Fields over here, mountains over there. Here is a river, there is a town. Today is really hot and then tomorrow, brr, so cold! And you can travel there by sea or by land.

. . . So, well: let's imagine that we have arrived in Peking. The first thing you see is the city's big gate. First surprise: What a gate! You may imagine that it is quite like the Arc de Triomf at the Saló de Sant Joan. Come on, my dear friends, how could that be! They are like chalk and cheese! It's so different that . . . well . . . how should I put it? Yes, well, it is completely different from the Arc de Triomf at the Saló de Sant Joan.

Pass through the gate and you are already inside. The first thing you bump into is a street . . . but what a street! All of you, who have never been away from Barcelona, may say: "Well, yes, this is a street just as our Carrer Nou or Carrer de la Princesa," right? Nothing could be further from the truth! They are very different. Completely different, do you understand? Oh, please do not come to think that the houses stand in the middle of the way and the path runs along the sides. Oh, no, not that different. This is a street where the path runs along the middle of the way and the houses stand on the side, one next to the other . . . but what houses!

The farce goes on for a few minutes and the accumulation of hollow statements turns hilarious. Peking and China get their meaning as realities well known for their difference—even if their reality never gets fully described, only circumvented through familiar references from the Catalan local context. Peking and China are nothing but an oxymoron: a familiar unknown.

Throughout the chapters of this book, we have followed China's transformation into this kind of familiar unknown across the West during the last decades of the nineteenth century and the first decades of the twentieth century. We have seen how a humorous gag at the time of the original publication of *Pekin* in 1900 turned out to be a tangible reality in the 1930s. In 1900, the humor of Mestres's piece relied upon a growing but still rather incipient knowledge of China. In 1932, however, China could mean anything indeed—not due to a lack of information about China, but rather due to the opposite. It is probably not a coincidence that *Pekin* was republished in 1932. It coexisted with the plethora of references to China in novels, films, poetry, comics, art, and the newspapers and magazines that we have encountered in the previous chapters. *Pekin* anticipates in 1900 the effects of the growing archive that we have encountered in the journey that, across the previous chapters, has taken us from the late nineteenth century to the 1930s.

We began our journey at Tolstoy's library in 1884. From there we saw the workings of a pattern that would remain in operation in future decades: the representations of China in Europe—and particularly in Spain—heavily relied upon materials written in English or French but pretended to pass either as firsthand accounts or as actual translations from English or French originals that never existed as such. These late nineteenth-century secondhand representations illustrate a phenomenon that has kept us company throughout our journey: the dependence on and the erasure of translation in representing China.

Our second stop was at St Paul's Cathedral in July 1900. We saw how a new awareness of China as a coeval reality in the world at the turn of the twentieth century generated new concerns for China—particularly a keen concern for the "truth" about the "real" China that was existing at that very same time on the other side of the planet. This awareness raised also new concerns for who represented China (in the two senses, "portrait" and "proxy," synthesized by Gayatri Spivak) and for the reliability of the voices who embodied that representation. In a noncentral Western context such as Spain, these new concerns for the truth about the real China were a somatic expression of a weak geopolitical position. The tensions underneath these representations of China illustrate how difficult it was to hold independent views on distant cultures given the indirect access to these cultures and the discursive hegemonies that regulated such indirectness. These tensions illustrate how a binary epistemology—enacted and camouflaged by translation—constrains our understanding of the heterogeneity of the world.

Our next stop was Nanjing, where John Dewey stayed during his sojourn in China in 1919. We saw how in the period between the 1910s and the mid-1920s the presence of China in the West increased exponentially. The quantity, diversity, and competition among the multiple, overlapping images of China stimulated a new economy of representation. We saw how Western citizens had available a catalog with plenty of Chinas ready to be used—more images, more diversity, involving more agents and agendas, rooted in new and old epistemologies. At the same time, we also saw how, in Spain, the indirect mechanisms for cross-cultural representation established in previous decades were still in operation—up to the point that even firsthand experiences in China remained subject to discourses published in other languages. Having a wider yet still dependent catalog of Chinas produced a new phenomenon: the trialectical relationship (China seen through Western discourses in a Spanish context) was seriously challenged for the first time. In the past, the three vectors had synthesized in harmony. Now the relationship lost coherence, and tensions appeared in the content or form of some of the Chinas represented by Spanish writers.

Our final stop took us to Hollywood in the mid-1920s and the 1930s. In Charlie Chan and Fu Manchu, we saw how a consumer code-switching facilitated the coexistence of the multiple images of China and the Chinese that saturated Western societies. It was a period when, in Spain, China came to be explained by figures such as Pearl Buck and André Malraux. These non-Spanish and non-Chinese agents were extremely influential in introducing new sensibilities toward the Chinese people. The connection between Western mediation and code-switching between opposite images of China intensified the instrumentality of "China," as we could see in the representations of China in the Catalan language: the same archive of images could be used for very different cultural and political purposes—even within the same nation-state.

Through our journey across half a century we have seen how the dependence on and the erasure of translation in representing China in Spain contributed to create two illusions that should raise questions in many fields in the humanities (from sinographies to postcolonial studies, from translation studies to comparative literature, from world literature to global studies), as they reveal important aspects of the politics of cross-cultural knowledge and representation. First, the dependence on and the erasure of translation fabricated the illusion of the West as a homogeneous, unified subject vis-à-vis a China that remained always an object to be discovered, explained, understood. Translation was an essential mechanism through which nations such as Spain, which were in the middle of a historical debacle and were geopolitically and discursively the Rest of the West, could identify as an integral part of the West. Translation was an essential mechanism through which the Rest of the West came to share an epistemology of the world that emanated from hegemonic Western centers. Second, the dependence on and the erasure of translation forged the illusion of translation as a neutral connection between cultures, as a direct pathway that gave us privileged access to other realities of the world. The archive we have explored in this book shows that this pathway was full of intermediate—and intermediary—stops. In fact, underneath the illusion of a direct contact, indirectness may very well be the natural condition for cross-cultural interactions across the vast majority of languages and cultural contexts around pivotal Western centers.

It may not be exaggerated to say that it all boils down to translation, then. After all, this has been a book about how translation helps us to make sense of the world and also about how, within the very same process of cross-cultural perception, translation creates a biased understanding of that world for us—which may not correspond to the complex and heterogeneous reality out there.

It has always seemed to me that translation holds a powerful lure for scholarship. Translation is a ductile concept, full of metaphoric connotations and rhetorical possibilities, which can already be sensed in titles such as *After Translation, Against Translation, Architecture in Translation, Memes of Translation, Prismatic Translation*, and, of course, *Lost in Translation*.[2] Translation can be both evocative and concrete. It can be highly philosophical and mundanely down-to-earth. It can sustain endless debates on many aspects of cross-cultural interactions of both a theoretical and applied nature. Translation can produce sophisticated, exuberant reflections indeed.[3] In fact, it is hard to find any field in the humanities that has not trumpeted translation as a crucial, organizing concept for the discipline. In anthropology, Talal Asad's reflections on cultural translation contributed to the debates held by postmodern anthropologists on the dangers of ethnographic writing and the limits of the discipline.[4] In postcolonial theory, Homi Bhabha and Gayatri Spivak wrote canonical pieces on translation, and Dipesh Chakrabarty's influential project for provincializing Europe explicitly relied on the politics of translation raised by Naoki Sakai and Vicente Rafael, among others.[5] In comparative literature, Susan Bassnett made programmatic claims to reassess the discipline's relation to translation studies, and Emily Apter equally argued for a new comparative literature connected to translation theory. World literature was originally established following David Damrosch's definition as works in translation, "circulating out into a broader world beyond its linguistic and cultural point of origin." More recently, modernist studies have identified translation as one of the sixteen words that configure a "new vocabulary for global modernism," and Gayle Rogers has claimed that "much contemporary work on the topic of translation in world and comparative literary studies has productively unsettled" the assumptions about originality, influence, and literary value that undergird canonical approaches.[6] Digital humanities have increased the interest in translation, taking advantage of the empirical potential of translation and "big" data. Meanwhile, inside the discipline of translation studies itself, the variety of approaches to translation is, obviously, equally broad—if not even broader.[7]

To be sure, studying translations has expanded our theoretical horizons and has enlarged our understanding of languages and literatures, cultures and societies. At the same time, dealing with translation in so many heterogeneous ways has developed an irresolvable contradiction between conceiving translation as a practice and conceiving translation as a site for reflection—two paradigms that, as I have argued elsewhere, can be as mutually exclusive as the pair of images contained in a Gestalt reversible figure: you can see either a young woman or an old woman, but you cannot see them both at the same time.[8] Scholars in the humanities who conceive of translation as a site for reflection tend to underestimate the constraints that define the daily reality of a professional translator. Scholars in translation studies who conceive of translation as a practice claim for more focus on interlingual equivalences and against the metaphors that create an inflationary use of the concept.[9]

While many of the interventions within these two paradigms have not been done uncritically, this book has pointed to what I see as a blind spot shared by most of their approaches to translation: the empirical tangibility and the metaphorical potential of translation often conceal the politics underneath cross-cultural interactions. This book has shown that in this blind spot created by translation's plasticity lay complex political negotiations and hierarchies across cultures generated by translation itself. In other words, we have seen that the reasons that may explain translation's lure (both as a resource for those who want to contact with another distant culture and as a concept for scholars who want to study these contacts) are also the reasons that explain the limitations for studying cross-cultural interactions on the basis of translation. Let me group these limitations in three clusters according to the ideas we have encountered across the previous chapters.

First, the study of translation usually presupposes a rather homogeneous range of texts (e.g., texts explicitly marked as translations) that leaves out a much broader corpus of representations of the cultural other that also rely heavily on translation. This broader corpus is much more heterogeneous and difficult to identify, categorize, and study. Most of the texts examined in the previous chapters would pass undetected under the radar of translation studies despite their heavy dependence on translation.[10]

Second, the study of translation has traditionally privileged the study of direct transfers from a source to a target text. But, as the texts examined in the previous chapters testify, cross-cultural interactions—and their power differentials—are in fact much more twisted: besides source and target there might be an intermediary that, for the target, may be more relevant than the source itself. While some approaches in translation studies have already started seriously examining indirectness and moving beyond the privileging of the source text, the intricacies of indirect translations and cross-cultural interactions remain to be fully explored—probably due to the assumption that, particularly outside the field of translation studies, still holds translations as inferior to originals.[11] This bears consequence at both the micro and macro level of analysis. At a micro level, work on relay translation, for instance, has mainly focused on showing how relay translations carry out twice the loss vis-à-vis the original. At a macro level, scholarship on polysystems and the sociology of translation have applied a similar logic to the relations between literary systems.[12] As a result, phenomena such as the ones explored in this book (i.e., representations across cultures in noncentral locations) remain underexamined as derivative or unqualified without enough power credentials to be thematized as issues of major, central importance—even if they affect an overall readership of hundreds of millions. The cases examined in this book hint at a fact that should make us reconsider this logic: indirect cross-cultural representation is probably the most common method to learn about other cultures around the world—especially about those cultures that, for us, are very distant ones.

Third, the study of cross-cultural interactions on the basis of translation imposes an epistemology and a correlation of concepts (authorship, mediation, circulation) on the relations between cultures that can be inadequate, insufficient, or misleading when it comes to describing the complexity of many cross-cultural phenomena that take place across languages. As translation creates difference under a regime or *schema* of co-figuration, the heterogeneity of each process of cross-cultural representation gets simplified under a binary ethnographic relationship in which the subject translates the object.[13] Understanding the heterogeneous cross-cultural representations that take place around the world through concepts that easily fit in the translation regime such as authorship, mediation, and circulation contributes to concealing the ethnographic gaze and the power relations at work. The texts examined in the previous chapters show that authorship, mediation, and circulation may be very ambiguous indeed. Most of the cross-cultural mediations encountered in the previous pages, for instance, would barely conform to standard criteria attributed to cultural mediators.[14] Such ambiguities are not casual eccentricities but rather systemic conditions that influence how we make sense of the world.

In sum, the lure of translation and the limitations of understanding the diversity of the world through translations lie in the comfort of a subject-object power relationship that is intrinsic to the ethnographic relationship to other, distant cultures. It seems to me that such complicity between translation and ethnography still tends to be taken too lightly.[15] It is my impression that the economy for representing China that we have seen at work throughout this book is also at work in most of the contemporary scholarship dealing with world, global, or transnational topics.

Where does all this leave us now? There may be important limitations for studying cross-cultural interactions on the basis of translation, but the fact of the matter is that translation is always in operation. We are inevitably subjected to translation. We make sense of the world's diversity thanks to translation. We live in translation. How should we continue producing knowledge—especially about foreign cultures and distant worlds—from the inside of the prison house of translation?[16] To be sure, this is a question that is impossible to answer in a single book. In fact, this is a question that should be posed to all the disciplines in the humanities and should therefore be answered—or, at least, confronted—collectively. Let me try to contribute with a final reflection and a methodological suggestion derived from my own experience in writing this book.

As I was approaching the end of this project, I realized what, for me, was a rather striking coincidence: just as Peking in Apel·les Mestres's monologue or, more generally, just as China in the West, translation can also mean pretty much anything. In this book we have seen how increasing the number of images of China in the West did not necessarily imply reaching a deeper, more critical engagement with China. Similarly, increasing the number of translations from foreign cultures—or increasing our scholarly attention to translation as a metaphor or as a practice—does not necessarily imply having a deeper, more critical engagement with the cultures being translated. Rather the opposite: an increased presence of China in the West condemned China to be a ductile, even empty reference, just as an increased presence of translation across the humanities condemns translation to be a ductile, even empty metaphor.[17] It may not be a coincidence, then, that translation and China have become a suitable resource for world literature, modernist studies, and comparative literature: translation and China fulfill the need for a broader conceptual and geographical reach without giving away the subject-object power relationship that characterizes the traditional ethnographic gaze. Ernesto Laclau claimed that terms such as justice, democracy, and independence could be used as empty signifiers to be filled up with appropriate meaning in order to build successful narratives for political hegemony.[18] Could it be the case that a similar kind of emptiness in China and translation—as well as in other non-Western geographies or flexible concepts—is being used across the humanities in order to retain hegemonic positions in the production of knowledge?

In this book I have confronted the question of how we should continue producing knowledge from the inside of the prison house of translation by trying to move beyond the limits of translation and of translation's correlates in two ways. On the one hand, I have tried to enlarge and diversify the archive with case studies that complicate our corpus. I have examined explicit translations but also other works that, in spite of being heavily dependent on translation, were not translations themselves. I have considered sinographies in a variety of texts and genres. I have included languages besides English and French. I have highlighted the connections between places like China and Spain or Catalonia—connections that do not often receive our scholarly attention. On the other hand, I have tried to challenge our epistemology of translation. I have examined the intricacies of the ethnographic gaze in translation—particularly when this gaze affects more than two contexts and creates cultural differences and hegemonies that get subsequently refracted through different languages. I have questioned who the subject and the object are in this indirect production of knowledge. I have exposed the inadequacy of East-West divisions. I have used trialectics—or the synthesis between perceived, conceived, and lived cultures—as a heuristic model to complicate our conventionally assumed binaries.

There is probably no need for more programmatic proclamations about the need for translation studies to open up to other disciplines in the humanities or about the need for the humanities to seriously incorporate translation in their developments. Instead, my suggestion is modest but, I hope, applicable in any of the many approaches that try to absorb translation into their discussions. If we want to emancipate ourselves from the cultural hegemonies that underlie the lure of translation and produce new and significant knowledge about the world based on a radical equality between cultures, we need to both diversify our archives *and* challenge our epistemologies.[19] To be sure, many enlargements and challenges wait to be exposed and explored. This, as I said, should be a collective project. More translations, more studies based on translations, more data, and new vocabularies will be very much welcome—but their results will be futile unless they are truly diverse in genres and languages *and* unless they truly imagine new possibilities for understanding the interactions between cultures around the world.

Notes

1. John Harrisson, "La China moderna: Cartas de un diplomático a su familia," *Hispania*, September 30, 1900; October 15, 1900; October 30, 1900; November 15, 1900; November 30, 1900; December 30, 1900; April 30, 1901.

2. T. S. H. Thompson, *El enigma del despertar de China*, trans. Fabián Casares (Barcelona: Apolo, 1931).

3. I. Worski-Riera, *El despertar de Asia: Japón, China, India, Persia, Turquía, Afghanistán* (Barcelona: Publicaciones Mundial, 1931).

4. Karol de Czola-Olai, *Cómo me escapé de Siberia y conocí a Chiang-Kai-Shek* (Madrid: Espasa Calpe, 1942); Karol de Czola-Olai, *Cómo funciona el espionaje soviético en Extremo Oriente* (Madrid: Espasa Calpe, 1942).

5. José Eugenio Borao Mateo, "Julio de Larracoechea (1901–1999): Vicecónsul en Shanghai (1932–1936) y novelista de la ciudad del Wangpú," *Encuentros en Catay* 12 (1999): 1–50.

6. For the case of Larracoechea, which is outside the chronological scope of this book, see: Carles Prado-Fonts, "'Que redundase en beneficio de sus compatriotas': Julio de Larracoechea, *Ramonchu en Shanghai* y la China modelable," *Journal of Iberian and Latin American Research* 22, no. 1 (January 2, 2016): 61–77.

7. For some works about how translation may depend on invisibility or how authors may prefer to pass as translators, James St. André quotes José Lambert, "La traduction, les langues et la communication de masse: Les ambiguïtés du discours international," *Target* 1, no. 2 (1989): 215–38; Gideon Toury, *Descriptive Translation Studies and Beyond* (Amsterdam: John Benjamins, 1995); Anthony Pym, "Twelfth-Century Toledo and Strategies of the Literalist Trojan Horse," *Target* 6, no. 1 (1994): 43–66; Tarek Shamma, *Translation and the*

Manipulation of Difference: Arabic Literature in Nineteenth-Century England (Manchester: St. Jerome Publishing, 2009). See: James St. André, *Translating China as Cross-Identity Performance* (Honolulu: University of Hawai'i Press, 2018), 6–7.

8. Enrique Bendito, *Un viaje a Júpiter: Obra escrita en español* (Valladolid: Imprenta, Librería y Encuadernación de Jorge Montero, 1899); Joan Crespi i Martí, *La ciutat de la por* (Barcelona: Les Ales Esteses, 1930).

9. I am following the synthesis provided in: Emily S. Rosenberg, introduction to *A World Connecting, 1870–1945*, ed. Emily S. Rosenberg (Cambridge, MA: Belknap Press of Harvard University Press, 2012), 3–28.

10. Rosenberg, introduction to *A World Connecting*, 3.

11. Two terminological clarifications are in need. First, "China," "Spain," "Europe," and "the West" should be understood as both geopolitical locations and discursive formations. In this book I problematize our understanding of these concepts and highlight the tension between their geopolitical and discursive meaning. I will nevertheless avoid an excessive use of scare quotes and limit them to the instances when I feel the need to emphasize their discursive meaning. Second, "Europe" and "the West" are often used quite interchangeably in the field of East-West studies since most of the main discourses on China (or the East) are shared between Europe and the United States. Throughout the book I tend to refer to "Europe" to stress the specific historical and geopolitical connection between Spain and other European contexts, and I refer to "the West" in a more general and discursive sense. To be sure, the specificity of the relationship between the United States and China should be considered too. For instance, debates on immigration policies (such as the Chinese Exclusion Act of 1882) in the late nineteenth century influenced the representations of China and the Chinese in the United States but had a lesser impact in Europe.

12. Eric Hayot, Haun Saussy, and Steven G. Yao, "Sinographies: An Introduction," in *Sinographies: Writing China*, eds. Eric Hayot, Haun Saussy, and Steven G. Yao (Minneapolis, MN, and London: University of Minnesota Press, 2008), vii. The analogy they use is the following: "sinography would be to sinology [which they understand as the knowledge about China] as historiography is to history, a reflection on the conditions, assumptions, and logic of a set of disciplinary and cultural practices" (vii).

13. Eric Hayot, *Chinese Dreams: Pound, Brecht, Tel Quel* (Ann Arbor: University of Michigan Press, 2003); Eric Hayot, *The Hypothetical Mandarin: Sympathy, Modernity, and Chinese Pain* (Oxford: Oxford University Press, 2009); Christopher Bush, *Ideographic Modernism: China, Writing, Media* (Oxford: Oxford University Press, 2010). Books in East-West studies and on the representations of China in the West have opened up new avenues to rethink China's position in Western cultural, literary, and intellectual history. I am indebted to all these contributions. Besides the works by Hayot and Bush, other important books on the subject are: Peter Kitson, *Forging Romantic China: Sino-British Cultural Exchange 1760–1840* (Cambridge: Cambridge University Press, 2013); Ross G. Forman, *China and the Victorian Imagination: Empires Entwined* (Cambridge: Cambridge University Press, 2013); Gordon H. Chang, *Fateful Ties: A History of America's Preoccupation with China* (Cambridge,

MA: Harvard University Press, 2015); Hua Hsu, *A Floating Chinaman: Fantasy and Failure across the Pacific* (Cambridge, MA: Harvard University Press, 2016); Richard Jean So, *Transpacific Community: America, China, and the Rise and Fall of a Cultural Network* (New York: Columbia University Press, 2016); Wendy Gan, *Comic China: Representing Common Ground, 1890–1945* (Philadelphia: Temple University Press, 2018). On slightly earlier modern contacts: David Porter, *Ideographia: The Chinese Cipher in Early Modern Europe* (Stanford, CA: Stanford University Press, 2002) and *The Chinese Taste in Eighteenth-Century England* (Cambridge: Cambridge University Press, 2010).

14. On this tension, see for instance: Hayot, *Chinese Dreams*, 186; Hayot, Saussy, and Yao, "Sinographies," xi; and Bush, *Ideographic Modernism*, 126 and throughout chapter 4.

15. For an example of this kind of alternative (non-Western) global imagined communities based on a shared historical experience, see: Rebecca E. Karl, "Creating Asia: China in the World at the Beginning of the Twentieth Century," *The American Historical Review* 103, no. 4 (1998): 1096–1118. These ideas are further developed and contextualized in Rebecca E. Karl, *Staging the World: Chinese Nationalism at the Turn of the Twentieth Century* (Durham, NC, and London: Duke University Press, 2002). The coexistence of the Civil War in Spain (1936–1939) and the War of Resistance against Japan in China (1937–1945) did produce a short-lived communion between the two countries in the late 1930s and will be examined in chapter 5. For an analysis of this connection, see: Andrés Herrera-Feligreras et al., *España y China 1937–2017: 80 aniversario del internacionalismo antifascista* (Granada: Comares, 2017).

16. Siwen Ning, "De la China legendaria al declive del Celeste Imperio: La representación de China y su imagen literaria en la España del siglo XIX" (PhD diss., Universitat Autònoma de Barcelona, 2015), published as *Fragmentos del Celeste Imperio: La representación de China y su imagen literaria en la España del siglo XIX* (Madrid and Frankfurt: Iberoamericana Vervuert, 2020).

17. Data taken from bibliographic lists at *Archivo China-España 1800–1950*, which includes about 120 books. As it was common that books published materials that had been published first by installments in journals or magazines, the data should therefore not be taken as a totality.

18. St. André, *Translating China*, 12.

19. Elisa Martí-López, *Borrowed Words: Translation, Imitation, and the Making of the Nineteenth-Century Novel in Spain* (Lewisburg, PA: Bucknell University Press, 2002); Lynn C. Purkey, *Spanish Reception of Russian Narratives, 1905–1939* (Suffolk: Tamesis Books, 2013), particularly 9–44. The representations of Russia and the translation of Russian literature in Spain certainly share some similarities with the cases examined in this book: Russian works also arrived in Spain indirectly through English and, especially, French translations. However, there are at least two aspects that make the Russian case significantly different. First, Russian literature and culture were popularized in late nineteenth-century Spain in a more patterned, systematic way, particularly after Emilia Pardo Bazán's three influential lectures given at the Ateneo de Madrid in April 1887. Her lectures were later published as a book: Emilia Pardo Bazán, *La revolución y la novela en Rusia: Lectura en el Ateneo de Madrid* (Madrid:

Publicaciones Españolas, 1961), which had four editions between 1887 and 1901. Her lectures were "highly derivative" of Viscount Eugène-Melchior de Vogüé's *Le Roman Russe* and Pardo Bazán herself explicitly acknowledged this source and many others (*La revolución y la novela en Rusia*, 24–26). Her book even includes a final section, "Libros consultados" (Works Consulted) with about eighty-five primary and secondary sources (279–81). Her book was translated into English but without the final list of sources: Emilia Pardo-Bazán, *Russia: Its People and Its Literature* (Chicago: McClurg, 1890). Second, Russian literature and, particularly, the Russian novel had a solid prestige in Spain in the late nineteenth century. The symbolic importance attached to the Russian novel conferred more intellectual respect for Russian society and history. Pardo Bazán's humble approach to Russia (see, for instance: *La revolución y la novela en Rusia*, 292–93) cannot be compared to the Spanish intellectuals' rather arrogant and patronizing attitudes toward China and Chinese culture that we will see in this book. In other words, Chinese culture was translated in Spain without a legitimized literary backup.

20. I thank Robert Bickers for this insight and these references.

21. Hayot's formulation is: "It matters that the mandarin is Chinese, because his being Chinese means that his being Chinese doesn't matter" (Hayot, *The Hypothetical Mandarin*, 35). Hayot defines the hypothetical mandarin (or the mandarin button or paradox) as "a philosophical conjecture that has remained, in a variety of derivative forms, a crucial figure of European thought over the last two centuries: What is the relative worth to you of harm done to a Chinese stranger? . . . How does spatial distance affect one's moral responsibility?" (4, 5). The hypothetical mandarin was introduced by Chateaubriand's *Génie du christianisme* in 1802, probably inspired by Diderot's "Entretien d'un père avec ses enfants" (1771). It was later popularized by Balzac's *Le Père Goriot* (1834–1835), where Rastignac asks Bianchon what he would do if he could make a fortune by killing an old mandarin in China by simply exerting his will, without a stirring from Paris. Quoted in Hayot, *The Hypothetical Mandarin*, 4. See also: Carlo Ginzburg, "Killing a Chinese Mandarin: The Moral Implications of Distance," *Critical Inquiry* 21, no 1 (1994): 46–60.

22. The politics of translation have been widely acknowledged. Postcolonial translation scholars have showed the intimate connection between colonialism and translation—how translation contributed to processes of colonization in non-Western contexts and also how translation contributed to processes of subordination, subalternity—perhaps even colonization—within the West itself. The classical works of postcolonial translation theory are: Vicente Rafael, *Contracting Colonialism: Translation and Christian Conversion in Tagalog Society under Early Spanish Rule* (Ithaca, NY: Cornell University Press, 1988); Eric Cheyfitz, *The Poetics of Imperialism: Translation and Colonization from The Tempest to Tarzan* (Oxford: Oxford University Press, 1991); Tejaswini Niranjana, *Siting Translation: History, Post-Structuralism, and the Colonial Context* (Berkeley, CA, and Los Angeles: University of California Press, 1992). For an excellent summary of the interrelation between translation studies and postcolonial theory and a survey of more recent contributions, see: Susan Bassnett, "Postcolonialism and/as Translation," in *The Oxford Handbook of Postco-*

lonial Studies, ed. Graham Huggan (Oxford: Oxford University Press, 2013), 340–58.

23. Edward Said considered that the Orientalist model based on the British or French colonizer against the Oriental colonized described in *Orientalism* did not fit in Spain, given that "el islam y la cultura española se habitan mutuamente en lugar de confrontarse con beligerancia" (Islam and Spanish culture inhabit each other instead of clashing with belligerence). Edward Said, "Prólogo a la nueva edición española," in *Orientalismo*, trans. María Luísa Fuentes (Barcelona: Debolsillo, 2003), 9–10. Many scholars have nevertheless reexamined Said's assumption from different angles. See, for example: Susan Martin-Márquez, *Disorientations: Spanish Colonialism in Africa and the Performance of Identity* (New Haven, CT: Yale University Press, 2008); Barbara Fuchs, *Exotic Nation: Maurophilia and the Construction of Early Modern Spain* (Philadelphia: University of Pennsylvania Press, 2009); Joan Torres-Pou, *Asia en la España del siglo XIX: Literatos, viajeros, intelectuales y diplomáticos ante Oriente* (Amsterdam: Rodopi, 2013); José Luis Venegas, *The Sublime South: Andalusia, Orientalism, and the Making of Modern Spain* (Evanston, IL: Northwestern University Press, 2018). This book shares with these works the attempt to understand the intricate, shifting connection between Spain and Orientalism—both of the orientalizing and orientalized kind. The representations of China in Spain examined in this book triangulate the politics of Orientalism in Spain with the politics of Orientalism in other Western contexts.

24. For instance, Laura Huerga, founder of the Catalan publishing house Raig Verd, openly acknowledged that reviewing original manuscripts in the Catalan language implies too much work and that she limits herself to publish only one Catalan original work per year—the rest of the works in Raig Verd's catalog are translations. See: Carles Geli, "Joves editors amb pas ferm," *El País*, May 11, 2017.

25. Ngũgĩ wa Thiong'o, *Globalectics: Theory and the Politics of Knowing* (New York: Columbia University Press, 2012), 60–61.

26. For the 1898 crisis see, for example: Sebastian Balfour, *The End of the Spanish Empire, 1898–1923* (Oxford: Clarendon Press, 1997). For the development of "the idea of Spain" or Spanish national consciousness, see, for example: José Álvarez-Junco, *Spanish Identity in the Age of Nations* (Manchester: Manchester University Press, 2013); Spanish original: José Álvarez Junco, *Mater Dolorosa: La idea de España en el siglo XIX* (Madrid: Taurus, 2001). For Spanishness in connection to nationhood and ethnicity, see, for example: Antonio Feros, *Speaking of Spain* (Cambridge, MA: Harvard University Press, 2017).

27. Josep Fradera, *The Imperial Nation: Citizens and Subjects in the British, French, Spanish, and American Empires*, trans. Ruth MacKay (Princeton, NJ: Princeton University Press, 2018). Spanish original: Josep Maria Fradera, *La nación imperial (1750–1918)*, 2 vols. (Barcelona: Edhasa, 2015).

28. Fradera, *The Imperial Nation*, 248.

29. Fradera, *The Imperial Nation*, 176.

30. Thus, while Fradera sustains that "the notion of [Spain's] inexorable decline overseen by ignorant friars and incompetent, cruel, and corrupt bureaucrats" may have existed "only because of the historiographic myth fabricated

in 1898 amid competition among imperial countries" (Fradera, *The Imperial Nation*, 176), the case studies examined in the following chapters suggest that, besides the myths fabricated by foreign historiographies, there were other cultural mechanisms that contributed to the narrative of Spain's decline.

31. As examples of the breadth and vitality of this trend that follow the pioneer work by scholars like Evelyn Hu-Dehart, Araceli Tinajero, Axel Gasquet, and Ignacio López-Calvo, see the following edited volumes and special issues: Ignacio López-Calvo, ed., *Alternative Orientalisms in Latin America and Beyond* (Newcastle: Cambridge Scholars Publishing, 2007); Araceli Tinajero, ed., *Orientalisms of the Hispanic and Luso-Brazilian World* (New York: Escribana Books, 2014); Zelideth María Rivas and Debbie Lee-Distefano, eds., *Imagining Asia in the Americas* (New Brunswick, NJ: Rutgers University Press, 2016); Jorge J. Locane and María Montt Strabucchi, eds., "Special Issue: Latin America-China Voyages," *Transmodernity: Journal of Peripheral Cultural Production of the Luso-Hispanic World* 9, no. 3 (2020).

32. Pedro R. Erber, *Breaching the Frame: The Rise of Contemporary Art in Brazil and Japan* (Oakland, CA: University of California Press, 2014). Ana Paulina Lee, *Mandarin Brazil: Race, Representation, and Memory* (Stanford, CA: Stanford University Press, 2018). Junyoung Verónica Kim, "Asia-Latin America as Method: The Global South Project and the Dislocation of the West," *Verge: Studies in Global Asias* 3, no. 2 (2017): 97–117.

33. Alejandro Mejías-López, *The Inverted Conquest: The Myth of Modernity and the Transatlantic Onset of Modernism* (Nashville, TN: Vanderbilt University Press, 2010).

34. Gayle Rogers, *Incomparable Empires: Modernism and the Translation of Spanish and American Literature* (New York: Columbia University Press, 2016). Inspired by Rogers's statement about the importance of translation in modernism and literary history and by his exploration of inter-imperiality through translation, I extend the statement and the exploration to the broader sphere of cross-cultural and historical connections. For inter-imperiality, see: Laura Doyle, *Inter-Imperiality: Vying Empires, Gendered Labor, and the Literary Arts of Alliance* (Durham, NC, and London: Duke University Press, 2020).

35. Besides Rosenberg, ed., *A World Connecting*, see, for instance: Christopher Bayly, *The Birth of the Modern World, 1780–1914: Global Connections and Comparisons* (Oxford: Blackwell, 2004); or Jürgen Osterhammel, *The Transformation of the World: A Global History of the Nineteenth Century* (Princeton, NJ: Princeton University Press, 2014).

36. An excellent summary of these contributions in historical scholarship, including world history, can be found in Rosenberg, introduction to *A World Connecting*, 9.

37. Stuart Hall himself pointed out that these terms are shorthand generalizations and that "the West has always contained many internal differences." Stuart Hall, "The West and the Rest: Discourse and Power," in *Modernity: An Introduction to Modern Societies*, eds. Stuart Hall et al. (Cambridge, MA: Wiley-Blackwell, 1996), 185, 188.

38. Sakai has claimed that "we are urged to acknowledge that the unity of the West is far from being unitarily determinable," arguing that what we under-

stand as "the West" is in fact ambiguous and incongruous. The ambiguity of the West can be claimed in relation to not only concepts such as class or ethnicity but also the different nations that are usually placed within this category. Naoki Sakai, "Dislocation of the West and the Status of the Humanities," in *Specters of the West and the Politics of Translation*, eds. Yukiko Hanawa and Naoki Sakai, Traces 1 (Hong Kong: Hong Kong University Press, 2001), 71–94. Hevia has called for the need to develop studies about the interactions between East Asia and Western countries based on non-Anglophone and non-Francophone sources as the first step to understanding the transnational patterns of these interactions. James L. Hevia, *English Lessons: The Pedagogy of Imperialism in Nineteenth-Century China* (Durham, NC: Duke University Press, 2003). Chakrabarty has claimed that "the Europe I seek to provincialize or decenter is an imaginary figure that remains deeply embedded in *clichéd and shorthand forms* in some everyday habits of thought that invariably subtend attempts in the social sciences to address questions of political modernity in South Asia" (italics in the original). Dipesh Chakrabarty, *Provincializing Europe: Postcolonial Thought and Historical Difference* (Princeton, NJ: Princeton University Press, 2009), 3–4.

39. I am following the insightful synthesis in Ignacio M. Sánchez Prado, *Strategic Occidentalism: On Mexican Fiction, the Neoliberal Book Market, and the Question of World Literature* (Evanston, IL: Northwestern University Press, 2018), 8–12.

40. Stefanie Gänger, "Circulation: Reflections on Circularity, Entity, and Liquidity in the Language of Global History," *Journal of Global History* 12, no. 3 (November 2017): 303–18. For an insightful critique of the circulation model and an inspiring counterproposal, see: Alexander Beecroft, *An Ecology of World Literature: from Antiquity to the Present Day* (London: Verso Books, 2015).

41. Sánchez Prado, *Strategic Occidentalism*, 8–12. Sánchez Prado refers to two different yet supplementary critiques to diffusionist or world-system theories: Aamir R. Mufti, *Forget English!: Orientalisms and World Literature* (Cambridge, MA: Harvard University Press, 2016) and Pheng Cheah, *What Is a World?: On Postcolonial Literature as World Literature* (Durham, NC: Duke University Press, 2016).

42. Subramanian Shankar, *Flesh and Fish Blood: Postcolonialism, Translation, and the Vernacular* (Berkeley, CA: University of California Press, 2012), 104.

43. I was particularly inspired by James St. André's more open conception of translation based on the relationship between translation, literature, and other activities. See: St. André, *Translating China*. I expand St. André's contribution by moving outside the Anglophone and Francophone contexts and by adding a new layer of complexity—the triangular relationship between texts.

44. Harald Kittel and Armin Paul Frank, *Interculturality and the Historical Study of Literary Translations* (Berlin: Eric Schmidt, 1991). This definition is taken from Maialen Marin-Lacarta, "Indirectness in Literary Translation: Methodological Possibilities," *Translation Studies* 10, no. 2 (May 4, 2017): 135. For a recent overview on indirect translation, see also: Alexandra Rosa, Hanna

Pięta, and Rita Bueno Maia, "Theoretical, Methodological and Terminological Issues Regarding Indirect Translation: An Overview," *Translation Studies* 10, no. 2 (May 4, 2017): 113–32.

45. James St. André, "Relay," in *Routledge Encyclopedia of Translation Studies*, eds. Mona Baker and Kirsten Malmkjær (London: Routledge, 1998), 230–32. See also: Martin Ringmar, "Relay Translation," in *Handbook of Translation Studies*, eds. Yves Gambier and Luc van Doorslaer, vol. 3 (Amsterdam: John Benjamins, 2012), 141–44. Indirect or relay translation has been defined as the translation of a translated text (either spoken or written) into a third language. Translation studies theorists have examined relay translation particularly in relation to linguistic aspects. But it remains a minor concept within the main concerns of the discipline. As both St André and Ringmar note, this is probably due to the generalized view that holds translations as inferior to originals.

46. Karen Laura Thornber, *Empire of Texts in Motion: Chinese, Korean, and Taiwanese Transculturations of Japanese Literature* (Cambridge, MA: Harvard University Asia Center, 2009), 23–24.

47. Thornber, *Empire of Texts in Motion*, vii.

48. Jacob Edmond, *A Common Strangeness: Contemporary Poetry, Cross-Cultural Encounter, Comparative Literature* (New York: Fordham University Press, 2012); Heekyoung Cho, *Translation's Forgotten History: Russian Literature, Japanese Mediation, and the Formation of Modern Korean Literature* (Cambridge, MA: Harvard University Asia Center, 2016).

49. Henri Lefebvre, *The Production of Space*, trans. Donald Nicholson-Smith (Oxford: Blackwell, 1991); Shu-mei Shih, "Is the Post- in Postsocialism the Post- in Posthumanism?," *Social Text* 30, no. 1 (110) (March 20, 2012): 31.

50. For Lefebvre these are *le perçu* (spatial practices and perceptions related to daily or urban reality), *le conçu* (representations or theories of space), and *le vécu* (representational spaces or symbolic, artistic, literary images of that space). *The Production of Space*, 38–39.

51. Lefebvre, *The Production of Space*, 40.

52. Naoki Sakai, "Translation," *Theory, Culture & Society* 23, no. 2–3 (May 1, 2006): 71. See also: Naoki Sakai, *Translation & Subjectivity: On "Japan" and Cultural Nationalism* (Minneapolis, MN: University of Minnesota Press, 1997).

CHAPTER 1

1. Quoted in Derk Bodde, *Tolstoy and China* (Princeton, NJ: Princeton University Press, 2015), 20.

2. Bodde, *Tolstoy and China*, 11.

3. Thomas Taylor Meadows, *The Chinese and Their Rebellions* (London: Smith, Elder, and Company, 1856); Eugène Simon, *La Cité chinoise* (Paris: Nouvelle Revue, 1885).

4. Bodde also mentions: Samuel Beal, Lafcadio Hearn, Paul Carus, Eugène Simon, Léon de Rosny, Charles de Harlez, Ernest Faber, Victor von Strauss, V. P. Vasilyev, Ku Hing-ming [Gu Hongming] and Liang Ch'i-cha'ao [Liang Qichao] (*Tolstoy and China*, 13).

5. Bodde, *Tolstoy and China*, 95–102. Data taken from Paul Birukoff, *Tolstoi und der Orient* (Zurich and Leipzig: Rotapfel-Verlag, 1925). These were the languages of the works owned or consulted by Tolstoy. Authors were British, American, French, Belgian, German, Austrian, Russian, Chinese, and Japanese.

6. Guillaume Pauthier, *China o descripción histórica, jeográfica y literaria de este vasto imperio, según documentos chinos* (Barcelona: Imprenta del Imparcial, 1845); Clément Pellé, *La China pintoresca: Historia, descripción, costumbres: Desde la más remota antigüedad hasta nuestros días* (Barcelona: Imprenta de Joaquín Verdaguer, 1845); and François Pétis de la Croix, *Los mil y un dias: Cuentos persas, indios, turcos y chinos* (Barcelona: Oliveres, edits. é impr., 1863).

7. As an example of the review articles, Fernando Araujo opens the section "Revista de revistas" in *La España Moderna* in the following way: "La *Revue Bleue*, de París; la *Nuova Antología*, de Roma; la *Review of Reviews*, de Londres, y otras muchas revistas, dedican al estudio de las sociedades secretas de China sendos artículos, cuya substancia procuraremos resumir del modo más claro y preciso para conocimiento de nuestros lectores" (*Revue Bleue* in Paris; *Nuova Antología* in Rome; *Review of Reviews* in London, and many other magazines, include articles about the study of the secret societies of China. We will try to summarize the substance of these studies in the clearest and most precise way for the knowledge of our readers). Fernando Araujo, *La España Moderna*, July 1900, 187.

8. For a summary of this topic, see: Kathleen E. Davis, "Translation, Plagiarism and Amplification in Mentaberry's *Impresiones de un viaje a la China*," *Bulletin of Spanish Studies* 94, no. 1 (2017): 75–90. Davis examines Adolfo de Mentaberry's *Impresiones de un viaje a la China*: "While a large part of the China section of *Impresiones* is an uncredited translation from the work of de Beauvoir, Mentaberry does make use of what De Quincey would consider amplifications, adding material and making changes in emphasis that may serve the work from being an example of culpable plagiarism, according to the definition of the term among Romantic authors" (77).

9. Siwen Ning's work provides a systematic analysis of this process in her study of four important illustrated journals in nineteenth-century Spain: *Semanario Pintoresco Español, El Museo Universal, El Mundo Pintoresco*, and *La Ilustración Española y Americana* ("De la China legendaria al declive del Celeste Imperio").

10. Ning, "De la China legendaria al declive del Celeste Imperio," 169.

11. The following example is analyzed in Davis, "Translation, Plagiarism and Amplification."

12. Pablo Martín Asuero, "Introducción," in *Impresiones de un viaje a la China*, by Adolfo de Mentaberry, ed. Pablo Martín Asuero (Madrid: Miraguano, 2008), 22.

13. Mentaberry, *Impresiones de un viaje a la China*, 192–93.

14. Ning, "De la China legendaria al declive del Celeste Imperio," 224.

15. Mentaberry refers explicitly to the following works: Joseph Marie Amiot, *Eloge de la ville de Moukden* (Paris: Tiliard, 1770); Eugène Buissonet, *De Pékin à Shanghaï, souvenirs de voyages* (Paris: Amyot, 1871); John Francis Davis,

La Chine, ou description générale des moeurs et des coutumes . . . de l'empire chinoise, trans. A. Pichard (Paris: Paulin, 1837); Antoine Gaubil, *Histoire de Gentschiscan et de toute la dinastie des Mongous* (Paris: Briasson, 1739); Jean Baptiste Grosier, ed., *Histoire générale de la Chine* , trans. Joseph-Anne-Marie de Moyriac de Mailla (Paris: Ph. D. Pierres and Clousier, 1777–1785, 13 vols); Jean Baptiste Grosier, *De la Chine, ou description générale de cet empire* (Paris: Pillet Ainé and Arthus Bertrand, 1818–1820); Évariste Régis Huc, *L'Empire chinois: Faisant suite à l'ouvrage intitulé souvenirs d'un voyage en Tartarie et le Thibet* (Paris: Gaume Frères, 1854); William Jones, *The Works of Sir William Jones* (London: G. G. and J. Robinson, 1799); M. Charles Lemire, *La Conchinchine* [sic] *Française et le Royaume de Cambodge, avec l'itinéraire de Paris à Saigon et à la capitale cambodgienne et deux cartes* (Paris: Bar-Sur-Aube Mme. Jardeaux, 1869); William Milne, *A Retrospect of the First Ten Years of the Protestant Mission to China* (Malacca: The Anglo-Chinese Press, 1820); Jean Pierre Pauthier, *Histoire des relations politiques de la Chine avec les puissances occidentales depuis les temps les plus anciens jusqu'a nos jours suivie de ceremonial observé a la cour de Pe-King pour la réception des ambassadeurs* (Paris: Firmin Didot, 1859, 1st ed. 1837); Marco Polo, *El libro de las maravillas* (no specific edition is given); Abel Rémusat, *Nouveaux mélanges asiatiques* (Paris: Éditions Schubart et Heideloff, 1829); M. de Saurigny, *Histoire de la Chine, du Japon, de la Perse, de l'Inde, de l'Arabie, de la Turquie, de l'Égypte, de l'Algérie, etc, depuis les temps les plus reculés jusq'en 1840* (Paris: Librairie Universelle, 1846). The list has been compiled in: Martín Asuero, "Introducción," 35–36.

16. These are closely examined in Davis, "Translation, Plagiarism and Amplification," 79–89.

17. St. André, *Translating China*, 1.

18. David B. Honey, *Incense at the Altar: Pioneering Sinologists and the Development of Classical Chinese Philology* (New Haven, CT: The American Oriental Society, 2001), 3.

19. It "went to thirty editions in various European languages before the century was out" and "it informed the work of many European thinkers and scholars, Francis Bacon for one, and inspired a like number of explorers, among them Sir Walter Raleigh." Honey, *Incense at the Altar*, 3–4.

20. For a general summary of these developments, see, for instance: Jonathan D. Spence, *The Chan's Great Continent: China in Western Minds* (New York: Norton, 1999), chapters 4 and 5. Other examples are discussed in, for instance, St. André, *Translating China*, chapters 1 and 2. For the sinological context, see: Honey, *Incense at the Altar*, chapter 1, section "Learned Laity and the First Professionals."

21. St. André, *Translating China*, 129.

22. Honey, *Incense at the Altar*, chapter 1.

23. For all these, see: St. André, *Translating China*, chapter 1.

24. I am summarizing here some aspects from Gregory Blue, "China and Western Social Thought in the Modern Period," in *China and Historical Capitalism: Genealogies of Sinological Knowledge*, eds. Timothy Brook and Gregory Blue (Cambridge: Cambridge University Press, 2002), 57–109; and Spence, *The Chan's Great Continent*, 71.

25. Spence, *The Chan's Great Continent*, 139.

26. Jonathan Spence, "Western Perceptions of China from the Late Sixteenth Century to the Present," in *Heritage of China: Contemporary Perspectives on Chinese Civilization*, ed. Paul S. Ropp (Berkeley, CA: University of California Press, 1990), 6. See, among many others: Rolf J. Goebel, "China as an Embalmed Mummy: Herder's Orientalist Poetics," *South Atlantic Review* 60, no. 1 (1995): 111–29; Young Kun Kim, "Hegel's Criticism of Chinese Philosophy," *Philosophy East and West* 28, no. 2 (1978): 173–80.

27. "Like its mirror image blackface, whiteface is a process whereby members of a secure social group create a caricature of some outside or marginalized group. The image of this outsider (Other) is set in strong contrast to the image of the in group (Self); the difference is that, rather than affirming one's own image at the expense of the other as in blackface (*luckily*, I am not that), whiteface functions as a criticism (*unfortunately*, I am not that). The Other is held up as possessing certain qualities, values, or strengths that one's own society lacks" (St. André, *Translating China*, 24).

28. David Martínez-Robles, "La participación española en el proceso de penetración occidental en China: 1840–1870" (PhD diss., Universitat Pompeu Fabra, 2007), 108–10. In fact, it is significant that some of the few scholarly works about China written by Spanish authors were originally written in French and published in France. See below the case of Sinibaldo de Mas.

29. Martí-López, *Borrowed Words*, 11. Martí-López argues that the success of popular (French) literature in Spain among both common readers and literatos can be explained because it was appropriate "to the particularly 'extreme situations'—the extreme vulnerability—that characterized the triumph of liberalism in Spain. The weakness of its industrialization process, the violence of the civil war, the unfinished character of its political revolution (the constant alzamientos), the well-rooted centrifugal forces of regionalism (the juntas undermining the authority of the state), and the loss of the empire (when the most prosperous European nations were busy building them) did not find a vehicle of expression in the 'solid and well-regulated world' that characterizes the 'Realistic temper' of both the British novel of social manners and, after the revolution of 1848, the new generation of French novelists. Thus, the narrative formula of melodrama—prone to unusual events and characters, to a clear-cut representation of conflicts and resolutions, and to the uncensured display of emotions—actively contributed to represent the *off-center* historical conditions of Spain with respect to the political and cultural hegemony of France and Britain" (136–37).

30. Ning, "De la China legendaria al declive del Celeste Imperio."

31. Ning, "De la China legendaria al declive del Celeste Imperio," 98, 117.

32. Joseph Méry, *Ingleses y chinos*, trans. Traductor [Ramon Martí i Alsina] (Barcelona: Imprenta de Juan Capdevila, 1848). I thank Xavier Ortells-Nicolau for bringing this text to my attention.

33. Conchi Chillón, "Onze textos de Ramon Martí i Alsina," in *De realisme: Aproximacions i testimonis*, eds. Josep M. Domingo and Anna Llovera (Lleida: Punctum, 2013), 299.

34. Ironically, on the topic of infanticide in China, after summarizing different points of view, the translator concludes that "en fin, para que opinión nos

decidiremos? . . . Es tan difícil convencerse de una verdad . . ." (anyway, what opinion will we follow? . . . It is so difficult to convince yourself of a truth . . .) and leaves the issue unresolved (Méry, *Ingleses y chinos*, 184).

35. Auguste Wahlen, *Moeurs, usages et costumes de tous les peuples du monde* (Bruxelles: Librairie Historique-Artistique, 1843); Dumont d'Urville et al., *Viaje pintoresco alrededor del mundo: Resumen jeneral de los viajes y descubrimientos de Magallanes, Tasman, Dampier . . .* , ed. Juan Oliveres (Barcelona: Imprenta y Librería de Juan Oliveres, 1841).

36. Luis Prudencio Álvarez y Tejero, *Reseña histórica del gran imperio de China* (Madrid: Imprenta de T. Fortanet, 1857). Hereafter I will add page numbers within parentheses after the quotations. I have gathered information about Álvarez y Tejero largely from Martínez-Robles, "La participación española," 108. According to the description in one of Álvarez y Tejero's books, he was "Abogado de los Tribunales Nacionales, Comendador de la Real orden Americana de Isabel la Católica, Secretario Honorario de S. M. la Reina Doña Isabel II, Ministro Honorario y Supernumerario de la Audiencia territorial de Filipinas, Socio corresponsal nacional de la Real Academia de Ciencias naturales de Madrid, individuo de número de la Sociedad económica de Amigos del Pais de la ciudad de Valencia, y Majistrado en propiedad de la Audiencia territorial de esta misma ciudad" (Lawyer of the Tribunales Nacionales, Commander of the Real Orden Americana de Isabel la Católica, Honorary Secretary of Her Majesty Reina Doña Isabel II, Honorary Minister and Supernumerary of the Territorial Court of the Philippines, National Correspondent Partner of the Real Academia de Ciencias naturales of Madrid, member of the Sociedad económica de Amigos del Pais of the city of Valencia, and Magistrate in property of the Audiencia territorial in Valencia). Luis Prudencio Álvarez y Tejero, *De las Islas Filipinas: Memoria* (Valencia: Imprenta de Cabrerizo, 1842), 1.

37. Álvarez y Tejero does not provide a printed list of subscribers as it was often the case in subscription publishing. But he does mention—and thank—subscribers and quotes the information previously given to them to attract their investment (Álvarez y Tejero, *Reseña histórica del gran imperio de China*, 214–15; 222).

38. Álvarez y Tejero, *Reseña histórica del gran imperio de China*, 97 ft 1; similar on 101 and 346. In this case, he refers to: Mariano Torrente, *Geografía universal física, política é histórica* (Madrid: Imprenta de Don Miguel de Burgos, 1828).

39. Johannes Fabian, *Time and the Other: How Anthropology Makes Its Object* (New York: Columbia University Press, 1983).

40. See, for instance: Juan Ferrando, *Historia de los pp. Dominicos en las Islas Filipinas y en sus misiones del Japón, China, Tung-Kin y Formosa* (Madrid: Rivadeneyra, 1871); Ramon Jordana y Morera, *La inmigración china en Filipinas* (Madrid: Tipografía de Manuel G. Hernández, 1888); VV.AA, *La inmigración china y japonesa en Filipinas: Documentos* (Madrid: Imprenta Luis Aguado, 1892); Alfredo Opisso, "La raza amarilla. China-Japón-Corea," in *Viajes a Oriente* (Barcelona: Librería de Antonio J. Bastinos, Editor, 1898–1899). Florentino Rodao has explored the impact of biological determinism and the increasingly racialized understanding of Filipino society, both in Spain

and in the Philippines themselves, during the last stages of Spain's colonial domination. See: Florentino Rodao, "'The Salvational Currents of Emigration': Racial Theories and Social Disputes in the Philippines at the End of the Nineteenth Century," *Journal of Southeast Asian Studies* 49, no. 3 (October 2018): 426–44.

41. Just as a general quantitative reference: "Europa" or "europeos" is mentioned on thirty pages. "España" is mentioned on three pages (163, 186, 267). Other terms such as "español" appear on four pages (20, 76, 160, 242), always in expressions such as "religioso español" or "misionero español." "Filipinas" appears on twelve pages.

42. Lord Salisbury, "The Primrose League: Speech by Lord Salisbury," *Times*, May 5, 1898.

43. Rosario de la Torre del Río, "La prensa madrileña y el discurso de Lord Salisbury sobre las 'naciones moribundas:' Londres, Albert Hall, 4 de mayo 1898," *Cuadernos de Historia Moderna y Contemporánea*, no. 6 (1985): 173–79.

44. Julián Casanova and Carlos Gil Andrés, *Historia de España en el siglo XX* (Barcelona: Ariel, 2009), 9.

45. Casanova and Gil, *Historia de España*, 5. For an account of the moral and emotional consequences in Spain's transition from empire to nation-state, see: Javier Krauel, *Imperial Emotions: Cultural Responses to Myths of Empire in Fin-de-Siècle Spain* (Liverpool: Liverpool University Press, 2013).

46. Casanova and Gil, *Historia de España*, 8.

47. Ai Qing, *Nostalgia imperial: Crónicas de viajeros españoles por China (1870–1910)* (Madrid: Miraguano, 2019).

48. Fradera, *The Imperial Nation*, 248.

49. "La cuestión palpitante, el asunto del día, la intervención europea en China, en ese Imperio desconocido en absoluto hasta ayer, y del que hoy tenemos ligerísmas noticias" (the burning question, the topic of the day, the European intervention in China, in that Empire completely unknown until yesterday, and of which we have slight news today). Francisco Peniche de Lugo, "China y Europa," *La España Moderna*, July 1900, xx.

50. Honey, *Incense at the Altar*, xiii.

51. Sinibaldo de Mas, *L'Angleterre et le Céleste Empire* (Paris: Henri Plon, 1857); Sinibaldo de Mas, *L'Angleterre, la Chine et l'Inde* (Paris: Jules Tardieu, 1858); Sinibaldo de Mas, *La Chine et les puissances chrétiennes* (Paris: Louise Hachette et Cie, 1861). For an exhaustive analysis of de Mas's biography and his significance, see: David Martínez-Robles, *Entre dos imperios: Sinibaldo de Mas y la empresa colonial en China (1844–1868)* (Madrid: Marcial Pons, 2018).

52. A good biographical sketch can be found in: Yolanda Molina-Gavilán and Andrea L. Bell, introduction to *The Time Ship: A Chrononautical Journey*, by Enrique Gaspar, trans. Yolanda Molina-Gavilán and Andrea L. Bell (Middletown, CT: Wesleyan, 2012), xi–xlii. Ning argues that Gaspar undertook the writing of science fiction (leaving aside the writing of zarzuelas and more realist works) due to his distancing from Spanish society. This kind of alienation, in fact, could also explain his writing on China in the travel account ("De la China

legendaria al declive del Celeste Imperio," 261). A similar argument is made by Molina-Gavilán and Bell, who mention that Gaspar's consular post in China produced his crisis as a playwright and he took to writing newspaper articles as a source of additional income (introduction to *The Time Ship*, xxvi).

53. Enrique Gaspar, *The Time Ship: A Chrononautical Journey*, trans. Yolanda Molina-Gavilán and Andrea L. Bell (Middletown, CT: Wesleyan, 2012). The introduction to the English translation by Molina-Gavilán and Bell includes a section that compares Gaspar's machine with Wells's. They also clarify that Edward Page Mitchell's "The Clock That Went Backwards," published in 1881, was the first work to link time travel to a mechanical device (introduction to *The Time Ship*, xvii–xxii; xiii).

54. Enrique Gaspar, *El Anacronópete; Viaje a China; Metempsicosis* (Barcelona: Daniel Cortezo y Cia., 1887). Hereafter I quote from this edition and will add page numbers within parentheses after the quotations. Translations into English are mine.

55. Ning, "De la China legendaria al declive del Celeste Imperio," 301.

56. Cesare Cantù, *Histoire universelle*, trans. Eugène Aroux and Piersilvestro Léopardi (Paris, 1845–1854). See the entry "Chine" in: Pierre Larousse, *Grand Dictionnaire universel du XIXe siècle. Tome quatrième* [vol. 4] (Paris: Administration du Grand Dictionnaire Universel, 1866).

57. Hermann Wagner and Ernst Behm, *Die Bevölkerung Der Erde. Jährliche Übersicht Über Neue Arealberechnungen, Gebietsveränderungen, Zählungen Und Schätzungen Der Bevölkerung Auf Der Gesammten Erdoberfläche* (Gotha: J. Perthes, 1872), I, monograph no. 33 in supplementary vol. 7; Armand David, "Voyage de l'Abbé David en Chine," *Bulletin de la Société de Géographie de Paris*, series 6, vol 2, December 1871, 468. The connection between the two works is made by: Bodde, *Tolstoy and China*, 39.

58. Juan Bautista Carrasco, *Mitología universal: Historia y explicación de las ideas religiosas y teológicas de todos los siglos, de los dioses de la India, el Thibet, la China, el Asia, el Egipto, la Grecia y el mundo romano, de las divinidades de los pueblos eslavos, escandinavos y germanos, de la idolatría y el fetichismo americanos y africanos, etc* (Madrid: Imprenta y Librería de Gaspar y Roig, 1864).

59. St. André, *Translating China*, 67. St. André summarizes here different contributions on authorship such as Foucault and Woodmansee.

60. Martí-López, *Borrowed Words*, 135.

61. See: Noemí Carrasco Arroyo, "Insinuado en el alma. El *japonismo* en las crónicas finiseculares de Emilia Pardo Bazán," in *La literatura de Emilia Pardo Bazán*, eds. José Manuel González Herrán, Cristina Patiño Eirín, and Ermitas Penas Varela (A Coruña: Real Academia Galega y Fundación CaixaGalicia, 2009), 229–37.

62. Emilia Pardo Bazán, "Agravante," in *Cuentos completos*, vol. 1 (La Coruña: Fundación Pedro Barrie de la Maza, Conde de Fenosa, 1990), 155–57; "El templo," in *Cuentos completos*, vol. 2 (La Coruña: Fundación Pedro Barrie de la Maza, Conde de Fenosa, 1990), 278–81. For an extended analysis of the two pieces see: Ning, "De la China legendaria al declive del Celeste Imperio," 369–80.

63. Pardo Bazán's reply was published with her next short story, "La hierba milagrosa" (The Magical Herb). See: Pardo Bazán, *Cuentos completos*, vol. 1, 158.

64. Fray Juan de Miguel, "Agravante y demás." *La Unión Católica*, November 3, 1892; Ricardo Axeitos Valiño, "Las agencias periodísticas y literarias a fines del siglo XIX: las colaboraciones de Emilia Pardo Bazán y Clarín" (PhD diss., Universidade da Coruña, 2017), 328–29.

65. "The influence that Far Eastern art, particularly Japanese print, had on modernism and art nouveau in the late 1800s and early 1900s is evident in the cover illustration [by Gómez Soler], which suggests wonder and exoticism through the portrait of an Asian woman (presumably the Empress Sun-che) gazing at the *Time Ship*, trapped within what appears to be its own private universe" (Molina-Gavilán and Bell, introduction to *The Time Ship*, xxxix).

66. September 26, 1878; October 8, 1878; March 14, 1879; April 19, 1879; April 30, 1879; November 18, 1879; March 26, 1880; January 30, 1881; September 26, 1881; March 10, 1882; and December 8, 1882.

67. I thank Xavier Ortells-Nicolau for helping me trace the origin of Gaspar's mention. For an analysis of *weixing* and other gambling practices in that historical period, see: En Li, "Betting on Empire: A Socio-Cultural History of Gambling in Late-Qing China" (PhD diss., Washington University–St. Louis, 2015), chapter 3.

68. Martí-López, *Borrowed Words*, 11; Molina-Gavilán and Bell, introduction to *The Time Ship*, xiv; Maximiliano Brina, "De la zarzuela a la ciencia ficción: *El anacronópete*, de Enrique Gaspar. Expansión de los límites de lo fantástico en la coyuntura del nacionalismo," *Studia Romanica Posnaniensia* 45, no. 2 (2018): 53.

69. In fact, Gaspar originally planned this work as a three-act, thirteen-scene zarzuela. He later adapted the manuscript as a novel but kept the structural conventions of the musical form: three parts or acts, scenes corresponding to different places and times, cast with paired voices, and so on. The zarzuela was never performed. Molina-Gavilán and Bell, introduction to *The Time Ship*, xxxi.

70. Similar scientific parenthetical disquisitions appear in other chapters, often disconnected from the plot and the narrative pace—"perhaps in the hope of emulating Flammarion" (Molina-Gavilán and Bell, introduction to *The Time Ship*, xv). These disquisitions also tried to establish verisimilitude and scientific plausibility. See: Brian J. Dendle, "Spain's First Novel of Science Fiction: A Nineteenth-Century Voyage to Saturn," *Monographic Review* 3, no. 1–2 (1987): 47.

71. Fabian, *Time and the Other*.

72. In *Viaje a China* Spain is mentioned in relation to physical distance: letters from home take many days to reach him and Gaspar expresses sorrow and emotion for being so far away from home (226). Later, he sends a telegram home from Hong Kong to say he has arrived safely, which is received only "pocos días después" (a few days later [253]).

73. *Hispania*: September 30, 1900; October 15, 1900; October 30, 1900; November 15, 1900; November 30, 1900; December 30, 1900; and April 30, 1901. Letters to Olga were numbers 1, 3, 5, and 7. Letters to Roberto were

numbers 2, 4, and 6. Hereafter I will add letter and page numbers in brackets after the translated quotations.

74. The English expression "nine-king" appears, for instance, in: *The Asiatic Journal and Monthly Register for British and Foreign India, China and Australasia*, vol. 12, 1833, 569. It also appears in the English translation of Du Halde's *Description géographique, historique, chronologique, politique, et physique de l'empire de la Chine et de la Tartarie chinoise*, originally published in 1735. See: Jean-Baptiste Du Halde, *The General History of China: Containing a Geographical, Historical, Chronological, Political and Physical Description of the Empire of China, Chinese-Tartary, Corea, and Thibet, Including an Exact and Particular Account of Their Customs, Manners, Ceremonies, Religion, Arts, and Sciences*, 3rd ed. (London: J. Watts, 1741), 277.

75. Menpes's paintings and writings had been published (through engravings) and discussed in Spain. See, for instance, in *La Ilustración Ibérica*: "Estudios sobre el arte japonés, por Mortimer Menpes" (July 7, 1888 and August 25, 1888), "Las tres pruebas a la punta seca, por Mortimer Menpes" (July 12 1890), and "Ilustración del Cardenal Manning" (November 12, 1898).

76. St. André, *Translating China*.

77. "A Xina. Ecos de la Guerra," *La Esquella de la Torratxa*, July 1900, 444–45. The piece is supplemented by a caricature of the Empress Dowager, which is acknowledged to be taken from "una revista extranjera" (a foreign magazine). I thank Xavier Ortells-Nicolau for bringing this text to my attention.

78. Many of these residents arrived from the Philippines and included Filipino aboriginals who worked as sailors, soldiers, or musicians, numbering in the hundreds in some ports. Data taken from Carles Brasó-Broggi and David Martinez-Robles, "Beyond Colonial Dichotomies: The Deficits of Spain and the Peripheral Powers in Treaty-Port China," *Modern Asian Studies* 53, no. 4 (July 2019): 1222–47.

79. *Hispania* was published in Barcelona between 1899 and 1903 in Spanish.

80. June 20, 1898; undated; July 8, 1898; August 1898; undated; September 10, 1898; and October 20, 1986 [sic, probably 1898].

81. When talking about missionaries, Harrisson mentions the progresses made and privileges obtained by missions in rural China (especially French missions). He briefly mentions the incidents in 1838 and 1840 (L7, 154), but he does not mention the Boxers in 1899. Similarly, he mentions princes who "se conforman con conspirar en el 'Nenúfar blanco' o en el Tsai-Ly-Hoei o 'Sociedad de la Verdad,' a la que pertenecen los rebeldes que los ingleses hemos bautizado con el nombre de boxers" (settle for conspiring in the "White Water Lily" or in the Tsai-Ly-Hoei or "Society of Truth," to which the rebels that in English we have baptized as boxers belong [L2, 362]). But he does not develop the Boxer topic beyond this.

82. Martí-López, *Borrowed Words*, 135.

83. This has been developed in the discussions around cultural translation and cross-cultural representation. See: Roger M. Keesing, "Conventional Metaphors and Anthropological Metaphysics: The Problematic of Cultural Translation," *Journal of Anthropological Research* 41, no. 2 (1985): 201–17; Talal Asad, "The Concept of Cultural Translation in British Social Anthropology," in

Writing Culture: The Poetics and Politics of Ethnography, eds. James Clifford and George E. Marcus (Berkeley, CA: University of California Press, 1986), 141–64.

84. Sakai, *Translation & Subjectivity*.

CHAPTER 2

1. *Daily Mail*, July 16, 1900; *New York Times*, July 16, 1900; *Times*, July 17, 1900. Conger's telegram was published in, for instance, the *New York Times*, July 21, 1900.

2. Peter Fleming, *The Siege at Peking* (New York: Harper, 1959), 134–39; Diana Preston, *The Boxer Rebellion* (New York: Berkley Books, 2000), 172–74; James L. Hevia, *English Lessons: The Pedagogy of Imperialism in Nineteenth-Century China* (Durham, NC: Duke University Press, 2003), 192–93.

3. Arthur H. Smith, *China in Convulsion*, vol. 1 (Edinburgh and London: Oliphant, Anderson, and Ferrier, 1901), ix.

4. Fleming, *The Siege at Peking*, 130–31.

5. Fleming, *The Siege at Peking*, 131.

6. The origin of the *Daily Mail* report lies on a dispatch from its special correspondent in Shanghai on July 16. It confirmed and amplified "the substance of the most horrific rumors already current. Authoritative Chinese sources were quoted and the story, soberly told, was buttressed with a mass of circumstantial detail. It was accepted, with rage, grief and horror, as the truth" (Fleming, *The Siege at Peking*, 134–35). Yet the report was false, and the identity of the *Daily Mail* special correspondent in Shanghai remained obscure for a few months. On October 20, George Morrison, correspondent for the *Times*, identified the author of the report as F. W. Sutterlee, an American fraudster "who had a track record of dubious business dealings in the East, including arms smuggling to the Philippine rebels" (Preston, *The Boxer Rebellion*, 174). Sutterlee was now living in Shanghai at the Astor House and acting as the trusted correspondent of the *Daily Mail*. See also: George Ernest Morrison, *The Correspondence of G. E. Morrison 1895–12*, vol. 1, ed. Hui-min Lo (Cambridge: Cambridge University Press, 1976), 148–49.

7. Fleming, *The Siege at Peking*, 137.

8. Hevia, *English Lessons*, 187.

9. In Madrid, it was reported in full in *La Correspondencia Militar*, July 16, 1900, 2; or in *Revista Contemporánea*, July 1900, 114. See also editions of July 16 in, among others: *El Correo Militar*, *La Correspondencia de España*, *El Día*, *Diario Oficial de Avisos de Madrid*, *La Dinastía*, *La Época*, *El Heraldo de Madrid*, *El Imparcial*, *El Liberal*, and *El País*. For Conger's telegram, see July 24 or July 25 editions of, among others: *El Correo Militar*, *La Correspondencia de España*, *El Imparcial*, and *El País*. In Catalonia, the biggest coverage for the Boxer Rebellion was in *La Publicidad*, *La Veu de Catalunya*, and *El Diluvio*. But the conflict was also mentioned in local publications such as *Sabadell Moderno*, *La Tomasa*, and *La Campana de Gràcia*.

10. *El Correo Militar*, July 16, 1900, 2; *La Correspondencia Militar*, July 16, 1900, 2.

11. "Chinese cruelty in general and against foreigners in particular was so strong" that when the report was published "most people believed it and responded with rage and calls for vengeance." Colin Mackerras, *Western Images of China* (Oxford: Oxford University Press, 1999), 60–61. An example is the fury of Kaiser Wilhelm II's exhortation to the German troops assembled in Bremerhaven on July 27 to be dispatched as part of the allied expeditionary relief force only two days after the memorial service. In a speech that deviated from the official text that had been prepared, the Kaiser declared: "Just as a thousand years ago the Huns under their King Attila made a name for themselves, one that even today makes them seem mighty in history and legend, may the name German be affirmed by you in such a way in China that no Chinese will ever again dare to look cross-eyed at a German." See: "Wilhelm II: 'Hun Speech' (1900)" in *German History in Documents and Images (GHDI)*, accessed November 25, 2021, https://ghdi.ghi-dc.org/sub_document.cfm?doc ument_id=755, which includes Thomas Dunlap's translation of both the official version of the speech and the unofficial but correct version of its troubling passage. The official version of the speech can also be found in Johannes Prenzler, ed., *Die Reden Kaiser Wilhelms in den Jahren 1896–1900*, vol. 2 (Leipzig: Reclan, 1904), 209–12. The unofficial version of the speech is also reprinted in Manfred Görtemaker, *Deutschland im 19. Jahrhundert: Entwicklungslinien* (Bonn: Bundeszentrale für Politische Bildung, 1989), 357.

12. *La Ilustración Artística*, July 16, 1900, 7.

13. *El Día*, July 16, 1900, 2.

14. "One preoccupation of translators of Chinese material in the early nineteenth century, then, was to establish the 'truth' of their translations in opposition to the pseudotranslations. Not surprisingly, 'truth' in translation became either a 'true representation of the Chinese' or a 'true and faithful' rendering of the original text. In other words, fidelity became the guarantor of truth" (St. André, *Translating China*, 68).

15. Back in 1861 Nemesio Fernández Cuesta had explicitly expressed the anxiousness facing the conundrum: Was it possible to accuse the United Kingdom and France of imperial aggressions and, at the same time, support imperialism and European expansionism? See: Ning, "De la China legendaria al declive del Celeste Imperio," 135–38. In 1880 Fernando Garrido had used a fictional visit to Spain by a Chinese writer to severely criticize both Spanish society and the British imperial project. Carles Prado-Fonts, "China como patriótico desahogo: Usos de la alteridad en los *Viajes del chino Dagar-Li-Kao* de Fernando Garrido," *Hispanic Review* 83, no. 3 (2015): 275–98.

16. Hevia, *English Lessons*, 187.

17. Julia Chang has showed how the opening of the Suez Canal brought about a new way of imagining the once-remote Philippines from Spain. The Suez Canal "profoundly changed the temporal-spatial contours of empire, prompted writers, artists and statesmen on both sides of the Pacific to imagine empire through the trope of intimacy." Julia Chang, "Between Intimacy and Enmity: Spain and the Philippines Post-Suez," *Journal of Spanish Cultural Studies* 17, no. 4 (October 1, 2016): 305–22.

18. For a survey of the development of the telegraph worldwide, see: Steven C. Topik and Allen Wells, "Commodity Chains in a Global Economy," in *A World Connecting, 1870–1945*, ed. Emily S. Rosenberg (Cambridge, MA: Belknap Press of Harvard University Press, 2012), section "Telegraphs, Underwater Cables, and Radios," 661–71. For more specific details about the telegraph in China, see: So, *Transpacific Community*, xxiii and 25.

19. Topik and Wells, "Commodity Chains in a Global Economy," 662.

20. Rosenberg, *A World Connecting*, 26. See also: Christopher Bayly, *The Birth of the Modern World, 1780–1914*. For the relationship between new media technologies and internationalism in the same period see also: Armand Mattelart, *La mondialisation de la communication* (Paris: Presses Universitaires de France, 1996).

21. Karl, "Creating Asia," 1101.

22. Talcott Williams, "Books on China," *Book News*, September 1900, 8.

23. St. André, *Translating China*, 180.

24. Arthur H. Smith, *Chinese Characteristics* (Shanghai: The North China Herald Office, 1890); Arthur H. Smith, *Village Life in China: A Study in Sociology* (New York, Chicago, and Toronto: F. H. Revell Company, 1899). Williams's praise can be found in: Talcott Williams, "Books on China," 8–9.

25. Ning, "De la China legendaria al declive del Celeste Imperio," 175. This interrelation shows that the factual information was soundly anchored in an interest in culture more related to fiction and stereotypes. See articles by Castelar discussed in: Ning, "De la China legendaria al declive del Celeste Imperio," 176–83. Chronicles by Pedro Prat and Fernando de Antón del Olmet, authors who will be discussed later, were also published in this journal.

26. Apel·les Mestres, *Mis vacaciones: Notas de viaje* (Barcelona: Imprenta de Salvat e Hijo, 1900).

27. See, for instance: Xavier Ortells-Nicolau, "China en el imaginario visual de la España de principios del siglo xx," *Hispanic Research Journal* 18, no. 5 (September 3, 2017): 411–38.

28. Rosenberg, *A World Connecting*, 851, 852, 855.

29. Rosenberg, *A World Connecting*, 887.

30. Rosenberg, *A World Connecting*, 894.

31. Carlos Mendoza, "¿A qué ocultarlo? La sección que se ve más concurrida por el público es la de la China: al público le gustan las chinerías," *La Ilustración Ibérica*, August 18, 1888. See also: "Yong Heng y la sección china," *Archivo China-España, 1800–1950*, accessed November 25, 2021, http://ace.uoc.edu/items/show/1057. For location, see: "Plano del Palacio de la Industria," *Archivo China-España, 1800–1950*, accessed November 25, 2021, http://ace.uoc.edu/items/show/1059. Although the Qing Empire declined to participate in the event, the organization of a China section was commissioned to the Cantonese merchant Yong Heng. The diplomat Juan Mencarini provided a collection of Chinese objects that were exhibited with great success.

32. Lumière's "Japanese films" shot in 1897 were shown in Barcelona as early as March 1898. See: Jon Letamendi and Jean-Claude Seguin, *Los orígenes del cine en Cataluña* (Barcelona: Euskadiko Filmategia / Generalitat de Cata-

lunya, Institut de les Indústries Culturals, 2004). I thank Teresa Iribarren for this reference.

33. For a complete survey of Gu's biography and contributions see: St. André, *Translating China*, chapter 5.

34. Pierre Loti, *Les Derniers jours de Pékin* (Paris: Calmann-Lévy, 1902), based on the letters he had published in *Le Figaro* between May and December 1901. On Conger, see: Spence, *The Chan's Great Continent*, 117. On Twain, see: Hsuan L. Hsu, *Sitting in Darkness: Mark Twain's Asia and Comparative Racialization* (New York: NYU Press, 2015) and Selina Lai-Henderson, *Mark Twain in China* (Stanford, CA: Stanford University Press, 2015).

35. Torres-Pou, *Asia en la España del siglo XIX*, 185–86.

36. See, for example: Bush, *Ideographic Modernism* and So, *Transpacific Community*.

37. *Diario Oficial de Avisos de Madrid*, July 16, 1900, 4; *La Ilustración Artística*, July 16, 1900, 7; *El País*, July 25, 1900.

38. Smith, *Chinese Characteristics*, 1.

39. The Battle of the Yalu River was closely reported in all major Western newspapers such as the London *Times* and the *New York Times*, which included information based on telegrams from foreign correspondents and from Japanese officers, as well as pieces discussing the battle in the Letters to the Editor section. For example: "The Lessons of the Engagement Off the Yalu," by a "Naval Officer," published in the *Times*, October 3, 1894, 4, responding to "The War in the East," published also in the *Times* a few days before (September 29, 1894, 5). Magazines such as *Harper's Bazaar* also included reports and analyses of the battle. See, for instance: Eustace B. Rogers, "The Story of War in Asia," *Harper's Weekly*, November 24, 1894, 1119–20. More specialized publications that analyzed the battle and that include the same data that Auñón uses are: "The Naval Battle of Haiyang," in J. H. Glennon, ed., *Proceedings of the United States Naval Institute* 20, no. 4 (Annapolis, MD: The US Naval Institute, 1894): 808–18; Hilary A. Herbert, "The Fight off the Yalu River," *North American Review* 159, no. 456 (1894): 513–28; or *US Army and Navy Gazette* issues on September 22 and 29, October 20, November 3, 10 and 17, December 1 and 8 in 1894. A piece published in Madrid is explicit about its sources and the channels followed by the information: "Un diario de Tien Tsin, el *Pekin and Tien-Txin Times*, ha publicado una reseña bastante completa del combate naval de Yalu, debida á un europeo que tomó parte en la acción; por otra parte, el capitán de ingenieros alemán Von Hannecken, consejero del almirante Ting, embarcado en el buque almirante, ha dado à oficiales extranjeros preciosos datos sobre los incidentes del combate y las averías de los buques chinos. De estas fuentes son los datos que apuntamos à continuación" (A journal in Tiajin, the *Peking* and *Tientsin Times,* has published a quite complete review of the naval combat in Yalu, given by a European who took part in the action; furthermore, the German captain of engineers Von Hannecken, counselor of admiral Ting, embarked in the admiral ship, has provided foreign officers precious information about the events in the combat and the damages suffered by the Chinese warships. The following information comes from these sources). *Revista de Navegación*

y Comercio, December 15, 1894, 539–41. Auñón's data and account coincides with all these sources.

40. Ramón Auñón y Villalón, *El combate naval de Ya-Lu entre chinos y japoneses: Conferencia* (Madrid: Establecimiento Tipográfico R. Álvarez, 1895), 51.

41. Auñón, *El combate naval de Ya-Lu*, 52.

42. Luis Valera, *Sombras chinescas: Recuerdos de un viaje al Celeste Imperio* (Madrid: La Viuda é Hijos de Tello, 1902), originally published by installments in *El Imparcial* in 1901; Torres-Pou, *Asia en la España del siglo XIX*, chapter 2.

43. Torres-Pou, *Asia en la España del siglo XIX*, 19.

44. Torres-Pou, *Asia en la España del siglo XIX*, 62.

45. "Je n'ai donc pu observer nos soldats que pendant la période de l'occupation pacifique; là, partout, je les ai vus bons et presque fraternels envers les plus humbles Chinois. Puisse mon livre contribuer pour sa petite part à détruire d'indignes légendes éditées contre eux!" (Thus, I was only able to observe our soldiers during the period of peaceful occupation; then, everywhere, I saw them nice and almost fraternal toward the humblest Chinese. May my book contribute by its small share to destroy unworthy legends published against them!) (Loti, *Les Derniers jours de Pékin*, ii, quoted in Torres-Pou, *Asia en la España del siglo XIX*, 79 n. 12).

46. Torres-Pou, *Asia en la España del siglo XIX*, 63.

47. "Civilizadas y por civilizar," *La Correspondencia Militar*, May 31, 1901, 1. Similar pieces were published in other media. See, for instance: *El Motín*, June 22, 1901, 1.

48. St. André, *Translating China*, 23. There is a long list of texts that feature a visitor from another more civilized country visiting France, England, or other European countries and passing judgment on various facets of their civilization. Among others in which the visitor comes from China: Marquis d'Argens, *Lettres chinoises* (1739–1740); Walpole, *Letter from Xo-Ho* (1757); and Goldsmith, *Citizen of the World* (1762). In Spain, Fernando Garrido, *Viajes del chino Dagar-Li-Kao por los países bárbaros de Europa, España, Francia, Inglaterra y otros* (Madrid: Manuel Minuesa de los Rios, 1880).

49. The life and works of Chen Jitong have been analyzed by Catherine Vance Yeh, "The Life-Style of Four Wenren in Late Qing Shanghai," *Harvard Journal of Asiatic Studies* 57, no. 2 (1997): 419–70; Yinde Zhang, "Pour une archéologie de la francophonie chinoise: le cas de Tcheng Ki-tong," *Revue de littérature comparée* 339, no. 3 (2011): 289–300; Jing Tsu, *Sound and Script in Chinese Diaspora* (Cambridge, MA: Harvard University Press, 2011), chapter 5; Ke Ren, "Fin-de-Siècle Diplomat: Chen Jitong (1852–1907) and Cosmopolitan Possibilities in the Late Qing World" (PhD diss., Johns Hopkins University, 2014); Ke Ren, "Chen Jitong, Les Parisiens Peints Par Un Chinois, and the Literary Self-Fashioning of a Chinese Boulevardier in Fin-de-Siècle Paris," *Esprit créateur* 56, no. 3 (2016): 90–103.

50. Jing Tsu, *Sound and Script in Chinese Diaspora*, 119.

51. *Les Chinois peints par eux-mêmes* (Paris: Calmann-Lévy, 1884), *Le Théâtre des Chinois: Étude de moeurs comparées* (Paris: Calmann-Lévy, 1886),

Contes chinois (Paris: Calmann-Lévy, 1889), *Les Plaisirs en Chine* (Paris: Charpentier et Cie, 1890), *Le Roman de l'homme jaune: Moeurs chinoises* (Paris: Bibliothèque-Charpentier, 1891), *Les Parisiens peints par un Chinois* (Paris: Charpentier, 1891), *Mon pays, la Chine d'aujourd'hui* (Paris: Charpentier et Fasquelle, 1892).

52. Arvède Barine, review of *Les Chinois peints par eux-mêmes*, *Revue politique et littéraire*, October 25, 1884, quoted in Ke Ren, "Fin-de-Siècle Diplomat," 89.

53. Ki-tong Tcheng [Chen Jitong], *The Chinese Painted by Themselves*, trans. James Millington (London: Field and Tuer, 1885); *Kina og Kineserne*, trans. M. Ottesen (København: Schou, 1886); *China und die Chinesen*, trans. Adolph Schulze (Dresden und Leipzig: C. Reissner, 1896). Some scholars mention a Swedish and an Italian version, but I have not been able to locate them.

54. *El Pabellón Nacional*, July 31, 1883, 3.

55. Chen's role as negotiator in the Sino-French War of 1894 was also widely reported. See: *La Publicidad*, August 25, 1884, 1; *La Época*, September 12, 1884, 3; *El Correo Militar*, February 14, 1885, 1; *La Época*, April 4, 1885, 1

56. *El Imparcial*, April 13, 1885, 4.

57. Tcheng-Ki-Tong [Chen Jitong], *La China contemporánea* (Madrid: La España Moderna, 1894); Chen's *Los chinos pintados por sí mismos* was published in a volume that also included Paul Bonnetain's *La China y los chinos: Viaje y descripción de aquel imperio* (China and the Chinese: Travel and Description of That Empire) (Madrid: Nuevo Mundo, 1901).

58. A typical example would be: "Son por demás curiosas é instructivas las noticias comunicadas por la prensa francesa acerca de una conferencia sobre la China, dada recientemente en París por el general Tcheng-ki-Tong [Chen Jitong]; y seguramente causarán extrañeza á los economistas, que no comprenden cómo un país cerrado, hasta hace pocos años, al comercio exterior, pueda haber crecido en riqueza y civilización. Hé aquí, sin embargo, lo que es aquel pueblo, generalmente mal conocido, y al que sólo le ha faltado un alfabeto para colocarse, desde muchos siglos ha, muy por encima de Europa. Mientras los pueblos de Occidente se legan sucesivamente los tesoros artísticos y literarios que les dan renombre, ha dicho el general conferenciante, nuestro pueblo se educa á sí mismo bajo la dirección de la naturaleza" (The news reported by the French press about a conference on China, recently given in Paris by General Tcheng-Ki-Tong [Chen Jitong], are curious and instructive. And they will surely cause surprise to economists, who do not understand how a country closed to foreign trade until only a few years ago can have grown in wealth and civilization. But here it is—a people generally poorly known and lacking only an alphabet to stand well above Europe as it was the case for many centuries. While the peoples of the West successively pass on themselves the artistic and literary treasures that make them famous, the general said in his lecture, our people educate themselves under the guidance of nature). Then the text goes on with a three-page literal quotation of Chen's speech. *El Eco de la producción*, December 25, 1885, 736–38. A similar text can be found in *El Diluvio*, December 26, 1885, 10311–13, with a three-page quotation.

59. *Diario Oficial de Avisos de Madrid*, August 5, 1889, 3; *La Justicia*, October 3, 1889, 2; *La Ilustración Española y Americana*, October 22, 1889, 14; and also in *El Diluvio*, October 22, 1889), with identical text.

60. *La Dinastía*, June 12, 1884, 3638–39; *Revista de España*, May–June 1884; *El Globo*, June 14, 1884, 1–2; *El Día*, June 22, 1884, 4; *Revista Contemporánea*, July–August 1884, 502–4. For example, a typical paragraph read: "En cuanto al periodismo, el agregado á la embajada dice, que en China no puede fundarse ningún diario, por la sencilla razón que no existe la libertad de imprenta. Sin embargo, añade, desde hace muchos siglos funciona un Consejo permanente compuesto de doce miembros, llamados censores, el cual Consejo, tiene por objeto presentar al Soberano, informes sobre el estado de la opinión en las diversas provincias del imperio. Estos informes constituyen un periódico cuyos únicos lectores son los altos dignatarios de la Corte. Más tarde, se dio mayor publicidad á los expresados escritos y hoy se insertan en *La Gaceta de Pekín*" (As for journalism, the attaché argues that no newspaper can be established in China, for the simple reason that there is no freedom of the press. However, he adds, for many centuries there has been a permanent Council made up of twelve members, called censors, whose aim is to present to the Sovereign reports on the state of opinion in the various provinces of the empire. These reports constitute a newspaper itself whose only readers are the highest dignitaries of the Court. Later, these writings were given wider publicity and today they are inserted in *Beijing Gazette*) (*La Dinastía*, June 12, 1884, 3639).

61. *La Época*, August 22, 1889, 4; *El Día*, September 28, 1890, 2.

62. *Les Plaisirs en Chine* was later translated in the journal *La España Moderna* as "Los placeres en China," published in four installments between September and December 1900: September 1900, 5–41; October 1900, 34–66; November 1900, 5–34; and December 1900; 28–55. Also: "La cocina china," *El Diluvio*, January 11, 1901, 4–5; "La jardineria en China," *El Diluvio*, January 21, 1901, 12–13; "La vida es sueño," *El Diluvio*, January 21, 1895, 4, translated later in *Revista Contemporánea*, January 15, 1904, 279–84, in this case with the annotation "Traducción de A. G.-B." (Translated by A. G.-B.).

63. "They moved in the direction of homogenizing tastes, prices, and technical and scientific advances, though there was resistance as well as acquiescence. Scandals, riots, and disasters as well as celebrities and fashion became known throughout the Western urbane world" (Topik and Wells, "Commodity Chains in a Global Economy," 662).

64. *El Liberal*, July 18, 1884, 1.

65. A typical example is: "*El Fígaro*, de París, publica una notable frase de Tcheng-Ki-Tong [Chen Jitong], el ingenioso agregado militar de China en Francia, que está publicando notables artículos acerca de su país en la *Revista de Ambos Mundos*. Hallábase en un salón donde la conversación había tomado un carácter muy tierno. Una dama que sabía que el diplomático militar posee con perfección varios idiomas, le preguntó que cuál empleaba con preferencia para hablar de amor. —Ninguno, señora, contestó Tcheng-Ki-Tong, en esos momentos el salvaje recobra sus derechos. Como se vé, no es muy platónico el amor á el chino, que no dejó de estar en boga alguna temporada en Madrid" (The *Figaro*

in Paris publishes a remarkable sentence from Tcheng-Ki-Tong [Chen Jitong], China's witty military attaché in France, who is publishing outstanding articles about his country in the *Revue des Deux Mondes*. Tcheng was in a room where the conversation had taken on a very delicate tone. A lady who knew that the military diplomat speaks several languages perfectly, asked him which language he preferred to speak of love. "None, ma'am," replied Tcheng-Ki-Tong, "when speaking of love the savage regains his rights." As you can see, the Chinese love is not very platonic, something which was also in vogue in Madrid for some time) (*El Día*, June 22, 1884, 4).

66. *La Época*, April 21, 1890, 2.

67. "De la noche á la mañana, el General fué llamado por su Gobierno á Pekín, y con motivo de su viaje han comenzado á correr en la capital de la vecina República los rumores más sinistros. El pobre General parece que á estas horas no debe tener muy segura la cabeza sobre sus hombros, si es que ya tiene hombros y cabeza" (Overnight, the General was called by his government to Beijing. On the occasion of his trip the most sinister rumors began to spread in the capital of our neighboring Republic. It seems that at this time the poor General's head may not be very safe above his shoulders, assuming that he still has shoulders and head) (*El Heraldo de Madrid*, July 6, 1891, 1). Similar news, sometimes with identic text can also be found in *El Diluvio*, July 9, 1891, 5665, under the title: "Como las gastan en China" (The Chinese Have a Nerve).

68. The report continued: "Es cierto que el General ha sido encarcelado á su llegada á Fon-Tcheou, hace seis semanas, y que se ha comenzado su proceso; pero aunque el Código chino tiene suplicios cruelísimos para los concusionarios, el Marqués no está amenazado ni de ser decapitado ni ahorcado. . . . Las faltas de Tcheng-Ki-Tong [Chen Jitong] consisten, sobre todo, en promesas imprudentes de concesiones, mediante comisión, por supuesto, y en deudas. Será degradado, desterrado, acaso condenado á algunos meses de prisión, pero nada más. Y hasta es posible que, teniendo en cuenta les progresos hechos por la civilización occidental en China, le acuerden sus jueces circunstancias atenuantes" (It is true that the General was imprisoned upon his arrival at Fon-Tcheou six weeks ago. And that his trial has begun. But although the Chinese laws include cruel torture for the extortioners, the marquis is not under threat of being beheaded or hanged. . . . Tcheng-Ki-Tong [Chen Jitong]'s faults consist, above all, of reckless promises of concessions, through commission, of course, and debts. He will be demoted, banished, perhaps even sentenced to a few months in prison, but nothing more. And it is even possible that, taking into account the progress made by Western civilization in China, his judges may grant him mitigating circumstances) (*El Heraldo de Madrid*, July 17, 1891, 1). Identical text in: *Diario Oficial de Avisos de Madrid*, July 20, 1891, 3.

69. *La Época*, June 6, 1895, 1.

70. *La Correspondencia de España*, March 12, 1907, 1–2; Fabián Vidal described Chen almost as a hero: "Ha muerto en Nankín el general chino Tcheng-Ki-Tong [Chen Jitong]. ¿Bueno—dirán mis lectores—y qué nos importa eso? A Dios gracias, nos separan de China mares lo bastante anchos para que no prestemos atención a lo que allí suceda. Pero es el caso, que Tcheng-Ki-Tong no era un chino como los otros" (Chinese General Tcheng-Ki-Tong [Chen Jitong] has

died in Nanking. Well—my readers will say—and what do we care about that? Thank God, there are seas wide enough to keep us separate from China, so let us not pay attention to what happens there. But it happens that Tcheng-Ki-Tong was not a Chinese like the rest).

71. See particularly: Ke Ren, "Fin-de-Siècle Diplomat," and Ke Ren, "Chen Jitong."

72. For example, when the Qing government declined the invitation to participate in the 1889 Exposition Universelle due to a lack of funds, Chen decided to act as China's representative in a Chinese pavilion put together at the last minute by a French architect. Chen also participated in a series of conferences and scientific talks that were part of the exhibition program. Ke Ren, "Fin-de-Siècle Diplomat," 190.

73. Ke Ren, "Chen Jitong," 92.

74. Ke Ren, "Chen Jitong," 91.

75. An example that synthesizes these points is the review: "The Chinese as They Are," *The Literary World: A Monthly Review of Current Literature*, May 20, 1885, quoted in Ke Ren, "Chen Jitong," 89.

76. Chen's case coincides with the strategy of "masquerade" that, according to James St. André, was followed by Lin Yutang and Gu Hongming as translators or cross-cultural performers "who found a voice in English through the conscious adoption of existing notions of Chineseness and Chinese culture" (St. André, *Translating China*, 162). "In order to have their works accepted by a European and American audience, both writers resorted to masquerade; effectively giving their publishers and readers what they wanted, they conformed to certain stereotypes of who the Chinese were, while at the same time betraying a certain anxiety about their 'Chinese' role" (160).

77. Tcheng [Chen], *Les Chinois peints par eux-mêmes*, vii, my emphasis.

78. Tcheng [Chen], *Les Chinois peints par eux-mêmes*, viii, languages not capitalized in the original.

79. Ke Ren, "Chen Jitong," 92.

80. Jing Tsu, *Sound and Script in Chinese Diaspora*, 121.

81. *La Época*, August 22, 1889, 4.

82. *El Día*, September 28, 2.

83. Tcheng [Chen], *La China contemporánea*.

84. A typical example would be: "El periódico alemán *Frankfurter Zeitung* publica una entrevista tenida por uno de los redactores con el general chino Lin-Tcheng, que marchaba a Londres" (The German newspaper *Frankfurter Zeitung* publishes an interview between one of the editors and the Chinese General Lin-Tcheng, who was leaving for London), which is followed by a translation of the interview. *El Diluvio*, September 23, 1894, 16–17.

85. As an example, Chen "no ha podido llevar con paciencia el concepto que la OBRA DE LA SANTA INFANCIA ha hecho formar de los padres y madres chinos, y ha querido rectificarlos, ilustrando á los europeos sobre las costumbres de su país" (has been unable to bear with patience the image that the OBRA DE LA SANTA INFANCIA has disseminated about the Chinese fathers and mothers; he wanted to correct them, showing to Europeans the customs of his country). Then the text quotes Chen himself, saying that the ideas spread

across Europe about Chinese families abandoning children are false. *El Liberal*, July 18, 1884, 1.

86. As an example: "Se quejó el general chino Tcheng-Ki-Tong [Chen Jitong], en la sesión de la Sorbona que hemos mencionado, de que las escuelas francesas de la China no admitan más que los conversos, se lamentó de que los chinos tuvieran que aprender el francés, leyendo obras contrarias a su religión, tratados políticos opuestos al régimen del Celeste Imperio, lo cual hace poco simpáticos a los franceses entre los naturales de su país. Invitó el diplomático chino los franceses que estudiaran su lengua, la más generalizada del mundo que la hablan más de 400 millones de hombres" (During the Sorbonne session that we have mentioned, the Chinese General Tcheng-Ki-Tong [Chen Jitong] complained that French schools in China only admit converts, he lamented that the Chinese had to learn French too, had to read works contrary to their religion, political treaties opposed to the regime of the Celestial Empire, something which makes the French unfriendly among the natives of his country. The Chinese diplomat also invited the French to study Chinese, the most widespread language in the world, spoken by more than 400 million people.) *El Barcelonés*, February 22, 1889, 1.

87. Tcheng [Chen], *Les Chinois peints par eux-mêmes*, iii and vi.

88. *La Monarquía*, August 8, 1890, 1. Similar claims in: *La Ilustración Artística*, July 23, 1900, 2.

89. Felipe Fernández-Armesto, *Pathfinders: A Global History of Exploration* (New York: Norton, 2006), 385.

90. Mentaberry, *Impresiones de un viaje a la China*, 7.

91. Garrido, *Viajes del chino Dagar-Li-Kao*, 15.

92. Valera, *Sombras chinescas*, 99.

93. Auñón, *El combate naval de Ya-Lu*, 10, my emphasis.

94. Fernando de Antón del Olmet, *El problema de la China* (Madrid: Imprenta y Litografía del Depósito de la Guerra, 1901), 21. Hereafter I will add page numbers within parentheses after the quotations.

95. Fernando de Antón del Olmet, "Un cotillón en Pekín," *La Ilustración Española y Americana*, August 22, 1900, 103.

96. See, for example: "Impresiones de un diplomático," *El Defensor de Córdoba*, July 31, 1900; "Los miembros del cuerpo diplomático en Pekín," *La Verdad*, August 8, 1900; "El Club de Pekín," *La Correspondencia de España*, August 11, 1900; "La prensa en China," *África: Periódico Semanal de Las Posesiones Españolas*, August 11, 1900; "La legación inglesa en Pekín," *La Correspondencia de España*, August 28, 1900; "Impresiones de un diplomático: Psicología china," *El Defensor de Córdoba*, August 31, 1900; "Impresiones de un diplomático: Costumbres chinas," *El Defensor de Córdoba*, September 18, 1900; "Recuerdos de China: Pao-Tieen-Fu," *El Guadalete*, September 23, 1900; "La legación de Francia en Pekín," *La Correspondencia de España*, November 15, 1900; "Recuerdos de Pekín: La legación de Alemania," *La Correspondencia de España*, November 28, 1900; "Recuerdos de China: La legación de Rusia," *La Correspondencia de España*, December 26, 1900; "Recuerdos de China: La legación de Italia," *La Correspondencia de España*, January 11, 1901; "Recuerdos de China: El Gran Hotel," *La Correspondencia de España*, February 19, 1901; "Recuerdos de China: El Templo del Cielo," *La Correspondencia de*

España, February, 28, 1901; "Recuerdos de China: El club de los maridos," *El Defensor de Córdoba*, April 16, 1901; "Recuerdos de China: La tumba de la princesa," *La Correspondencia de España*, May 22, 1901.

97. Real Sociedad Geográfica, *Boletín de la Real Sociedad Geográfica*, vol. 43, 1901.

98. He mentions: Conde de la Viñaza, *Escritos de los portugueses y castellanos referentes á las lenguas de China y el Japón*; Cobo, *Beng-Sim-po-cam ó Espejo rico del claro corazón*; González de Mendoza, *Historia de las cosas más notables, sitios y costumbres del gran reino de la China*; Fernández de Navarrete, *Tratados históricos, políticos, éticos y religiosos de la Monarquía de la China*; Ribadeneyra, *Historia de la China y la Tartaria*; Herrera Dávila, *Lecciones de historia del Imperio Chino*; Mas, *La Chine et les puissances chrétiennes*; de Aguilar, *El intérprete chino*; Toda, *La vida en el Celeste Imperio*; Mentaberry, *Impresiones de un viaje a la China*; Marqués de Prat, *Serie de cartas sobre China*; Álvarez y Tejero, *Reseña histórica del gran imperio de China*.

99. "El famoso escritor Pierre Loti, de la Academia francesa, en una de sus correspondencias escritas y fechadas . . . en Pekín (Martes 22 de Octubre), publicadas en *Le Fígaro* (núm. de 25 de Agosto), relata su entrada en el Panteón imperial de Palacio. Describe primero las maravillas inimaginables que contempla, hundiendo sus pies en medio metro de polvo formado por los restos de joyas de nácar y de perlas, y luego exclama: '¡Penetro en uno de los Santuarios más sagrados—el del Emperador Kuang-Sü—cuya gloria resplandecía en los comienzos del siglo XVIII! . . .' Kuang-Sü es el nombre del Emperador actual, y, por lo menos, desde 1600 hasta hoy, no ha habido en China Emperador alguno de tal nombre" (The famous writer Pierre Loti, member of the French Academy, in one of his correspondences . . . written and dated in Beijing [Tuesday, October 22] and published in *Le Figaro* [August 25 issue], describes his entry in the Pantheon of the Imperial Palace. He first describes the unimaginable wonders he is contemplating while he sinks his feet into half a meter of dust formed by the remains of pearls and mother-of-pearls, and then he exclaims: "I am entering one of the most sacred Shrines— that of the Emperor Kuang-Sü—whose glory was already shining at the beginning of the eighteenth century! . . ." Kuang-Sü is the name of the current Emperor, and, at least from 1600 until today, there has been no Emperor of this name in China) (113).

100. Rosenberg, *A World Connecting*, 851.

101. Antón del Olmet quotes: *Antiguas relaciones de la China de dos viajeros mahometanos* (he explicitly mentions that it was published by Renaudot in 1718), *El libro de Marco Polo* (he mentions Pauthier's version of 1863), and Ibn-Battuta's diary.

102. Antón del Olmet lists the following works: Webbs, *Ensayo histórico*; Chambers, *Dibujos chinos*; Isbrants, *Tres años en China*; Anderson, *Relación de la embajada de Lord Macartney*; Oliphant, *China y el Japón*; Staunton, *Viaje al interior de la China*; Edkins, *Religión en China*; Davis, *China*; Gilles, *Esbozos chinos*; Mooreroft, *Investigaciones asiáticas*; Martin, *Los chinos*; Williamson, *Viajes al Norte de China*; Meadows, *Los chinos y sus rebeliones*; Hodgson, *Ensayo sobre la lengua, la literatura y la religión del Tibet*; Barrow, *Viajes á China*; Milne, *Vida real en China*; Allen, *Informe sobre los tribunales mixtos*

de Shanghai; Kaw, *Descripción de la China*; Cooper, *China*; Chalmers, *Origen de los chinos*; List, *China y Japón*; Williams, *El Imperio del Medio*; Lord Beresford, *La China abierta*; Chester Holcombe, *El verdadero hombre chino*; and Smith, *Características chinas*. He also mentions the following authors: Bridgman, Langdon, Gill, Wade, King, Wolseley, Lord Curzon, and Robert Hart. Here and in the following references Antón del Olmet mentions their titles in Spanish, even if these works had not been published in Spanish—a practice that indicates how naturally accepted the reliance upon foreign sources was.

103. He lists the following works: Trigault, *Historia de la China*; *Memorias de los Misioneros de Pekín*; *Cartas edificantes*; Du Halde, *Descripción del Imperio de la China*; Mailla, *Historia general de la China*; Vojeu de Brunem, *Conquista de la China*; Helman, *Victorias y conquistas del Imperio chino*; Rémusat, *Ensayo y Descripción de la China*; Jurien de la Gravière, *Viaje*; Pellé, *La China pintoresca*; Pauthier, *La China*; Girard, *Vida pública y privada de los chinos*; Paléologue, *El arte chino*; Lavollée, *La China contemporánea*; Marqués de Moges, *Recuerdos de una embajada China*; Mgr. Reynaud, *Una China distinta*; Robin, *Instituciones de la China*; Rousset, *A través de la China*; Conde d'Escayrac de Lauture, *Memorias sobre la China*; Amiot, *Memorias referentes á los chinos*; Huc, *El Imperio chino* and *Recuerdos de un viaje á China*; Conde de Rochechouart, *Pekín y el interior de la China*; Lecomte, *Nuevas memorias sobre el estado de China*; Simón, *Relaciones de un viaje á China*; David, *Diario de un tercer viaje á China*; Pallu, *Relación de la expedición de China*; Poussielgue, *Viaje á la China*; Bard, *Chinos* and *Los Chinos en casa*; and Mgr. Favier, *Pekín*. He also mentions the following authors: Leroy-Boileau, Bazancourt, Montrecy, Labrosse, Biot, Julien, Bazin, and Champion.

104. He lists the following works: Halde, *China*; Barón de Hübner, *Viaje por la China*; Bretschneider, *La llanura pekinesa*; Bastian, *Viaje á China*; Ritter, *Asia*; Hiekisch, *Los tungusos*; Schott, *Kitay y Kiarakitay*; Plath, *La agricultura de los chinos*; Neumann, *Historia del Asia Oriental*; Pzimaier, *La Corea*; Richthofen, *China*; Katschen, *Cuadros de la vida china*; Werner, *La expedición prusiana en China*; Hesse-Wartegg, *El Shantung y la China alemana*; and Franzius, *Kiochao*. He also mentions the following authors: Köppen, Von Brandt, Meyen, Schlagintweit, Walker, Regel, Klöden, Schiern, Finsch, and Ratzel. He also mentions the following Austrian authors: Szecheni and Kreiner.

105. He lists the following works: Piasetsky, *Viaje á China*; Vasilijev, *Historia de la literatura china*; Zakharov, *Trabajos de la Legación rusa en Pekín*; Semonov, *Suplemento á la obra de Ritter*; Intorcetta, *La Misión china*; Orazio della Penna, *Breve notícia del reino del Tibet*; Viviani, *Historia de la China*; Gherdardini, *Relación*; Ferrari, *China y Europa*; Barón Vitale, *Rimas pekinesas (folklore chino)*; Caldeira, *China*; and Van Braan, *China*. He also mentions the following authors: Fedtchenko and Koupatkin (on Turkestan), Sosnowsky and Prjevalsky (on Mongolia), Metchikow, Syrsky, Martino Martini, and Ricci. He also refers to Conde de la Viñaza's bibliography of works written by Portuguese missionaries.

106. It includes: "Memoria presentada á las Cortes Constituyentes, 24 de febrero de 1869" (Report presented to the Constituent Assembly, February 24, 1869); "Protocolo presentado a Li-Hun-Chang y el Príncipe Ching, Plenipo-

tenciarios de China, por el Cuerpo Diplomático en Pekín en la Nota colectiva de 22 de Diciembre" (Protocol presented to Chinese Plenipotentiaries Li Hong-zhang and Prince Qing by the Diplomatic Corps in Peking in the Collective Note on December 22); "Sobre: 'Una correspondencia desde Pekín' de Pierre Loti;'" (About: Pierre Loti's "A Correspondence from Peking"); and "Texto, en extracto, del Tratado entre Alemania y la China, relativo á la cesión del arrendamiento (bail) de Kiaochao, 6 de Marzo de 1898" (Abstract of the Treaty between Germany and China, related to the leased territory of Jiaozhou, March 6, 1898).

107. María Dolores Domingo Acebrón, *Rafael María de Labra: Cuba, Puerto Rico, Las Filipinas, Europa y Marruecos, en la España del sexenio democrático y la restauración (1871–1918)* (Madrid: Editorial CSIC, 2006).

108. On page 20 he quotes works by H. Cordier, Leroy de Beulien, Courant, L'Abbé Huc (French); John H. Gray, Krause, Parker, Holcombe (English and American); and Enlers (German).

109. Antón del Olmet would later publish *El alma nacional: Genealogía psicológica del pueblo español* (Madrid: Imprenta Cervantina, 1915), where he claims for a Spanish national regeneration based on Iberian nationalism and the "afirmación de nuestra personalidad castiza, la reintegración de nuestra espiritualidad, la vuelta a nuestro pasado histórico" (affirmation of our pure-blood personality, the reintegration of our spirituality, the return to our historical past). Vicente Blasco Ibáñez, "Cartas Inéditas de Vicente Blasco Ibáñez a Fernando Antón del Olmet (1924–1926)," ed. José Luis Molina Martínez (Alicante: Biblioteca Virtual Miguel de Cervantes, 2017), 112. According to his own views in the correspondence with Vicente Blasco Ibáñez, Antón del Olmet conceived this movement in 1900 after his experience in Beijing and the reflections included in *El problema de la China*.

CHAPTER 3

1. John Dewey, Harriet Alice (Chipman) Dewey, and Evelyn Dewey, *Letters from China and Japan* (New York: E. P. Dutton Company, 1920), 184.

2. Dewey, *Letters from China and Japan*, 184.

3. An excellent summary can be found in: Jessica Ching-Sze Wang, *John Dewey in China: To Teach and to Learn* (Albany, NY: State University of New York Press, 2007).

4. Wang, *John Dewey in China*, 4.

5. Wang, *John Dewey in China*, 3.

6. Wang, *John Dewey in China*, 5.

7. Wang, *John Dewey in China*, chapter 3. See also: Han-Liang Chang, "Hu Shih and John Dewey: 'Scientific Method' in the May Fourth Era-China," *Comparative Criticism* 22 (2000): 91–103; Takeuchi Yoshimi, *What Is Modernity?: Writings of Takeuchi Yoshimi*, ed. and trans. Richard Calichman (New York: Columbia University Press, 2005), chapter 4.

8. Wang, *John Dewey in China*, especially chapter 5.

9. Wang, *John Dewey in China*, 7.

10. Tom Buchanan, *East Wind: China and the British Left, 1925–1976* (Oxford: Oxford University Press, 2012), ix, viii–xix.

11. Blue, "China and Western Social Thought in the Modern Period," 84.

12. Albert Einstein, *The Travel Diaries of Albert Einstein: The Far East, Palestine, and Spain, 1922–1923*, ed. Ze'ev Rosenkranz (Princeton, NJ, and Oxford: Princeton University Press, 2018), for example: 125, 129, 131, 133, 135.

13. St. André, *Translating China*, 17, 57.

14. William Somerset Maugham, *On a Chinese Screen* (London: Vintage, 2000), 2.

15. *North China Herald*, December 22, 1923, 840.

16. Maugham, *On a Chinese Screen*, 34.

17. Rosenberg, *A World Connecting*, 960.

18. Rosenberg, *A World Connecting*, 900, 938. Rosenberg mentions specifically the popularity of Arthur de Gobineau's *Essai sur l'inégalité des races humaines*, originally published in 1853.

19. Paul Smethurst, introduction to *Travel Writing, Form, and Empire: The Poetics and Politics of Mobility*, eds. Julia Kuehn and Paul Smethurst (New York and London: Routledge, 2008), 2; Steve Clark, introduction to *Travel Writing and Empire: Postcolonial Theory in Transit*, ed. Steve Clark (London and New York: Zed Books, 1999), 3.

20. X. Y. Z. [Amado Nervo], "La China vieja y la nueva: Un país en transformación," *Por Esos Mundos*, December 1911, 7.

21. X. Y. Z. [Amado Nervo], "La China vieja y la nueva," 7–8.

22. X. Y. Z. [Amado Nervo], "La China vieja y la nueva," 17.

23. X. Y. Z. [Amado Nervo], "La China vieja y la nueva," 17.

24. These juxtapositions became a global tendency derived from the use of photography for domination and the spread of Western civilization: "juxtapositions of traditional lifestyles with the machines of modernity—autos, cameras, record players—became stock favorites" (Rosenberg, *A World Connecting*, 854).

25. X. Y. Z. [Amado Nervo], "La China vieja y la nueva," 16.

26. So, *Transpacific Community*. See also: Hsu, *A Floating Chinaman*.

27. Charles Burdett and Derek Duncan, introduction to *Cultural Encounters: European Travel Writing in the 1930s*, eds. Charles Burdett and Derek Duncan (New York and Oxford: Berghahn Books, 2002), 5. For a quick outline of Chinese migration to Europe, see: Frank N. Pieke, introduction to *The Chinese in Europe*, eds. Gregor Benton and Frank N. Pieke (London: Palgrave Macmillan, 1998), 3–9.

28. Tagore traveled to Europe in June 1912. He was awarded the Nobel Prize for Literature in November 1913. He then became a global phenomenon as he visited Europe, the United States, and Latin America in different travels: 1916–1917, 1924, and 1930, respectively.

29. Jonathan D. Spence, *The Search for Modern China* (New York: Norton, 1999), 285–88.

30. Buchanan, *East Wind*.

31. X. Y. Z. [Amado Nervo], "La China vieja y la nueva," 17.

32. As we will see, Blasco Ibáñez's depictions of China were translated into English and French, and Oteyza's novel had also a significant trajectory in translation.

33. Ricardo Llopesa, "Orientalismo y Modernismo," *Anales de Literatura Hispanoamericana* 25 (1996): 171–80.

34. The quotation is from Lorca's last interview before being killed at the beginning of the Spanish Civil War: "Diálogos de un caricaturista salvaje: Federico García Lorca habla sobre la riqueza poética y vital mayor de España," *El Sol*, June 10, 1936, 5. I thank Yue Zhang for bringing this interview to my attention. The presence of Chinese imagery in Lorca's works has only recently been studied. See: Yue Zhang, "'El chino lloraba en el tejado.' La mitad marginada en *Danza de la muerte* de Federico García Lorca," in *Nuevas Perspectivas Literarias y Culturales II*, eds. Rocío Hernández Arias, Gabriela Rivera Rodríguez, and María Teresa del Préstamos Landín (Vigo: MACC-ELICIN, 2017), 33–41; Yue Zhang, "Evolución de las imágenes chinas en la poesía de Lorca," *Círculo de Lingüística Aplicada a la Comunicación* 74 (June 1, 2018): 133–46. For the role played by China in Catalan poetry around the same time, see chapter 4.

35. Juvencio Hospital, *Notas y escenas de viaje: Cartas del Extremo Oriente* (Barcelona: Nicolás Poncell, 1914); Agustín Melcón, *Páginas de la última revolución china* (Madrid: Imprenta del Asilo de Huerfanos del S.C. de Jesús, 1914); Antonio de Santa María, *Relación de la persecución en China (1644–1666)* (Madrid: Gabriel López del Horno, 1915); Dominicos del Santísimo Rosario de Filipinas, *Los Dominicos en el Extremo Oriente: Relaciones publicadas con motivo del séptimo centenario de la confirmación de la Sagrada Orden de Predicadores* (Barcelona: Seix Barral, 1916); Otto Maas, *Cartas de China: Documentos inéditos sobre misiones franciscanas del S. XVII y XVIII* (Sevilla: Antigua Casa de Izquierdo y Compañía, 1917); Enrique Heras, *La dinastía manchú en China: Historia de la última dinastía imperial y en particular de sus relaciones con el cristianismo y la civilización europea* (Barcelona: Lib. y Tip. Católica de Hijo de M. Casals, 1918); Bernardo Martínez, *Historia de las misiones agustinianas en China* (Madrid: Imprenta del Asilo de Huérfanos del S.C. de Jesús, 1918); Lorenzo Pérez, *Origen de las misiones franciscanas en la provincia de Kwang-tung (China)* (Madrid: Imprenta de G. López del Horno, 1918); José María de Iruarrizaga, *Religiones dominantes en China: Observaciones hechas y tomadas sobre el terreno por el P. José María Iruarrizaga, franciscano misionero apostólico en Shensi* (Guernica: Goitia y Hermaechea, 1922); Joseph Spillmann, *Los Hermanos Yang y los Boxers: Episodio de los últimos desórdenes ocurridos en China* (Friburgo de Brisgovia: Herder, 1923); Zenón Aramburu, *El vicariato de Ngan-hoei, China* (Shanghai: Zikawei, 1924); Jaime Masip, *Por tierras del extremo Oriente (China. Japón. Indochina): Conferencias sobre las misiones católicas en tierras de infieles* (Madrid: B. del Amo, 1929).

36. Francesc Darder i Llimona, *Piscicultura fluvial y doméstica en China* (Barcelona: Imprenta Hijos de D. Casanovas, 1913); Carlos de Sostoa, *La industria casera de las pajas trenzadas en China* (Madrid: Centro de Información Comercial del Ministerio de Estado, 1913); Pedro Cerezal, *Breve estudio sobre la música china* (Madrid: Imprenta del Asilo de Huérfanos, 1914); Gaudencio Castrillo, *El comercio en el Extermo Oriente* (Madrid: Asilo de Huérfanos, 1918); Julio Palencia y Tubau, *El haba soya de Manchuria* (Madrid: Imprenta

del Ministerio de Estado, 1919); Joan Sacs, *El mueble de la China* (Barcelona: Librería Catalonia, 1920).

37. Richard Wilhelm, *Kung-Tsé*, trans. A. García-Molins (Madrid: Revista de Occidente, 1926); Richard Wilhelm, *Laotsé y El Taoismo*, trans. A. García-Molins (Madrid: Revista de Occidente, 1926). Other works providing general surveys on religious topics: Confucio. *El evangelio de Confucio* (Barcelona: B. Bauzá, ca. 1920); Arthur Arnould, *Las creencias fundamentales del Budismo* (Barcelona: Editorial Teosófica, 1922).

38. Augusto Riera, *La guerra ruso-japonesa: Del Yalú al Mukden* (Barcelona: Maucci, 1915); Augusto Riera, *La guerra ruso-japonesa: De Mukden a la paz* (Barcelona: Maucci, 1915); Albert Londres and Gonzalo de Reparaz, *China en ascuas: El peligro amarillo en marcha* (Barcelona: Mentora, 1927); José Revuelta Blanco, *La Revolución comunista en China: Sus causas y efectos* (El Escorial: Imprenta del Real Monasterio, 1927); Juan Andrade, *China contra el imperialismo* (Madrid: Ediciones Oriente, 1928); Augusto Riera, *China en llamas* (Barcelona: Iberia, 1928).

39. Princesa Der Ling, *China: Dos años en la Ciudad Prohibida. Vida íntima de la emperatriz Tzu Hsi*, trans. José Pérez Hervás (Barcelona: Montaner y Simón, 1913); *Chung-Kuei, domador de demonios* (Madrid: Revista de Occidente, 1929); John Colton, *Shanghai: Comedia dramática, en tres actos*, trans. Arturo Mori (Madrid: Rivadeneyra, 1930). Other similar works: Emilio Sevilla Richart, *La hija del cielo: Memorias de una emperatriz: Novela china* (Madrid: Hijos de R. Álvarez, 1912); Domingo de Abril y Alegre, *La boda de Bada con Buda: Antigua leyenda de China* (Madrid: La Novela Alegre, 1920); Pierre Loti, *Pekín* (Barcelona: Cervantes, 1923); *Cuentos populares de China* (Madrid: Revista de Occidente, 1925); Federico García Sanchiz, *La comedianta china (Cantón, 1830)* (Madrid: La Novela Mundial, 1926); Lewis Stanton Palen, *El dragón rojo*, trans. Teodosio Leal y Quiroga (Madrid: M. Aguilar, 1926); Augusto Martínez Olmedilla, *El collar del chino* (Madrid: Atlántida, 1929).

40. Bertrand Russell, *The Problem of China* (London: George Allen and Unwin, 1922), 9.

41. Russell, *The Problem of China*, 9.

42. Russell, *The Problem of China*, 18.

43. Russell, *The Problem of China*, 12, 209.

44. Russell, *The Problem of China*, 213.

45. Russell, *The Problem of China*, 17.

46. Buchanan, *East Wind*, 9, 8.

47. José Ortega y Gasset, "El problema de China. Un libro de Bertrand Russell," *Revista de Occidente* 3 (September 1923): 157.

48. Ortega y Gasset, "El problema de China," 157–58.

49. Ortega y Gasset, "El problema de China," 159.

50. Ortega y Gasset, "El problema de China," 158.

51. Ortega y Gasset, "El problema de China," 160.

52. *El Mercantil* was the most important newspaper read by the Spanish residents in Manila. It was published between 1902 and 1930. José María Romero Salas, *España en China (Crónica de un viaje)* (Manila: García Bosque, Pomar, 1921).

53. Carl Crow, *Four Hundred Million Customers: The Experiences—Some Happy, Some Sad, of an American in China, and What They Taught Him* (New York: Harper and Brothers, 1937).

54. Castrillo, *El comercio en el Extremo Oriente.*

55. Romero Salas, *España en China*, 80, my emphasis.

56. Romero Salas, *España en China*, 77.

57. Romero Salas, *España en China*, 80. The Spanish community in Shanghai at the time was, officially, of 180 residents. However, only thirty were originally from Spain; the rest were natives of the Philippines (16–23).

58. Romero Salas, *España en China*, 81.

59. See, for instance: Romero Salas, *España en China*, 7, 28–29.

60. Eduardo González Calleja and Fredes Limón Nevado, *La hispanidad como instrumento de combate* (Madrid, Consejo Superior de Investigaciones Científicas, Centro de Estudios Históricos, 1988), 8; Joshua Goode, *Impurity of Blood: Defining Race in Spain, 1870–1930* (Baton Rouge, LA: Louisiana State University Press, 2009), 13–14.

61. St. André, *Translating China*, 192. He quotes Elazar Barkan, *The Retreat of Scientific Racism: Changing Concepts of Race in Britain and the United States Between the World Wars* (Cambridge: Cambridge University Press, 1992), 1–6. See also: William H. Tucker, *The Science and Politics of Racial Research* (Urbana, IL, and Chicago: University of Illinois Press, 1994).

62. Stanley Payne, *The Franco Regime, 1936–1975* (Madison: University of Wisconsin Press, 1987), 402 n. 19.

63. In the representations of China by Blasco Ibáñez, García Sanchiz, and Oteyza we can already find, for instance, the same combination that underlies Ramiro de Maeztu's section on the East: the regret for Spain's colonial decadence and the awareness of the dangers of communism are blended with recurrent manifestations of racial incommensurability. Ramiro de Maeztu, *Defensa de la Hispanidad* (Madrid: Ediciones Fax, 1941), 138, 131. In fact, Maeztu argues that Catholicism was the necessary legacy to develop civilization, since Catholicism is based on a hierarchy and enlightened domination that characterize the Spanish method of domination. In contrast, the British method would apparently be more generous but "en realidad, se funda en el absoluto desprecio del pueblo dominador al dominado, ya que lo abandona a su salacidad y propensiones naturales" (in fact, it is based on the dominating people's absolute contempt for the dominated people, since the former abandons the latter to its own lewdness and natural tendencies) (132–34).

64. The competition between García Sanchiz and Blasco Ibáñez was publicly stated by the media. See: "La vida inquieta y compleja de Changhai ha inspirado al novelista español Federico García Sanchiz," *Caras y Caretas*, March 4, 1926. Other works of travel writing that included references to China: Baldomero García Sagastume, *En el extremo Oriente de Tokio á Pekin* (Madrid: Clásica Española, 1916); Juan Potous Martínez, *Mi viaje por China y Japón* (Madrid: Hércules, 1925); Adolfo Bonilla y San Martín, *Viaje a los Estados Unidos de América y al Oriente* (Madrid: Imprenta Viuda e Hijos de Jaime Ratés, 1926); Alexandra David-Neel, *A través de la China misteriosa: Viaje a pie . . . a través del Tibet*, trans. Alejandro Ben (Barcelona: Joaquín Gil, 1929).

65. I have consulted the following contemporary edition: Vicente Blasco Ibáñez, *China* (Madrid: Gadir, 2011). Hereafter I will add page numbers within parentheses after the quotations.

66. Federico García Sanchiz, *La ciudad milagrosa (Shanghai)* (Madrid: V. H. Sanz Calleja, 1926), 10. Hereafter I will add page numbers within parentheses after the quotations.

67. Julio Rodríguez Puértolas, *Historia de la literatura fascista española* (Madrid: Akal, 2008).

68. El Profeta, "D. Federico García Sanchiz en Filipinas," *España y América*, September 30, 1925, 276.

69. El Profeta, "D. Federico García Sanchiz en Filipinas," 277.

70. "Federico García Sanchiz: Semblanza Biográfica," *ABC*, June 12, 1964, 79.

71. José Montero Alonso, "Federico García Sanchiz lleva a su próxima novela la vida inquieta y compleja de Shanghai," *La Libertad*, December 18, 1925, 5.

72. Buchanan, *East Wind*; Manabendra Nath Roy, *Revolución y contrarrevolución en China*, trans. Mariano Alarcón (Madrid: Cénit, 1932).

73. Salvador Garmendia, "Por la ruta imaginaria de Luis de Oteyza," in *Luis de Oteyza, Obras Selectas*, vol. 1 (Caracas: Universidad Católica Andrés Bello, 2000), 15.

74. Oteyza would later publish similar works such as *El tapiz mágico* (1929), *Anticípolis* (1931), and *La tierra es redonda* (1933). He traveled frequently across Latin America both as a diplomat and journalist. After the Spanish Civil War, he finally settled down in Venezuela.

75. Scholars mention two English translations (published by Cassell in London and F. A. Stokes in New York) as well as other translations into Italian, Portuguese, Romanian, Hungarian, Japanese, French, Czech, German, Yugoslavian, and Bulgarian. José Antonio Pérez Bowie, "Presentación," in Luis de Oteyza, *El diablo blanco* (Badajoz: Diputación de Badajoz, 1993), 30. I haven't been able to trace most of these editions. They might have been used by *La Publicidad* to advertise Oteyza's novel at the time of publication. I have traced the following: *The White Devil*, trans. Frederic Taber Cooper (New York: Frederick A. Stokes, 1930); *The White Devil*, trans. Frederic Taber Cooper (London: Cassell and Co., 1931); *A fehér ördög: Regény*, trans. Balogh Barna (Budapest: Légrády, 1931); *Le diable blanc*, trans. Paule Marcel-Lami (Paris: Éditions Colbert, 1947).

76. It was published in the McMillan Hispanic Series in 1932. The edition includes notes, exercises, and vocabulary. Luis de Oteyza, *El diablo blanco*, ed. Willis Knapp Jones (New York: The Macmillan Company, 1932). The foreword and introduction are highly praiseful: "A novel to make students of Spanish wish they did not have to put it down unfinished" (v). References to the novel's verisimilitude are particularly interesting: "There are many people who will consider the story highly exaggerated. Certainly it does not give the all-around picture of China found in such a novel as Pearl S. Buck's *The Good Earth*, but as in all the novels of Oteyza, chapter and page reference is available for practically every incident. It may not be the usual thing, but it happened. . . . But even if this yarn were set on Mars and purely imaginary, it would still be what one

critic termed it, 'the most absorbing and thrilling story of adventure I have read in any language in several years'" (5–6).

77. Pérez Bowie, "Presentación," 16.

78. Garmendia, "Por la ruta imaginaria de Luis de Oteyza," 28.

79. Garmendia, "Por la ruta imaginaria de Luis de Oteyza," 28.

80. Quotations will be from *Luis de Oteyza, Obras selectas*, vol 1 (Caracas: Universidad Católica Andrés Bello, 2000), 39–211. Hereafter I will add page numbers within parentheses after the quotations.

CHAPTER 4

1. Jill Lepore, "Chan, the Man," *New Yorker*, August 9, 2010.

2. The three previous movies were: *The House Without a Key* (1926, silent film serial directed by Spencer G. Bennet and produced by Pathé), *The Chinese Parrot* (1927, silent film directed by Paul Leni and produced by Universal), and *Behind That Curtain* (1929, directed by Irving Cummings and produced by Fox Film).

3. For a complete study of the Fu Manchu phenomenon, see: Christopher Frayling, *The Yellow Peril: Dr Fu Manchu & The Rise of Chinaphobia* (New York: Thames and Hudson, 2014). Quotations are from Julia Lovell, "The Yellow Peril: Dr Fu Manchu & the Rise of Chinaphobia by Christopher Frayling – Review," *Guardian*, October 30, 2014.

4. Frayling, *The Yellow Peril*.

5. Jeffrey Richards, *China and the Chinese in Popular Film: From Fu Manchu to Charlie Chan* (London and New York: I. B. Tauris and Co., 2017), chapter 3.

6. Richards, *China and the Chinese in Popular Film*, 91. See: Cay Van Ash and Elizabeth Sax Rohmer, *Master of Villainy: A Biography of Sax Rohmer* (Bowling Green, OH: Bowling Green University Popular Press, 1972).

7. Van Ash and Rohmer, *Master of Villainy*, 298.

8. Ron Goulart, *The Funnies, 100 Years of American Comic Strips* (Holbrook, MA: Adams Publishing, 1995), 104, 106.

9. Biggers quoted in Richards, *China and the Chinese in Popular Film*, 409.

10. John T. Soister and Henry Nicolella, *Down from the Attic: Rare Thrillers of the Silent Era through the 1950s* (Jefferson, NC: McFarland, 2016), 83–84.

11. Lepore, "Chan, the Man."

12. Earl Derr Biggers, *The House Without a Key* (New York: Bobbs-Merrill, 1925); *The Chinese Parrot* (New York: Bobbs-Merrill, 1926); *Behind That Curtain* (New York: Bobbs-Merrill, 1928); *The Black Camel* (New York: Bobbs-Merrill, 1929); *Charlie Chan Carries On* (New York: Bobbs-Merrill, 1930); *Keeper of the Keys* (New York: Bobbs-Merrill, 1932).

13. Tino Balio, *Grand Design: Hollywood as a Modern Business Enterprise, 1930–1939* (Berkeley, CA: University of California Press, 1995), 316–17.

14. Yunte Huang, *Charlie Chan: The Untold Story of the Honorable Detective and His Rendezvous with American History* (New York: Norton, 2010), 265–66; William H. Young and Nancy K. Young, *The Great Depression in America: A Cultural Encyclopedia* (Westport, CT, and London: Greenwood Publishing Group, 2007), 128.

15. Hsu, *A Floating Chinaman* and So, *Transpacific Community*. Both works focus on the United States, but their views can be applied to other Western contexts.

16. Rosenberg, *A World Connecting*, 985.

17. Lisa Jarvinen, *The Rise of Spanish-Language Filmmaking: Out from Hollywood's Shadow, 1929–1939* (New Brunswick, NJ: Rutgers University Press, 2012), 123–24.

18. Charles P. Mitchell, *A Guide to Charlie Chan Films* (Westport, CT: Greenwood Press, 1999), 153–54.

19. Xu Guangping, *Huiyi Lu Xun: Shinian Xieshou Gong Jianwei* (Shijiazhuang: Hebei Jiaoyu Chubanshe, 2000), 79.

20. Don Marion, "Charlie Chan in China," *The Chinese Mirror: A Journal of Chinese Film History*, May 2008.

21. Marion, "Charlie Chan in China."

22. Rosenberg, *A World Connecting*, 986. Rosenberg quotes from Miriam Silverberg, *Erotic Grotesque Nonsense* (Berkeley, CA: University of California Press, 2006).

23. An example of the amount and type of references available in Spanish bookstores can be found in the following catalog: Pedro Vindel, *Biblioteca oriental: Comprende 2.747 obras relativas a Filipinas, Japón, China y otras partes de Asia y Oceanía* (Madrid: P. Vindel, 1911–1912).

24. Joan Sacs, "Barcelona i l'Extrem-Orient," *La Publicitat*, December 6, 1929, 1, my emphasis.

25. Rosenberg, *A World Connecting*, 971. For an example of the interest raised in Spain by Chinese circuses, see: "Troupe See-Hee," *Eco Artístico*, January 5, 1919. For an example of advertisements of the Troupe See-Hee in Spain between 1915 and 1922, see several images at "Anuncios de la troupe See-Hee," *Archivo China-España*, accessed November 25, 2021, http://ace.uoc.edu/items/show/302.

26. Jerome Ch'en, *China and the West: Society and Culture, 1815–1937* (London: Hutchinson, 1979), 55.

27. Hergé, *Le Lotus bleu* (Brusselles: Casterman, 1936). Before being published as a volume, *Le Lotus bleu* was serialized in the children's supplement *Le Petit Vingtième* (attached to the newspaper *Le Vingtième Siècle*) between August 1934 and October 1935.

28. St. André, *Translating China*, 202.

29. Mackerras, *Western Images of China*, 65.

30. In the period between 1911 and 1926 there were at least forty-seven monograph publications. In the period between 1927 and 1940 the number increased to fifty-eight. See: "Publicaciones históricas," *Archivo China-España*, accessed November 25, 2021, http://ace.uoc.edu/publicaciones-historicas.

31. Elisenda Casas, "Impressions d'un viatge autèntic a la Xina," *Revista Garbí*, nos. 13–19, March 1935 to February 1936; Juan Marín Balmas, *De París a Barcelona passant per Honolulu* (Barcelona: Llibreria Catalònia, 1929); Ricardo Martorell Téllez-Girón, *Trece crónicas de viaje por China, Mongolia, Japón, Filipinas, Bali, Siam y la India.* (Madrid: Estanislao Maestre, 1933).

32. An illustrative example is the coverage of the Bias Bay incident in 1927. Chinese pirates hijacked foreign ships and the British legation decided to send their army to solve this diplomatic conflict. On March 30, 1927, *La Vanguardia*'s international page devoted three out of four columns to China and this particular subject, even if there were no Spanish vessels or citizens affected. Again, sources were either foreign press releases (Reuters, United Press, Havas) or based on them (Fabra based on Havas).

33. For example, the exhibitions held at the art gallery that belonged to the company Uralita, Barcelona, May 1926; Círculo de Bellas Artes, Madrid, September 1932; and Museu de les Arts Decoratives, Barcelona, 1935. These exhibitions showed many pieces from private collections owned by Alfonso Rodríguez Santamaría, Jerónimo Megías, and Damià Mateu.

34. In 1925, Margarita Xirgu and her company premiered Giovachino Forzano's *Tian-Hoa* at Teatre Tívoli in Barcelona and later at Teatro Español in Madrid. An example of the acclaimed reception of these plays can be found in Rodolfo de Salazar's review: "El Teatro, revista de espectáculos," *ABC*, April 12, 1925, 67–70. In 1930, Teatre Romea premiered the Catalan version of John Colton's *The Shanghai Gesture*, which had also been successfully adapted in Madrid. See: John Colton, *Xang-Hai*, trans. Alfons Fernández Burgas y Rodríguez-Grahit (Barcelona: Editorial Bistagne, 1930); John Colton, *Shanghai: Comedia dramática, en tres actos*, trans. Arturo Mori (Madrid: Rivadeneyra, 1930); Ezequiel Enderiz, "Shanghai, el éxito de una comedia exótica," *Nuevo Mundo*, June 20, 1930. In 1934, Jacinto Capella and Luis de Lucio's comedy *Fu-Chu-Ling* was received with great acclaim by audiences in Madrid and Barcelona. See: Jacinto Capella and José de Lucio. *Fu-Chu-Ling: Farsa cómica en tres actos* (Madrid: La Farsa, 1935). In 1936, Franco Padilla's comedy *Son . . . naranjas de la China* also had great success at Teatre Còmic del Paral·lel in Barcelona. See: Franco Padilla, *Son . . . naranjas de la China: Fantasía cómica en tres actos, con música de Quirós y Soriano* (Barcelona: Cisne, 1936).

35. "Otra manifestación de la cultura china en los escenarios españoles es la que ofrecieron diferentes troupes de artistas chinos. La más famosa de estas en España fue la troupe See-Hee, que llegó a España hacia 1915 y durante cuatro años estuvo actuando a lo largo y ancho de la Península" (Different troupes of Chinese artists offer another manifestation of Chinese culture on Spanish stages. The most famous of these in Spain was the See-Hee troupe, which arrived in Spain around 1915 and spent four years performing throughout the Peninsula). Xavier Ortells-Nicolau, "Itinerario: China en España: artes escénicas," *Archivo China-España, 1800–1950*, accessed November 25, 2021, http://ace.uoc.edu/exhibits/show/china-en-espana/china-artes-escenicas.

36. Traditional dancing or processional "gegants" (giants) are hollow statues made of wood and papier-mâché about three or four meters tall, carried from within the frame by someone who makes them dance. They usually represent historical figures or archetypes. In 1896 a pair of Chinese gegants was added to the celebrations in Lleida. In this case, the Chinese couple was built thanks to a popular donation that wanted to pay homage to the Roman Catholic missionaries that were still working in China.

37. See: "Fotografías del Cabaret Wu-Li-Chang, *Archivo China-España, 1800–1950*, accessed November 25, 2021, http://ace.uoc.edu/items/show/561. Martín Gala, "Los candidatos de la próxima temporada," *La Lidia*, July 27, 1926; Clemente Cruzado, "De mandarín chino a matador de toros," *Mundo Gráfico*, July 16, 1930; "Un torero chino," *La Fiesta Brava*, May 16, 1930; José Benavides, "Ha llegado a España un torero chino . . . ," *Estampa*, June 10, 1930.

38. *La Vanguardia*, June 23, 1929, 29. For the image, see: "El Pueblo Oriental en la Exposición Internacional," *Archivo China-España, 1800–1950*, accessed November 25, 2021, http://ace.uoc.edu/items/show/179.

39. See, for instance: "Tarjetas postales de misiones," *Archivo China-España, 1800–1950*, accessed November 25, 2021, http://ace.uoc.edu/items/show/353; or "Niñas disfrazadas de chinas y japonesas," *Archivo China-España, 1800–1950*, accessed November 25, 2021, http://ace.uoc.edu/items/show/182.

40. Pedro de Répide, "Paginario de la Exposición: Pueblo Oriental y pabellones europeos," *La Libertad*, September 29, 1929.

41. Francesc Trabal, *L'home que es va perdre* (Sabadell: La Mirada, 1929).

42. Moisès Llopis i Alarcon, "Paròdia i conflicte d'identitat en 'L'home que es va perdre' de Francesc Trabal," in *Actes del Dissetè Col·loqui Internacional de Llengua i Literatura Catalanes: Universitat de València, 7–10 de juliol de 2015* (Barcelona and València: Associació Internacional de Llengua i Literatura Catalanes, 2017), 339–48.

43. In fact, this was not an isolated reference to China in Trabal's production. Between 1926 and 1927 Trabal may have published several pieces (some of them anonymously) about China or that referred to China in *Diari de Sabadell*: "L'admirable aventura," February 4, 1926; "L'aprofitament de les ondes," March 17, 1926; "El jeroglífic xinès," August 20, 1927; "El perill groc," March 29, 1927. I thank Teresa Iribarren for these references.

44. Joan Alavedra, "El 'perill groc' a Barcelona," *Mirador*, June 26, 1930, 2.

45. Ramon Pei, "El camí del nord: De Primorskaia a Harbin," *Mirador*, October 26, 1933; "Sota les llums del gran Xang-hai," *Mirador*, November 23, 1933; "El camí del sud: De Port Said a Singapur," *Mirador*, November 30, 1933.

46. "24.378 'coolies' de 'rickshaw,'" *Mirador*, January 2, 1936.

47. Sheng Tcheng [Sheng Cheng], *Ma mère* (Paris: Éditions Victor Attinger, 1928); *Ma mère et moi* (Paris: Éditions Victor Attinger, 1929). Spanish translations: Cheng Tcheng, *Mi madre*, trans. J. G. Gorkín (Madrid: Cénit, 1929); *Mi madre y yo a través de la revolución china*, trans. Antonio Buendía Aragón (Madrid: Cénit, 1929).

48. Marilyn A. Levine, *The Found Generation: Chinese Communists in Europe during the Twenties* (Seattle, WA: University of Washington Press, 1993), 89–90, 232.

49. Annika A. Culver, "Sheng Cheng's *Ma Mère* (1928): An Interwar Period Search for Unity Between East and West," *Contemporary French and Francophone Studies* 21, no. 1 (January 1, 2017): 58. Between 1929 and 1933 they were translated into Spanish, Dutch, Yiddish, English, and Chinese: *Mijn moeder* (The Hague: Servire, 1929); *Mayn muter* (Warsaw: Bibliyotek M. Rakovski, 1929); *A Son of China* (New York: Norton, 1930); *Wode muqin* (Shanghai: Zhonghua shuju, 1933).

50. Levine, *The Found Generation*, 89–90.

51. Sergio Villani, *Paul Valery on War, Power, and Civilization* (Toronto: Canadian Scholars Press, 1991), 25, quoted in Culver, "Sheng Cheng's *Ma Mère*," 59.

52. Culver, "Sheng Cheng's *Ma Mère*," 54.

53. Culver, "Sheng Cheng's *Ma Mère*," 59.

54. *El Sol*, April 7, 1929; *La Voz*, October 26, 1929, 4; *La Revista Blanca*, February 1, 1931, 22. Similar reviews: *La Gaceta Literaria*, April 1, 1929, 3; *La Revista Blanca*, August 1, 1929, 33; *El Sol*, September 22, 1929, 2.

55. *La Veu de Catalunya*, April 11, 1935, 9.

56. Juan Andrade, *China contra el imperialismo* (Madrid: Ediciones Oriente, 1928); Warrack Wallace, *En la China de los bolcheviques* (Madrid: Prensa Moderna, ca. 1930); Worski-Riera, *El despertar de Asia*; Andreu Nin, *Manchuria y el imperialismo* (Valencia: Cuadernos de Cultura, 1932); Karl August Wittfogel, *El despertar de China*, trans. José Goicolea (Madrid: Dédalo, 1932); Roy, *Revolución y contrarrevolución en China*.

57. Rana Mitter, *Forgotten Ally: China's World War II, 1937–1945* (New York: Houghton Mifflin Harcourt, 2013), 9. For a detailed analysis of these synergies, see: Herrera-Feligreras et al., *España y China 1937–2017*. See also: Carles Brasó-Broggi, *Los médicos errantes: De las Brigadas Internacionales y la revolución china a la guerra fría* (Barcelona, Crítica, 2022).

58. Jaime Menéndez, "Dos millones de soldados chinos," *Estampa*, August 28, 1937, quoted in Xavier Ortells-Nicolau, "Itinerario: Conexiones en el comunismo internacional," *Archivo China-España, 1800–1950*, accessed November 25, 2021, http://ace.uoc.edu/exhibits/show/conexiones-comunismo-internaci/wuhan-sera-madrid.

59. Hwei Ru Tsou and Len Tsou, *Los brigadistas chinos en la guerra civil: La llamada de España*, coord. Laureano Ramírez Bellerín, trans. Liu Jian, Maialen Marín-Lacarta, and Sun Jiakun and Wang Jun (Madrid: Editorial Catarata, 2013).

60. Mao Zedong, "Letter to the Spanish People" (dated May 15, 1937), published in *Jiefang*, June 1937; a longer version was published as "The People of China Express Solidarity with Spain," *International Press Correspondence*, 17, no. 26, June 19, 1937. Mao Zedong, "For the Mobilization of All the Nation's Forces for Victory in the War of Resistance," August 25, 1937, a piece for the propaganda organs of the Central Committee of the Chinese Communist Party. Mao Zedong, "On Protracted War," May 1938, a series of lectures delivered at the Yan'an Association for the Study of the War of Resistance Against Japan. References retrieved from Ortells-Nicolau, "Itinerario: Conexiones en el comunismo internacional."

61. Luisa Carnés, "Seis estudiantes chinos van a luchar por la independencia de su patria," *Estampa*, October 23, 1937.

62. Sun Peiyuan's *Baowei Madeli* (Defend Madrid): "Lanzad granadas de mano de gran poder explosivo / contra Franco, incendiario y asesino. / ¡Álzate, álzate, pueblo español! / Por tu hogar y libertad, / por tu independencia; / refuerza el frente de la lucha y / de la libertad. / ¡Defiende Madrid! / ¡Defiende la paz del mundo entero! (Throw high-explosive hand grenades / against Franco,

arsonist and murderer. / Stand up, stand up, Spanish people! / For your home and freedom, / for your independence; / reinforce the front of the battle and / of freedom. / Defend Madrid! / Defend the peace of the whole world!). Menéndez, "Dos millones de soldados chinos."

63. "Publicaciones históricas," *Archivo China-España*, accessed November 25, 2021, http://ace.uoc.edu/publicaciones-historicas.

64. See references to Shaw's travels in the following pieces, among others: *La Vanguardia*, March 9, 1933, 25; *La Vanguardia*, March 11, 1933, 28; *La Vanguardia*, April 3, 1933, 2; *El Diluvio*, March 9, 1; *La Veu de Catalunya*, March 9, 1933, 11; *La Publicitat*, March 9, 1933, 7; *La Humanitat*, March 9, 1933, 6; *La Humanitat*, February 28, 1933, 10; *Flama*, April 14, 1933, 8.

65. "Bernard Shaw, a Xina: divendres volarà damunt la Gran Muralla," *La Humanitat*, February 22, 1933, 3.

66. For a work that attempts to conceptualize the role of translators as cultural mediators, see for instance: Diana Roig-Sanz and Reine Meylaerts, eds. *Literary Translation and Cultural Mediators in "Peripheral" Cultures: Customs Officers or Smugglers?* (New York: Palgrave Macmillan, 2018). In the volume, the cultural mediator is defined as "a cultural actor active across linguistic, cultural and geographical borders, occupying strategic positions within large networks and being the carrier of cultural transfer" (3).

67. *La Vanguardia*, April 2, 1933, 2.

68. *Flama*, April 14, 1933.

69. See: *La Vanguardia*, March 9, 1933, 25; *La Humanitat*, March 9, 1933, 6; *La Publicitat*, March 9, 1933, 7; *La Veu de Catalunya*, March 9, 1933, 11; *El Diluvio*, March 9, 1933, 1. The close association between Shaw and the diffusion of his actions was even remarked in *La Veu de Catalunya*: "El Japó es veié visitat per l'home de lletres les impressions del qual són noticies mundials que les agències informatives escampen arreu" (Japan was visited by the man of letters whose impressions are world news that press agencies spread everywhere), *La Veu de Catalunya*, May 13, 1933, 1.

70. *La Vanguardia*, March 11, 1933, 28; *La Humanitat*, February 28, 1933, 10. *La Vanguardia*: "Si no hubiera sido Shaw el que pronunció dicho discurso, seguramente habría sido detenido por incitar al pueblo a rebelarse contra la autoridad. Así se dice cuando menos en los círculos de la colonia inglesa en Hongkong" (Had the speech been given by someone other than Shaw, that person would surely have been arrested for inciting the people to rebel against the authorities. So it is said at least among the circles of the English colony in Hong Kong).

71. See, for example: *La Veu de Catalunya*, April 12, 1935, 9. Similar reviews: *El Sol*, April 2, 1929, 2; *La Gaceta Literaria*, April 1, 1929, 3; *La Revista Blanca*, August 1, 1929, 33; *El Sol*, September 22, 1929, 2.

72. St. André, *Translating China*, 209–10. St. André notes that these views "can be traced back to John Dewey's visit to China and his description of it as 'a potential democracy.'" See also: Karen J. Leong, *The China Mystique: Pearl S. Buck, Anna May Wong, Mayling Soong, and the Transformation of American Orientalism* (Berkeley, CA: University of California Press, 2005); and T. Christopher Jespersen, *American Images of China, 1931–1949* (Stanford, CA: Stanford University Press, 1999).

73. Daniel Sanderson, "Sentimental Educators: British and American Women's Writing on China," in *The Chinese Chameleon Revisited*, ed. Yangwen Zheng (Newcastle upon Tyne: Cambridge Scholars Publishing, 2013), 184.

74. Buck's influence over the images of China that circulated across the West has been widely examined. See particularly: Sanderson, "Sentimental Educators," 174–99; and Leong, *The China Mystique*. See also: Xiongya Gao, *Pearl S. Buck's Chinese Women Characters* (Selinsgrove, PA: Susquehanna University Press, 2000); Hsu, *A Floating Chinaman*; So, *Transpacific Community*.

75. Sanderson, "Sentimental Educators," 176.

76. Sanderson, "Sentimental Educators," 175.

77. Sanderson, "Sentimental Educators," 176.

78. Sanderson, "Sentimental Educators," 177.

79. Other books on China by Western women writers that were translated in the 1940s were: Elizabeth Foreman Lewis, *A orillas del alto Yangtze*, trans. Maria Sepúlveda (Barcelona: Editorial Juventud, 1935); Emily Hahn, *Las hermanas Soong*, trans. Senén Talarn (Barcelona: Serra y Russell, 1946).

80. *La buena tierra*, trans. Elisabeth Mulder (Barcelona: Editorial Juventud, 1935); *Viento del este, viento del oeste*, trans. G. y L. Gosú (Barcelona: Selecciones Literarias y Científicas, 1942); *La primera mujer de Se Yuan*, trans. Margarita Bernad (Barcelona: Albón, 1945); *La estirpe del dragón*, trans. Juan G. de Luaces (Barcelona: Aymá, 1947); *La promesa*, trans. Alfredo Gallart (Barcelona: Aymá, 1948); *La madre*, trans. Carlos Martínez-Barbeito (Barcelona: Aymá, 1949); *Un revolucionario en China*, trans. Eduardo Prado (Madrid: Revista Literaria, 1950).

81. P. S. Buck, *La Première Femme de Yuan*, trans. Germaine Delamain (Paris: Stock, 1935). The Spanish translation would appear in 1945: *La primera mujer de Se Yuan*, trans. Margarita Bernad (Barcelona: Albón, 1945).

82. Focius [J. V. Foix], "Panorama universal de les lletres," *La Publicitat*, February 25, 1936, 2, my emphasis. See also: Josep Maria Miquel i Vergés, *La Publicitat*, February 25, 1936; or Ramon Esquerra, "Pearl. S. Buck, novel·lista de la Xina: Testimonis," *Mirador*, August 15, 1935, 6.

83. Ramon Esquerra, "Testimonis: Pearl S. Buck, novel·lista de Xina," *Mirador*, August 15, 1935, 6; "Xina, en cos i ànima, evocada per l'escriptora Pearl S. Buck: Un llibre formidable," *La Humanitat*, September 15, 1935, 5. Similar opinions were held about other women writers. See: Ramon Esquerra, "Llibres de viatges," *Esplai. Il·lustració catalana setmanal*, August 19, 1934, 397. Esquerra also mentions that Nora Waln "ens ha donat un document interessantíssim sobre la vida de la Xina contemporània, particularment interessant per trobar-se a Xina durant la darrera revolució i la guerra xino-japonesa, que tanta importància ha tingut en la política de l'extrem Orient" (has offered a very interesting document about the life in contemporary China, particularly interesting for having been in China during the last revolution and the Sino-Japanese War, which have been so important in the politics of the Far East).

84. Marcela de Juan (Huang Masai, 1905–1981) was born in La Havana. Her father, Huang Lühe, was a Chinese diplomat; her mother, Juliette Broutá-Gilliard, was Belgian. The family later lived in Madrid and Beijing. In 1928 Marcela de Juan went back to Spain where she spent the rest of her life and

became a popular and prestigious journalist, translator, and interpreter. See: Manuel Pavón-Belizón, "Itinerario: Marcela de Juan," *Archivo China-España, 1800–1950*, accessed November 25, 2021, http://ace.uoc.edu/exhibits/show/galeria-de-personajes/marcela-de-juan. Marcela de Juan has nowadays become almost an icon as the first direct cross-cultural mediator between China and Spain. Most of her professional trajectory and her anthologies and memoirs were published during the Franco regime in a political context that remains out of the chronological boundaries of this book: *Breve antología de la poesía china* (Madrid: Revista de Occidente, 1948); *Segunda antología de la poesía china* (Madrid: Revista de Occidente, 1962); *Poesía china: Del siglo XXII a. C. a las canciones de la Revolución Cultural* (Madrid: Alianza Editorial, 1973); *La China que ayer viví y la China que hoy entreví* (Barcelona: Luis de Caralt, 1977). However, it must be noted that, as research by Jiawei Wang has showed, Marcela de Juan's translations were often equally indirect, mostly based on French translations by Marquis d'Hervey de Saint-Denys and Louis Laloy. Marcela de Juan's case demonstrates the impact of the mechanisms under study in this book. See: Jiawei Wang, "Versiones-puente de la traducción de poesía clásica china por Marcela de Juan," *Sinología hispánica* 12 (2021): 91–108.

85. Ramon Vinyes, "Xina," *Meridià*, August 12, 1938, 5.

86. Vinyes, "Xina," 5.

87. André Malraux, *Los conquistadores*, trans. José Viana (Madrid: Argos Vergara, 1931).

88. Jaume Miravitlles, "Ressenya de *Les conquérants*," *L'Opinió*, August 1929, 8. See also, later: Ramon Esquerra, "Malraux i el nihilisme," *El Matí*, March 7, 1934, 9.

89. See, among other reviews: *La Veu de Catalunya*, August 5, 1933, 7; *Mirador*, January 18, 1934, 4; *Nosaltres sols*, February 3 1934, 4; *La Humanitat*, February 11, 1934, 12; *La Humanitat*, June 5, 1935, 4; *El Matí*, July 19, 1934, 7. The Spanish translation (by César A. Comet) was first published in 1936 by Ediciones Sur in Buenos Aires. It was not published in Spain until 1971 by EDHASA. The Catalan translation (by Salvador Vives) was published in 1966 by Edicions Proa.

90. "*Els conqueridors* foren traduïts a l'anglès a instàncies d'Aldous Huxley, en 1929, però l'obra no tingue èxit ni a Anglaterra ni als Estats Units. Alguns crítics, però, l'elogiaren. Edmund Wilson digué que el llibre era com un far que, inesperadament, aclaria una regió que abans apareixia llunyana i fosca. . . . Per fi, quan *La condició humana* fou publicada, pel juny del 1934, als Estats Units, sota el títol *Man's Fate*, Malraux aconseguí la més alta celebritat i els crítics més eminents digueren que la seva novel·la era la millor publicada als Estats Units durant l'any 1934" (*Les Conquérants* was translated into English at the request of Aldous Huxley in 1929, but the work was not successful in either England or the United States. Some critics, however, praised it. Edmund Wilson said the book was like a beacon that unexpectedly illuminated a region that had previously appeared distant and dark. . . . Finally, when *La Condition humaine* was published in the United States in June 1934 under the title of *Man's Fate*, Malraux achieved the highest celebrity and the most eminent critics said that it

was the best novel published in the United States during the year 1934.) Josep Sol, *La Humanitat*, June 5, 1935, 4.

91. See particularly: Ramon Esquerra, "Malraux i el nihilisme," *El Matí*, March 7, 1934, 9; Ramon Esquerra, "Llibres sobre la Xina," *La Veu de Catalunya*, January 24, 1936, 6. On Malraux in Catalonia, see: Clarissa Laus, "*La condition humaine, L'espoir y Antimémoires*. Los primeros pasos de la recepción crítica de André Malraux en España," in *Traducción, (sub)versión, transcreación*, eds. Assumpta Camps, Jacqueline Hurtley, and Anna Moya (Barcelona: PPU, 2005), 165–75. On Esquerra, see: Guillem Molla Rodríguez, *Ramon Esquerra, geografia crítica d'un esperit comparatista* (Barcelona: Publicacions de l'Abadia de Montserrat, 2015).

92. JMV, *La Veu de Catalunya*, August 5, 1933, 7.

93. "Els grans esdeveniments històrics a la Xina han fet d'aquest país un centre d'interès, *també literari*, com en Malraux" (The great historical events in China have made this country a center of interest, *also literary interest*, as in Malraux.) Ramon Esquerra, "Llibres sobre la Xina," 6, my emphasis.

94. Josep Sol, *La Humanitat*, June 5, 1935, 4, my emphasis.

95. José Gabriel López Antuñano, *Mario Verdaguer, un escritor proteico* (Madrid: Editorial Pliegos, 1994), 33, 251. "Cuando se trata de obras de tipo comercial y destinadas al mercado editorial de gran consumo, Verdaguer no explicita su identidad o incluso la disfraza, como ocurre con asiduidad en el caso de 'La Novela Mensual.' En cambio, cuando el autor traducido ha sido ya legitimado por las instituciones—academias, premios, colecciones o revistas con capacidad para la consagración—el escritor menorquín descubre su identidad para favorecer asimismo su propio ascenso, no solo en el sistema literario nacional sino también en otros campos como el alemán" (When it comes to works of a commercial nature and destined for the mass publishing market, Verdaguer does not explain his identity or even disguises it, as is often the case in "La Novela Mensual." On the other hand, when the translated author has already been legitimized by the institutions—academies, prizes, collections, or magazines with the capacity for consecration—the Menorcan writer reveals his identity to promote his own rise, not only in the national literary system but also in other fields like the German). Diana Sanz Roig, "Los proyectos editoriales de Mario Verdaguer: la revista Mundo Ibérico y las editoriales Lux y Apolo," *Revista de Literatura* 75, no. 149 (June 30, 2013): 202.

96. I have not been able to locate the specific sources used by Verdaguer. However, the transliteration of names and other details clearly points to a French origin.

97. "Notas y noticias sobre libros," *Nosotros*, no. 75, 1932: 205–6; "O valor economico da China," *O Observador Economico e Financeiro*, no. 88, 1943: 56–68.

98. I am echoing Miriam Silverberg's use of the term in Silverberg, *Erotic Grotesque Nonsense*.

99. Among others: Manel Ollé, "La pluja de Du Fu en la poesia de Carner i Manent," in *Gèneres i formes en la literatura catalana d'entreguerres (1918–1939): I Simposi sobre traducció i recepció en la literatura catalana contemporània*, eds. Miquel M. Gibert and Marcel Ortín (Lleida: Punctum and Trilcat,

2005), 11–26; Manel Ollé, "Àsia Oriental en les lletres catalanes del segle xx: Versions, ficcions i afeccions," in *Antoni Saumell i Soler. Miscel·lània in Memoriam*, ed. Josep Maria Delgado (Barcelona: Universitat Pompeu Fabra, 2007), 617–40; Jordi Marrugat, *Marià Manent i la traducció* (Lleida: Punctum, 2009); Manel Ollé, "El veïnat xinès i l'exotisme literari," *452oF* 13 (2015): 167–86. See also: Carles Prado-Fonts, "Del xinès al català, traduccions per generació espontània," *Quaderns: Revista de Traduccio* 6 (2001): 107–17.

100. Ollé, "La pluja de Du Fu," 14.

101. Ollé, "El veïnat xinès i l'exotisme literari."

102. Ollé, "La pluja de Du Fu," 14–15.

103. Apel·les Mestres, *Poesia xinesa* (Barcelona: Llibreria de Salvador Bonavia, 1925); Marià Manent, *L'aire daurat: Interpretacions de poesia xinesa* (Barcelona: Atenas, 1928); Marià Manent, *Com un núvol lleuger: Més interpretacions de la lírica xinesa* (Barcelona: Proa, 1967); Josep Carner, "La passejada pels brodats de seda," *La Nostra Terra*, July 1932, 256–70; Josep Carner, *Lluna i llanterna* (Barcelona: Proa, 1935).

104. Josep Maria de Sagarra, "Poetes de la Xina," *La Publicitat*, September 6, 1923.

105. Ollé, "La pluja de Du Fu," 13.

106. Ollé, "La pluja de Du Fu," 20.

107. The most evident example is Marià Manent's own translation into Spanish of his Catalan interpretations of Chinese poetry as *El color de la vida* in 1942. In a postface, Manent lists the following references: Henry Baerlin, *The Singing Caravan* (London: John Murray, 1910); Laurence Binyon, *The Flight of the Dragon* (London: John Murray, 1918); Abel Bonnard, *En Chine* (Paris: Artème Fayard et Cie., 1924); L. Cranmer-Byng, *The Rose-Garden of Sa'adi* (London: John Murray, 1910); L. Cranmer-Byng, *A Lute of Jade* (London: John Murray, 1918); Herbert Giles, *The Civilization of China* (London: Williams and Norgate, 1919); James Legge, *The Chinese Classics* (London: Henry Frowdge, 1871); Singh Puran, *The Spirit of Oriental Poetry* (London: Kegan Paul, Trench, Trubner, and Co., 1926); Shigeyoshi Obata, *The Works of Li Po* (London and Toronto: J. M. Dent and Sons, 1923); Georges Soulié de Morant, *Florilège des poèmes song* (Paris: Librairie Plon, 1923); James Teackle Dennis, *The Burden of Isis* (London: John Murray, 1918); Tsen Tsonming, *Essai historique de la poésie chinoise* (Lyon: Joannès, Desvigne, and Cie., 1923); Helen Wadell, *Lyrics from the Chinese* (London: Constable and Co., 1919); Arthur Waley, *A Hundred and Seventy Chinese Poems* (London: Constable and Co., 1920); Arthur Waley, *More Translations from the Chinese* (London: George Allen and Unwin, 1920).

108. Carner, "La passejada," 256–57.

109. Carner, "La passejada," 257.

110. Ollé, "La pluja de Du Fu," 17.

111. Eugeni d'Ors, *La Veu de Catalunya*, May 6, 7, 9, 11, 12, and 13, 1914. Republished in Eugeni d'Ors, *Glosari 1912–1913–1914* (Barcelona: Quaderns Crema, 2005).

112. "Llegir això és emocionant. Déu meu, Déu meu, com ens esforcem, aquí i allà de la terra els pobres homes! Com repetim, a tanta distància, en medi

tan diferent, les mateixes coses, aquestes coses" (Reading that is so moving. Oh, my God, my God, how hard we try, all across the earth, us poor humans! How we repeat, so far apart from each other, in such a different place, the very same things, these things) (D'Ors, *Glosari*, 810). D'Ors's reflections were in fact spurred by Albert Maybon's *La République chinoise*, which he read in the original French version, published in 1914, during a trip to France. Albert Maybon, *La République chinoise* (Paris: A. Colin, 1914).

113. In 1920 Sacs published the catalog *El mueble de la China*. In 1927 he translated into Catalan the third chapter of Sinibaldo de Mas's *La Chine et les puissances chrétiennes* that had been originally published in French. In 1931 he published, under the pen name Apa, a cartoon that criticized the League of Nation's lack of reaction following Japan's occupation of Manchuria. In 1933 he introduced the works of two contemporary Chinese painters, Chen Handi and Xu Beihong, in "Pintura moderna xinesa," published in *Mirador*. Joan Sacs, *El mueble de la China* (Barcelona: Librería Catalonia, 1920); Sinibald de Mas, *La Xina*, trans. Joan Sacs [Feliu Elias] (Barcelona: Col·lecció Popular Barcino, 1927). The original was: *La Chine et les puissances chrétiennes* (Paris: Hachette, 1861), 2 vols. See: *Mirador*, November 26, 1931. See also: "Caricatura sobre la invasión japonesa de Manchuria," *Archivo China-España, 1800–1950*, accessed November 25, 2021, http://ace.uoc.edu/items/show/821. Joan Sacs, "Pintura moderna xinesa," *Mirador*, May 18, 1933 and May 25, 1933.

114. Josep Maria de Sagarra, "La Poesia Extrem-Oriental," *La Nova Revista*, 1927; Josep Lleonart, "Notes xineses," *La Nova Revista*, January to May 1929.

115. *La Nova Revista*, September 1928, 91. The series was never materialized.

116. *La Nova Revista*, April 1928, 331.

117. *La Nova Revista*, July 1928, 286. Sacs refers to Charles Vignier (1863–1934). Proud to have received the attention of an Orientalist such as Vignier, Sacs is then keen to share how they have followed Vignier's guidelines to design the book covers in the series: "Per indicació expressa del gran orientalista Mr. Vignier, hem enllestit les dues marques decoratives que figuraran en les portades de la nostra col·lecció Orient i Extrem-Orient. Hi haurà dos models: un pels llibres i àlbums que tractin o que es relacionin amb l'Orient i un altre pels que es refereixin a l'Extrem-Orient. Per l'Extrem-Orient hem fet reproduir la clàssica cigala estilitzada de jade, que hem extret de l'obra d'A. de Tizac: *L'art chinois classique*. Per l'Orient pròpiament dit, hem pres un altre motiu ornamental clàssic a base—oh! deliciosa recordança de Saâdi i d'Hafiz—d'un clavell i d'un xiprer combinats, *d'après* les ceràmiques i els teixits de la millor època persana" (By specific indication of the great Orientalist Mr. Vignier, we have completed the two decorative signs that will appear on the covers of our East and Far East series. There will be two models: one for books and albums that deal with or relate to the East and another for those that deal with the Far East. For the Far East series, we have reproduced the classic stylized jade locust, which we have taken from the work by A. de Tizac: *L'art chinois classique*. For the East series, we have taken another classic ornamental motif based—oh, such a delicious reminder of Saâdi and Hafiz—on a combination of a carnation and a cypress, *d'après* the pottery and fabrics of the best Persian period.) *La Nova Revista*, September 1928, 9.

118. Joan Sacs, "Àsia," *La Nova Cultura* 1 (January 1927): 69–75. Hereafter I will add page numbers within parentheses after the quotations.

119. Crespi i Martí, *La ciutat de la por*. The novel was republished by Pòrtic in 1987 and by Editorial Males Herbes in 2016. I will quote from the Pòrtic 1987 edition and hereafter I will add page numbers within parentheses after the quotations.

120. For example, in *La Publicitat* it was qualified as a sensational work (January 24, 1930) and in *Mirador* as a grandiose success (January 30, 1930).

121. See, for example: Marín Balmas, *De París a Barcelona*, with many scenes and passages matching Crespi i Martí's representations—for instance, the river full of sampans or the architecture and aesthetics of the temples.

122. In 1866, for instance, the Spanish version of *De la Terre à la Lune* was published only a year after the original publication in French, while the Catalan translation did not appear until 1926.

123. Ramon Pinyol, "La recepció de Verne a Catalunya," *Serra d'Or*, March 2005, 17.

124. Pinyol, "La recepció de Verne a Catalunya," 17.

125. Josep Maria Folch i Torres, *Aventures den Bolavà en el país dels xinos: Memories íntimes d'un detective aixerit* (Barcelona: Bagunyà, 1912).

126. Folch i Torres, *Aventures den Bolavà*, 68.

127. José Ortega y Gasset, "Prólogo," in *La Decadencia de Occidente*, by Oswald Spengler, trans. Manuel García Morente (Madrid: Calpe, 1923), 12.

128. Carl Antonius Lemke Duque, "La Biblioteca de las Ideas del Siglo XX, la *Revista de Occidente* (1922–1936): Prefiguración de la reintegración de España en Europa," in *Ortega y la cultura europea*, ed. Christoph Rodiek (Frankfurt am Main: Lang, 2006), 159–90.

129. Ramiro de Maeztu, "La Decadencia de Occidente," *El Sol*, November 15, 1923.

130. Carl Antonius Lemke Duque, "El concepto de 'Europa," en la *Revista de Occidente* (1923–1936) y su recepción en José Ortega y Gasset," *Política y Sociedad* 52, no. 2 (2015): 562.

131. Gaziel, "Les viles espirituals," presentation given in Girona, October 26, 1923. The presentation was later published in: Gaziel, *Hores viatgeres: Assaigs* (Barcelona: Guinart y Pujolar, 1926).

132. Pérez Bowie, "Presentación," 21.

CONCLUSION

1. Apel·les Mestres, "Pekin," in *Monólechs: Siluetas barceloninas* (Barcelona: Antoni López, ca. 1900), 51–60. The piece was republished in 1913 and 1932. I am quoting from this later edition: *Monòlegs* (Barcelona: Llibreria Millà, 1932), 29–34. I thank Xavier Ortells-Nicolau for bringing this piece to my attention.

2. Ignacio Infante, *After Translation: The Transfer and Circulation of Modern Poetics Across the Atlantic* (New York: Fordham University Press, 2013); Alan Shapiro, *Against Translation* (Chicago: University of Chicago Press, 2019); Esra Akcan, *Architecture in Translation: Germany, Turkey, and the Modern House* (Durham, NC: Duke University Press, 2012); Andrew Chesterman, *Memes of*

Translation (Amsterdam and Philadelphia, PA: John Benjamins, 1997); Matthew Reynolds, ed., *Prismatic Translation* (Cambridge: Legenda, 2019); Homay King, *Lost in Translation: Orientalism, Cinema, and the Enigmatic Signifier* (Durham, NC: Durham University Press, 2010).

3. Rebecca Walkowitz's *Born Translated* is an example of such scholarly virtuosity. Walkowitz juggles the notions of translation as a metaphor (that constitutes world literature), translation as a topic (that characterizes contemporary novels), and translation as an interlingual practice (that deconstructs identity, even within the English language alone). Rebecca L. Walkowitz, *Born Translated: The Contemporary Novel in an Age of World Literature* (New York: Columbia University Press, 2015).

4. The term *cultural translation* originated from a critical intervention in anthropology. In 1985 and 1986 Roger Keesing and Talal Asad pointed out to the differentials of power in cross-cultural representation. Their contributions opened the way for a broader discussion on the limits of anthropology. Keesing, "Conventional Metaphors and Anthropological," Asad, "The Concept of Cultural Translation in British Social Anthropology."

5. Homi K. Bhabha, "How Newness Enters the World: Postmodern Space, Postcolonial Times, and the Trials of Cultural Translation," in *The Location of Culture*, 212–35; Gayatri Chakravorty Spivak, "The Politics of Translation," in *Outside in the Teaching Machine* (London and New York: Routledge, 1993), 179–200; Chakrabarty, *Provincializing Europe*, 17–18; Sakai, *Translation & Subjectivity*; Vicente Rafael, *Contracting Colonialism: Translation and Christian Conversion in Tagalog Society under Early Spanish Rule* (Ithaca, NY: Cornell University Press, 1988), chapter 1, "The Politics of Translation."

6. Susan Bassnett, *Comparative Literature: A Critical Introduction* (Oxford: Blackwell, 1993); Emily Apter, *The Translation Zone: A New Comparative Literature* (Princeton, NJ: Princeton University Press, 2006); David Damrosch, *What Is World Literature?* (Princeton, NJ: Princeton University Press, 2003), 6; Eric Hayot and Rebecca Walkowitz, eds. *A New Vocabulary for Global Modernism* (New York: Columbia University Press, 2016); Gayle Rogers, "Translation," in *A New Vocabulary for Global Modernism*, eds. Eric Hayot and Rebecca Walkowitz (New York: Columbia University Press, 2016) 249.

7. In translation studies, James S. Holmes is usually quoted as the first scholar who, in the 1970s, attempted to map out such heterogeneity—including theoretical, descriptive, and applied approaches. See: James S. Holmes, "The Name and Nature of Translation Studies," in *Translated!: Papers on Literary Translation and Translation Studies* (Amsterdam: Rodopi, 1988), 66–80. Anthony Pym has insightfully explained and developed this map according to different "paradigms." Anthony Pym, *Exploring Translation Theories* (New York: Routledge, 2009).

8. Carles Prado-Fonts, "Embodying Translation in Modern and Contemporary Chinese Literature (1908–1934 and 1979–1999): A Methodological Use of the Conception of Translation as a Site." (PhD diss., Universitat Autònoma de Barcelona, 2005). An insightful exploration of this gap can be found in Anthony Pym, "Doubts about Deconstruction as a General Theory of Translation," *Tradterm* 2 (1995): 11–18.

9. For a critical view of these metaphorical uses, see for instance: Anthony Pym, "Emily Apter. *The Translation Zone: A New Comparative Literature*," *Target* 19, no. 1 (2007): 177–82; and Lawrence Venuti, "Hijacking Translation: How Comp Lit Continues to Suppress Translated Texts," *Boundary* 2 43, no. 2 (2016): 179–204.

10. A canonical definition of translations as texts that are considered translations (or "as facts") in the target culture can be found in Gideon Toury, *Descriptive Translation Studies and Beyond* (Amsterdam and Philadelphia, PA: John Benjamins, 1995), chapter 1.

11. St. André, "Relay;" Ringmar, "Relay Translation." In fact, for James St. André, relay translation (the translation of a translated text, either spoken or written, into a third language) "remains one of the most understudied phenomena in translation studies today, and one that could and should receive more attention from theoreticians and historians alike." St. André, "Relay," 232. Relay translation is part of a terminological amalgam that describes with slightly different nuances phenomena that resemble the cases examined in this book: indirect translation, retranslation, support translation. For a recent overview on indirect translation, see also: Rosa, Pięta, and Bueno, "Theoretical, Methodological, and Terminological Issues Regarding Indirect Translation: An Overview." The work of Maialen Marín-Lacarta provides important insights on indirectness and mediation in literary translation. See, for instance: Maialen Marin-Lacarta, "Indirectness in Literary Translation: Methodological Possibilities," *Translation Studies* 10, no. 2 (May 4, 2017): 133–49.

12. Besides Toury, *Descriptive Translation Studies*, see, for instance: Johan Heilbron, "Towards a Sociology of Translation: Book Translations as a Cultural WorldSystem," *European Journal of Social Theory* 2, no. 4 (1999): 429–44.

13. Sakai, *Translation & Subjectivity*.

14. For a definition of an "extended argument or model on cultural transfer and cultural mediator," particularly in peripheral spaces, see: Roig-Sanz and Meylaerts, *Literary Translation and Cultural Mediators*.

15. For a lucid exploration of the relationship between translation and ethnography, see: Kate Sturge, *Representing Others: Translation, Ethnography, and the Museum* (London and New York: Routledge, 2007).

16. I could have used the original term in Nietzsche's aphorism alluded to in Jameson's famous title: *Zwange* or "constraint"—which Nietzsche applies to language and I resituate in translation. However, I consider that the stronger connotation rendered by the metaphor of the prison house (ironically a mistranslation—or, at least, a debatable one—of Nietzsche's words by Erich Heller, which was given more circulation in Jameson's book) should help us think more critically about the points I am trying to argue in this conclusion and that have been developed throughout the book. The uncomfortable feeling (which I have experienced myself) upon seeing a dear practice or discipline such as translation being metaphorically connected to a prison may be indicative of both the power of translation's lure and the strength of our assumptions. For the loose rendering of Nietzsche's aphorism, see: David Lovekin, *Technique, Discourse, and Consciousness: An Introduction to the Philosophy of Jacques Ellul* (Bethlehem, PA: Lehigh University Press, 1991), 209.

17. A memorable example of such vagueness can be found in the position paper by Boris Buden and Stefan Nowotny on cultural translation followed by a series of responses from a variety of disciplines published in *Translation Studies* in 2009 and 2010. See: Boris Buden, Stefan Nowotny, Sherry Simon, Ashok Bery, Michael Cronin, "Cultural Translation: An Introduction to the Problem, and Responses," *Translation Studies* 2, no. 2 (2009): 196–219; and Mary Louise Pratt, Birgit Wagner, Ovidi Carbonell i Cortés, Andrew Chesterman, Maria Tymoczko, "Translation Studies Forum: Cultural Translation," *Translation Studies* 3, no. 1 (2010): 94–110. The vague use of cultural translation in this forum has been insightfully summarized by Sarah Maitland, *What Is Cultural Translation?* (London: Bloomsbury Academic, 2017), chapter 1.

18. Ernesto Laclau, *Emancipation(s)* (London: Verso, 1996), chapter 3, "Why Do Empty Signifiers Matter to Politics?"; and *On Populist Reason* (London: Verso, 2005), chapter 4, "The 'People' and the Discursive Production of Emptiness." See also the notion of "floating signifier" as "a signifier that absorbs rather than emits meaning" as defined in: Ian Buchanan, *A Dictionary of Critical Theory* (Oxford: Oxford University Press, 2020).

19. Inspiring works that argue for an expansion of the archive and a challenge of the epistemologies are: Susan Stanford Friedman, *Planetary Modernisms: Provocations on Modernity Across Time* (New York: Columbia University Press, 2015); and Eric Hayot, *On Literary Worlds* (Oxford: Oxford University Press, 2012). My point is that our expansions onto the planetary or our imagining of new literary worlds should not be mere "provocations" or "excursions" (as in Stanford Friedman's subtitle or the title of chapter 1) or "experiments" (as in Hayot's depiction of his own book, 8), but an inalienable duty for contemporary scholars—particularly for those who work on comparative, cross-cultural, transnational, world, or global issues.

Index

FLASHPOINTS